studies in jazz

Institute of Jazz Studies
Rutgers—The State University of New Jersey
General Editors: Dan Morgenstern and Edward Berger

1. BENNY CARTER: A Life in American Music, *by Morroe Berger, Edward Berger, and James Patrick,* 1982
2. ART TATUM: A Guide to His Recorded Music, *by Arnold Laubich and Ray Spencer,* 1982
3. ERROL GARNER: The Most Happy Piano, *by James M. Doran,* 1995
4. JAMES P. JOHNSON: A Case of Mistaken Identity, *by Scott E. Brown;* Discography 1917–1950, *by Robert Hilbert,* 1986
5. PEE WEE ERWIN: This Horn for Hire, *as told to Warren W. Vaché, Sr.,* 1987
6. BENNY GOODMAN: Listen to His Legacy, *by D. Russell Connor,* 1988
7. ELLINGTONIA: The Recorded Music of Duke Ellington and His Sidemen, *by W. E. Timner,* 1988; 4th ed., 1996
8. THE GLENN MILLER ARMY AIR FORCE BAND: Sustineo Alas/ I Sustain the Wings, *by Edward F. Polic;* Foreword *by George T. Simon,* 1989
9. SWING LEGACY, *by Chip Deffaa,* 1989
10. REMINISCING IN TEMPO: The Life and Times of a Jazz Hustler, *by Teddy Reig, with Edward Berger,* 1990
11. IN THE MAINSTREAM: 18 Portraits in Jazz, *by Chip Deffaa,* 1992
12. BUDDY DeFRANCO: A Biographical Portrait and Discography, *by John Kuehn and Arne Astrup,* 1993
13. PEE WEE SPEAKS: A Discography of Pee Wee Russell, *by Robert Hilbert, with David Niven,* 1992
14. SYLVESTER AHOLA: The Gloucester Gabriel, *by Dick Hill,* 1993
15. THE POLICE CARD DISCORD, *by Maxwell T. Cohen,* 1993
16. TRADITIONALISTS AND REVIVALISTS IN JAZZ, *by Chip Deffaa,* 1993
17. BASSICALLY SPEAKING: An Oral History of George Duvivier, *by Edward Berger;* Musical Analysis *by David Chevan,* 1993
18. TRAM: The Frank Trumbauer Story, *by Philip R. Evans and Larry F. Kiner, with William Trumbauer,* 1994
19. TOMMY DORSEY: On the Side, *by Robert L. Stockdale,* 1995
20. JOHN COLTRANE: A Discography and Musical Biography, *by Yasuhiro Fujioka, with Lewis Porter and Yoh-ichi Hamada,* 1995
21. RED HEAD: A Chronological Survey of "Red" Nichols and His Five Pennies, *by Stephen M. Stroff,* 1996

The *Annual Review of Jazz Studies* is edited by **Edward Berger, David Cayer, Henry Martin, Dan Morgenstern, and Lewis Porter. This special issue on Jazz Theory has been edited by Henry Martin.** The *Annual Review of Jazz Studies* is published by Scarecrow Press for the Institute of Jazz Studies at Rutgers, The State University of New Jersey.

Authors should address manuscripts and editorial correspondence to:

> The Editors
> *Annual Review of Jazz Studies*
> Institute of Jazz Studies
> Dana Library
> Rutgers, The State University of New Jersey
> Newark, New Jersey 07102

Review copies of books should be sent to this address by publishers and marked to the attention of the Book Review Editor.

Authors preparing manuscripts for consideration should follow *The Chicago Manual of Style*. In particular: (1) manuscripts should be original typed or word-processed copies; (2) except for foreign-language quotations, manuscripts must be in English; (3) *all* material (text, quotations, endnotes, author's biographical note) must be neat, *double-spaced,* and with adequate margins; (4) notes must be grouped together on separate pages at the end of the manuscript and should be complete references following the samples in *The Chicago Manual of Style;* (5) on a separate sheet, authors should provide a one- or two-sentence biographical note, including current affiliation; (6) musical examples must be on separate sheets in camera-ready form, preferably computer-copied; (7) authors should take the size of the *ARJS* page into account in assembling their examples; (8) authors are encouraged to submit a 3.5-inch computer diskette of their article (Word or WordPerfect, Macintosh or PC); and (9) a cassette tape of any examples transcribed or reproduced from recordings must be included; this is to facilitate reading the paper and checking the accuracy of the transcriptions (a cassette is not necessary for printed music or examples composed by the author).

Authors alone are responsible for the contents of their articles.

ANNUAL REVIEW OF JAZZ STUDIES 8 1996

edited by
Henry Martin

Special Edition on Jazz Theory

**Institute of Jazz Studies
Rutgers—The State University
of New Jersey
and
The Scarecrow Press, Inc.
Lanham, Md., & London
1997**

SCARECROW PRESS, INC.

Published in the United States of America
by Scarecrow Press, Inc.
4720 Boston Way
Lanham, Maryland 20706

4 Pleydell Gardens, Folkestone
Kent CT20 2DN, England

ISSN 0731-0641

ISBN 0-8108-3199-6 (cloth : alk. paper)

♾ ™ The paper used in this publication meets the minimum requirements of
American National Standard for Information Sciences—Permanence of
Paper for Printed Library Materials, ANSI Z39.48–1984.
Manufactured in the United States of America.

CONTENTS

PREFACE

Jazz scholarship has borne witness to a dramatic increase in the study of theory during the last two or three decades. In recognition of this growing interest in the field among both musicians and jazz scholars, we at the *Annual Review of Jazz Studies* thought it would be timely to showcase recent professional work with this special issue devoted entirely to articles of a theoretical nature.

There is a wide range of work represented in the pages to follow, spanning jazz in the 1920s (Dodds) to the 1960s (Coltrane and Hancock). A pedagogical section offers suggestions for ear training, a technique for using a CD player for transcription, and a method for exploring the outer boundaries of tonality in improvisation. The contributors range from scholars involved in jazz theory to professional musicians, with, of course, much overlap.

It is in the spirit of the growing interest and professionalization of work and research into the structures of jazz, its analysis and improvisation, that I am pleased to announce the recent foundation of a group of musicians and scholars, primarily members of the Society for Music Theory, with a special interest in jazz theory. There are plans for an analysis symposium at the annual meeting of the Society for Music Theory in 1997, and work has begun on a catalog of available transcriptions.

Several members of the Special Interest Group in Jazz Theory have contributed articles to this issue of ARJS, i.e., Strunk, Waters, Larson, and Martin. I organized the Group and am its current chair. Anyone interested in receiving information on membership should write me at 11 Riverside Drive, Apt. 3JW, New York, NY 10023 or send me an email message at martinh@newschool.edu.

Henry Martin

JAZZ THEORY: AN OVERVIEW

Henry Martin

I. JAZZ THEORY AND WHAT JAZZ THEORISTS DO

In the beginning of an overview of jazz theory,[1] the first question that comes to mind is, naturally, just what is it? An expected follow-up question might be "If there is such a thing as jazz theory, then is someone who does it a jazz theorist?" If we assume that we can define jazz theory and justify the existence of jazz theorists, then how can we distinguish what they do from what jazz historians do? Or critics? Or ethnomusicologists? While none of the answers adduced below is expected to be definitive, it is hoped that they may at least help frame subsequent discussion.

Music theory, having undergone extensive evolution in Western culture since the writings of Aristoxenus, largely concerns itself with discovering (and sometimes inventing) sets of rules that model various kinds of musical structure. These models attempt to show how a piece "works" or how music in some given style is written or performed. The rules are sometimes inferred from the musical sounds themselves, other times from notation, itself already a model of sound structure. Groups of related and overlapping theoretical models delimit substyles within broader musical genres. In addition to these activities that directly address pieces and performance practices, there is a long tradition of philosophical analysis and speculation in music theory that continues unabated in our time. Those musicians and scholars with a special interest in these issues as they apply to jazz performance and composition are jazz theorists. These brief remarks and definitions beg many questions, to be sure, but for our purposes they should suffice.

There are two principal ways that jazz theory (or any music theory, in fact) can be pursued. The first is from the point of view of the player or

composer: what is the necessary information that a musician needs in order to produce jazz in some given style? This "musician-based" theory
teaches musicians models containing tools for composition or improvisation, and can be divided into a basic vs. higher-level component. At the
basic level, "musician-based" theory is "pedagogical": it concentrates on
the rudiments virtually any musician needs to know. At the higher level
such theory becomes "speculative," since it assumes knowledge of rudiments and purports to suggest creative strategies musicians may wish to
pursue as either writers or improvisers. An overview of pedagogical and
speculative jazz theory follows below in section III.

The second general type of theory can be called "analytical," an activity of generally more recent vintage in the jazz world than pedagogical theory. An analytical theorist takes a listener's rather than a musician's point of view and thereby explicates "what is heard" by showing
elements of structure, general stylistic trends, or connections to other
pieces by the same or stylistically similar artists. In taking a cue from
theorists working with Western concert music, the analytical jazz theorist may raise philosophical or aesthetic issues of relevance to either written or improvised jazz.

While it is convenient to differentiate analytical from pedagogical and
speculative theory, these viewpoints often overlap. For example, a theorist may adopt an analytical point of view in order to ascertain elements
of style in a given artist, then switch to a pedagogical point of view in order to show how the style of that artist may be emulated. Although this
terminology is implicit in what has been defined so far, let us agree to follow what seems to be common practice by viewing analysis, pedagogy,
and speculative theory as branches of music theory broadly conceived.
An overview of analytical jazz theory appears below in Section IV.

It must be noted that jazz historians have tackled theoretical issues as
well, and often have explored them cogently. What then separates jazz
theorists from their more history-minded colleagues? The principal difference, I would suggest, is that theorists tend to concentrate on the
"more technical" areas, as against matters of historical import, such as
biography and discography. Further, jazz historians, like their counterparts in Western concert music, have often explicated music as historical and social process, as relating to other trends in either the social sciences or arts and letters. Theorists, on the hand, while certainly in no way
disavowing the importance of history, social issues, or humanistic concerns, have tended to focus on the music as music, that is, on the details
of the technical issues raised by the notes themselves.

Jazz critics form a third vital grouping. Before the 1950s, most writing on jazz consisted of criticism in which recordings, concerts, and artists were routinely evaluated, compared, and (in some instances) rated numerically. Critics, indeed, were among the first jazz historians, alongside fans and record collectors. There is also a remarkable professional correspondence between critics and analytical theorists in that both groups often evaluate pieces or musicians for intrinsic merit; theorists, however, usually approach the works technically whereas critics most often write for the popular media.

During the last two decades or so, the divide between critics and other jazz scholars has, if anything, been widening, since the latter, often involved professionally as musicians or academics, usually approach their projects with longer-term goals in mind. Still, jazz historians (and theorists) will sometimes write for the popular media when appropriate. To this end, jazz scholars during the last two decades or so have often authored liner notes, particularly of reissued recordings of historical importance, where their expertise can be of great interest. In general, jazz historians are more involved in such work than theorists.

The difference between theorists and historians in jazz strongly recalls an alignment in the study of Western concert music where theorists and composers, with their shared interests in musical structure, have often been one and the same. Indeed, almost all music theory before the twentieth century seems to have been written by active, practicing musicians. Is it possible, then, that jazz theorists, as our ranks continue to grow, will largely be drawn from musicians themselves? As will be noted below, much notable jazz theory, from at least the 1950s to the present, has been produced by musicians, so the analogy with theorists of Western concert music so far seems to be borne out. Jazz historians, on the other hand, are less likely to be practicing musicians. Instead, they have often seen themselves aligned with historians and scholars of other disciplines—again, like their counterparts studying Western concert music.

A somewhat more distinct group of scholars studying jazz consists of ethnomusicologists, who, more generally, have traditionally focused on the study of non-Western musical cultures. I write "cultures" because ethnomusicologists have largely seen their discipline as in partnership with anthropology. Ethnomusicologists in recent years have been studying jazz as well (not to mention other Western musics) and have produced very fine work, some of which is of great relevance to jazz theory. Indeed, an ethnomusicological point of view has been quite common in much recent jazz scholarly writing.

One characteristic of the ethnomusicological approach that usually distinguishes it from other kinds of writing on jazz is that it tends to avoid critical judgments of either artists or music. This can be seen as deriving from an anthropological desideratum that cultural description be "objective," not tinged by evaluation that may be inappropriate for an outside observer. It remains to be seen whether these jazz ethnomusicologists remain more comfortable in the anthropologists' camp, with their cultural concerns; aligned with musicologists and their emphasis on historical process; or with theorists and their more technical models of musical structure. Theorists themselves profit from ethnomusicological work whenever its descriptions of cultural behavior enlighten the specific rules of music making.

Again, in parallel to recent events in musicology and general music theory, the dramatic rise in jazz theoretical studies in recent years has triggered a counter-response from humanistically inclined scholars investigating jazz from other viewpoints. These writers have suggested that, historically, jazz criticism—by which they mean to include theoretical work—has been excessively concerned with the music simply as music and has not shown sufficient attention to the social processes and tensions involved in the production of jazz or in its relationships to other disciplines.

While it is not pertinent to this essay to engage in a broad defense of music theory, it comes as a surprise to many of us to find the study of jazz as centered on the music itself under attack.[2] If nothing else, I would like to point out that what leads most listeners and players to jazz *is* its music, not its connections to other disciplines. This is not to say that the social, historical, commercial, and other issues, are unrelated to what forms the music takes and how it functions. They are extremely critical to a fuller understanding of jazz as a product of Western cultural history. As such, we look forward to any studies that shed new light on the many controversies that have involved jazz since its inception. To paraphrase a familiar quotation, the house of jazz is large and has many mansions.

But we should never neglect what brought us to jazz itself: the music, and our emotional and aesthetic response to it. Theorists do not spurn the larger-scale issues; they simply prefer applying their expertise: attempting to fathom what is happening sonically, to the extent that it can be pinned down. To that end, we welcome the continuing increase in the activity of jazz theorists—whether they be active musicians, scholars from the academy, or both—and hope that they will continue to pursue a closer scrutiny of how jazz *works* as music.

II. EARLY JAZZ THEORY

The development of jazz theory has sometimes been considered a modern phenomenon, stemming perhaps from the 1950s—that key juncture when jazz itself was evolving from a mainstay of popular culture into a music with an artistic conscience. But a music theory does not spring into existence ex nihilo; a given musical style in any culture presupposes a set of rules that lets the music cohere—that lets the style be defined as a style—even if the theory is not designated as such and even if the musicians are unaware of what they have internalized. For example, many writers on the origins of jazz have granted critical formative influence to legendary musicians who played by "ear," without recourse even to written music, much less codified theory. But as all musics have rules, so there must have been a theory to the earliest jazz. Indeed these folk pioneers engaged in theoretical behavior by learning to play within the context of an oral tradition. Working by ear, they would pick out chords at the piano, experiment with the effect of various melodies and patterns over them, and later, after the rise of recording technology, copy solos from records. A skillful player could internalize much theory and then reproduce it in the music without necessarily being aware of doing so.

Thus, players who play "by ear" are not without theory, a claim seemingly at odds with the definitions listed above, all of which refer to cognitive models of music. "Ear training," to be sure, is pedagogical theory, so that a player "with good ears" has, in a sense, internalized that theory, though it may be unarticulated. For example, a jazz musician who "hears" and can play the changes of a blues, but knows nothing of functional harmony, would not understand a reference to the "subdominant in the fifth bar" despite being able to play the effect of the chord change. This player, then, "knows" or—perhaps better—"hears" the theory, but is unable to present this knowledge verbally. To put it another way, it can be argued that in learning to play by ear, a player internalizes rules in the broad sense, but does not learn terms or engage in the linguistic conventions commonly associated with those rules. Nor can such a player develop speculative models to extend musical ideas beyond what can be heard informally.

Recent scholarship has questioned the extent of aural culture's formative relationship to early jazz, since many of the pioneering musicians did have considerable instruction in the European tradition (Jelly Roll Morton, et al.). Such musicians would have applied whatever European music theory they knew to the music slowly metamorphosing into "jazz." Early jazz arranger-composers, such as Morton, Henderson, Challis, or Ellington, surely knew European "form and harmony" at varying levels of sophistication. And some important players not involved in arranging, such as Louis Armstrong, were literate enough to supply lead sheets of jazz compositions for copyright purposes. Whether such theoretical knowledge was "studied" or "picked up" is irrelevant.

Nevertheless, despite acknowledging that intuitive players have hands-on theoretical awareness, structural models of music constitute what we normally designate as theory. Because pianists, guitarists, and banjoists have traditionally been responsible for the harmonic underpinning of the jazz performance, it was necessary for them early on to identify chords. The talented horn player "with good ears" could get away with less solid grounding. So the earliest form of jazz theory was simply the study of European harmony, the formal backbone of jazz. After learning to read music, spelling and identifying chords were surely the most common forms of theory in early jazz. Investigation as to what important early jazz players studied or acquired informally in the way of European harmony would take us beyond the scope of this essay.

As noted above, we can simplify discussion of the subsequent genesis of cognitive jazz theory by separating the topic into the pedagogical, the speculative, and the analytical. Since the 1960s these three streams have intersected often.

III. PEDAGOGICAL AND SPECULATIVE JAZZ THEORY

As noted above, harmony generally directs the jazz musician's first forays into theory outside, perhaps, of reading music and learning basic scales. (And these latter, it can be argued, are necessary for the mastery of the player's instrument and so precede a study of theory qua theory.) Spelling chords and learning to identify the harmonic implications of musical passages continue to form the pedagogical bedrock of jazz education. Since harmony provides the basis of jazz theory, and since the harmony of jazz has been derived from the European tradition, it seems clear that early jazz musicians learned or acquired European harmony and adapted it to the conditions of playing jazz. This approach seems in line with the derivation of much early jazz from ragtime and the marching band–dance band repertory.

Improvisation in the jazz styles of the 1920s and 1930s was fairly dependent on arpeggiation. This is what would be expected of a style that was diatonically based and rooted in its usages on European harmony. Of course, the extent of the arpeggiation depended on the instrument, occurring more often, say, on piano or clarinet, and less on trumpet and trombone. Deviations from arpeggiation could be heard in the blues, which was more linear and modally based than the circle-of-fifths dependency of jazz as applied to the popular song. The more nonfunctional basis of the blues surely derived from its being closer to its African origins, where harmony in the European sense was not a factor in the music's structure. Indeed, the tension between the form and harmony of the European tradition and the linear, rhythmic focus of African music was perhaps a key to the foundation of jazz.

With books on improvisation decades away, most aspiring players learned how to improvise by ear. Yet there were some "transcriptions" available early on, for example, Louis Armstrong's *50 Hot Choruses for Cornet* and *125 Jazz Breaks for Cornet,*[3] from 1927. These may have been improvised by Armstrong for the company itself, since they were not transcriptions of his extant recordings. It is also possible that staff writers simply created solos in Armstrong's style. Nevertheless, the publisher was clearly satisfying a demand from players who wished to emulate Armstrong and could read music. Melrose followed up with books of transcriptions by other players. Throughout the 1930s and 1940s, transcription books continued to appear, while some periodicals, such as *Down Beat,* began to publish them to enhance their appeal to professional players. Thus improvisation before the 1950s was based on learning licks or complete solos from records, acquiring a knowledge of harmony, and, less commonly, using published transcriptions as guides. Today, these pedagogical methods remain as popular as ever.

Beginning in the 1950s, other pedagogical materials began to appear, partly as a result of the evolution of jazz style. The more linear approaches of the younger jazz players—beginning, arguably, with Lester Young and continuing through the beboppers—precipitated an approach to improvisation that relied less on the arpeggio. Not only was bebop more linear, but the modal and "cool" jazz styles of the 1950s eschewed arpeggiation in favor of more scalar melodic lines. Further, the gradual acquisition of fine-art status by at least some of these jazz substyles created an atmosphere in which the introduction of written materials seemed a natural consequence.

As gradually became clear to the theorists of early modern jazz, the essential note-choice problem for any improvising player is this: if a given harmony defines a passage, what notes, in addition to the ones of

the chord, are melodically compatible with that chord and are stylistically appropriate? In 1953, the first work of decided theoretical sophistication to tackle this problem head-on was published, *The Lydian Chromatic Concept of Tonal Organization for Improvisation* by George
Russell.[4] This landmark volume established the concept of chord-scale
theory in jazz composition and improvisation. Its decided twist was that
it was based on a unusual system of relationships between chords and
families of Lydian scales. This distinctive, and still controversial, approach stamped the method as more than pedagogical: it was the first
work of speculative jazz theory.

The second important work based on chord-scale theory appeared in
1959, John Mehegan's *Jazz Improvisation:* Volume 1: *Tonal and Rhythmic Principles;* the remaining volumes in the series soon followed as
Volume 2: *Jazz Rhythm and the Improvised Line* (1962); Volume 3:
Swing and Early Progressive Piano Styles (1964); and Volume 4: *Contemporary Piano Styles* (1965).[5] The first volume of the series featured
a short preface by Leonard Bernstein, who at the time was well known
not only as conductor, composer, and pianist, but also as a musician vi-
tally interested in jazz and theater music. Bernstein's comments clearly
showed the evolution of the status of jazz in the 1950s: not only was the
music becoming more respectable, but its theoretical study, as recom-
mended by Bernstein, was also fully sanctioned.

The Mehegan series codified much of what is now taken for granted
in jazz theory. In the first volume, for example, Mehegan designated seventh chords as normative (11), insisted on Roman numeral designation
to simplify description of function (11), located the five now-standard
seventh-chord qualities (25), described the now-standard seven diatonic
modes (81), and related chord type to various scales and modes (84–98)
in ways that still underlie much jazz theory. Volume 2 was useful for its
transcriptions, which together displayed a cumulative history of the jazz
line. Volumes 3 and 4 extended the harmonic principles and, otherwise,
contained much that was helpful to pianists trying to develop individual
styles. It is perhaps not unfair to say that while some may disagree with
much of Mehegan's work, or feel that its theory is dated or could be more
cogently described, there was still so much that has been adopted that its
influence has perhaps been decisive.

Thus, while *The Lydian Chromatic Concept* had its admirers, it was
the Mehegan series that set the stage and defined the terms for the pedagogical jazz works to follow. While this is not the place to go into an extensive comparison of these materials, a few early landmarks should be

listed, since in the 1960s and 1970s their numbers expanded enormously. Jerry Coker's *Improvising Jazz* (1964),[6] though brief, had much in common with Mehegan's four-volume study. An extensive series of monographs, *Reihe Jazz,* on various aspects of jazz theory were published by Universal Edition under the editorship of Joe Viera in the early 1970s.[7] Also of significance were the David Baker volumes, *Jazz Improvisation*[8] and *Advanced Improvisation,*[9] which extended chord-scale theory considerably; indeed, the second volume contained much material that could be thought of as speculative.

No discussion of pedagogical work in jazz can leave unmentioned the popular "play-along" methods. While there was material along jazz lines issued in the 1950s and early 1960s,[10] these methods became very popular in the late 1960s and 1970s when the field was taken up and creatively expanded by Jamey Aebersold.[11] With dozens of recordings currently available, play-along methods are now well established among student musicians.

It is probably not coincidental that the increase in pedagogical materials, begun in the late 1950s and vastly extended in the 1960s and 1970s, coincided with the establishment of college-level jazz programs. Among the pioneers were the University of North Texas, the Lenox School of Jazz, Indiana University, Rutgers University, the Berklee College of Music, and the University of Massachusetts at Amherst. Andrew Jaffe, a writer associated with the latter two schools, contributed what is probably the first theoretical text intended for college classroom use, *Jazz Theory,* in 1983.[12] In 1984 the first college text for classes on improvisation appeared: Benward and Wildman's *Jazz Improvisation in Theory and Practice.*[13] By the 1990s, programs of jazz studies, often leading to degrees, were to be found in many universities and conservatories throughout the world.

In keeping with the increase in college-level jazz teaching, the National Association of Jazz Educators (now renamed as the International Association of Jazz Educators) was founded in 1968. By 1993, the numerous offerings of jazz education led to the formation of a complementary professional group, the International Association of Schools of Jazz, which by its very existence documented that jazz education had expanded well beyond the United States. Serious university-level study of jazz, both in the United States and throughout the world, is increasing. In most college programs, the core of the theory curriculum is pedagogical, while analytical and speculative studies, which require greater theoretical acumen, are usually among the electives.

IV. ANALYTICAL JAZZ THEORY

Analytical jazz theory is a more recent phenomenon. As defined above, this approach to theory is descriptive and often critical, the music studied as an end in itself rather than as a guide to performance or composition.[14] In many cases analytical and speculative jazz theory overlap and most assuredly inform the other, but the first order of business in analytical theory is to provide deeper readings of the music or artists in question through ways that the analyst finds cogent. These often extend beyond pedagogical or performance-oriented insights, since, by the nature of pedagogy itself, those insights must be immediately applicable by the improvising player or composer. In analysis, on the other hand, much of "what's there" in the music is beyond the conscious intention of the musicians; the analyst instead aims to show how the music works in and of itself.

Appearing early on in jazz history, one work stood head and shoulders above the rest in its attention to musical detail and analytical depth, Winthrop Sargeant's *Jazz, Hot and Hybrid,* of 1938.[15] Sargeant was among the first to note that jazz in the late 1920s was influenced by "barbershop harmony" in which "[voice-leading] movement is by chromatic half-steps. Seventh- and ninth-chords are as common as, if not more common than, triads" (198). Further, "In jazz harmonization one can say that the seventh- or ninth-chord is the rule; the triad the exception" (202).

After Sargeant, there was really not much in the way of jazz analytical study for almost two decades.[16] Despite the emergence and rapid growth of jazz criticism, most of the material produced was not especially useful in terms of explicating musical structure. Yet André Hodeir's fine book, *Jazz, Its Evolution and Essence,*[17] first published in English in 1956—while largely a critical rather than analytical study—had a major impact on the world of jazz scholarship. In addition to helping define the canon of great jazz recordings, it also included enough musical discussion of specific pieces to focus attention on the fact that jazz was ripe for more sophisticated theoretical and analytical investigation. It may be the case that the next important analytical work on jazz, by Gunther Schuller, owed much to Hodeir's inspiration. Schuller's famous essay "Sonny Rollins and the Challenge of Thematic Improvisation," written in November 1958, for the first issue of the *Jazz Review,*[18] was possibly the first piece of jazz writing to analyze a work in musical detail for the sole purpose of showing its structural depth and, by implication, the depth of fine jazz improvisation more generally.

In 1968 Schuller continued his pioneering work with the important publication of *Early Jazz, Its Roots and Development*.[19] This volume, the first in what is intended as a multivolume jazz history, contained much musical analysis and specific study and transcription of individual pieces and improvisations. *The Swing Era,* Schuller's second volume, which appeared in 1989,[20] continued the musical exegeses of specific pieces, players, bands, and arrangers. While Schuller has been criticized for concentrating on recordings to the exclusion of other issues of historical import, he is, after all, one of the most prominent composer-conductors of our time; it is surely preferable that he write on musically germane issues than be sidetracked to more general topics. While there is much in these large books that can be contested, so many genuine musical insights animate the discussion that Schuller's comments offer a valuable first recourse to anyone investigating the jazz of these periods from music-analytical perspectives.

Beginning in the 1970s, jazz theory expanded into the academy at the doctoral level with two important breakthroughs, written virtually at the same time and illustrating, in a nutshell, what we might call the macroscopic-microscopic gamut often seen in music-theoretical work. The macroscopic principle, examining a large body of music for general conclusions, was illustrated by Thomas Owens's 1974 doctoral dissertation, "Charlie Parker: Techniques of Improvisation."[21] This two-volume work transcribed and analyzed hundreds of Parker solos in order to demonstrate Parker's use of melodic formula. For a work delineating the function of formula in jazz improvisation, it has not been surpassed. The theoretical microcosm, analyzing a smaller body of material in greater detail, was demonstrated in Milton Stewart's dissertation on Clifford Brown's "I Can Dream, Can't I?"[22] Stewart, using a Schenkerian-based analytical method, concentrated on a single solo and tellingly revealed the depth of Brown's improvisational invention. These two fine dissertations helped jazz scholarship make serious inroads into the academy, so that by the 1980s it was thoroughly accepted as a legitimate specialization in musical research. As a result, doctoral dissertations on jazz theory (and other aspects of jazz research) began to appear with greater regularity.[23]

The rapidly rising interest in jazz scholarship led to the foundation, in the late 1960s and early 1970s, of the two principal journals of jazz research. First, in 1969, was *Jazzforschung (Jazz Research),*[24] which in its first issue contained a short preface by the eminent musicologist Hellmut Federhofer pointing out, almost grudgingly, that an understanding of the role of jazz was essential to any comprehensive overview of twentieth century music. This first issue of *Jazzforschung* began a tradition of offering articles of a music-theoretical nature as well as work documenting numerous approaches to jazz research, including the ethnomusicological.

Shortly after the foundation of *Jazzforschung,* the *Journal of Jazz Studies,* the forerunner of the present *Annual Review of Jazz Studies,* began publication[25] in 1973. Beginning in 1974, articles of a analytical nature[26] began to appear in the *Journal of Jazz Studies.* The establishment of the general theoretical journal *In Theory Only* at the University of Michigan in 1973 was significant in that editorial policy encouraged articles on jazz. Since that breakthrough by a general interest music journal, many scholarly music journals now occasionally publish articles of interest to jazz theorists.[27]

With dissertations and scholarly articles on topics of relevance to jazz theory no longer rare, it might be expected that analytical studies of jazz artists and music should be widely available.[28] Such is not the case, however, at least with respect to book-length studies; and this lacuna is probably symptomatic of the general scarcity of music-analytical studies in any genre.[29] Thus, among the few studies available devoted principally to analysis are Ken Rattenbury's *Duke Ellington, Jazz Composer* (1990),[30] Paul Berliner's *Thinking in Jazz: The Infinite Art of Improvisation* (1994),[31] and Henry Martin's *Charlie Parker and Thematic Improvisation* (1996).[32]

V. JAZZ THEORY AND THE FUTURE

Let me conclude this overview of jazz theory by pointing out that we are fortunate to be working at a time when the field is young and interest is growing. Jazz theory has been around long enough to establish a presence, but not so long that the mine's most promising veins have been exhausted. In this respect, while there is much to be done and much to be desired, the situation is far more positive than negative. I expect jazz theory in the future largely to follow the three main genres established in past work, the pedagogical, speculative, and analytical.

With respect to pedagogy, a serious study of the numerous instructional materials available should be undertaken. The amount of material is staggering, extending back to the Melrose transcriptions noted above. A cursory search of the computer catalog of the Performing Arts Library at Lincoln Center yielded almost 100 works—and I merely entered "jazz instruction" as keywords. Further, this incomplete listing contained items mostly from the 1970s and later. Cogent organization and evaluation of this material would be very welcome.

Yet, while there is no shortage of pedagogical material, its quality needs to be upgraded. In the area of general theory, for example, there is very little that is much more sophisticated than the Mehegan series from the early 1960s. Perhaps the time is ripe for the pedagogical expertise developed over the past centuries in European music to be adapted to the special needs of jazz education.

Speculative jazz theory is in a curious state. As one thinks back through history, it becomes clear that the Golden Age of speculative theory was the 1950s and 1960s, for that was when actual, well-articulated ideas shaped performance and experiment within the jazz and allied traditions. For example, Russell's Lydian Chromatic Concept affected much jazz at the time, as did the "third stream" movement. One is hard pressed to think of any creative thought in music theory having as much power in jazz since. Perhaps this is because musicians nowadays prefer putting their ideas directly into practice—one thinks of Ornette Coleman's harmolodics—rather than publishing material about them.[33] Or perhaps there is currently such a plethora of speculative ideas on musical composition and performance that none of them has been able to win the recognition enjoyed by the Lydian Chromatic Concept. In the 1950s Russell, quite simply, had the field to himself.

In any event, I think jazz musicians might welcome new ideas about how to conceive of their music, both as improvisation and composition. For example, we are all aware of an influential group of musicians and theorists who for decades now have been immersed in the 12-tone method and its ramifications, and who continually suggest new modes of musical organization to each other. They have established a formidable body of work, a basis for many twentieth-century compositions. We could use something of this in jazz and its related musical practices: there has been no sense of jazz theory "advancing" in any sense comparable to 12-tone theory in concert music.[34]

There is especially great opportunity for growth and improvement in jazz analysis. It is only within recent years that scholars have begun to apply analytical techniques long established in concert music to jazz. And, further, we need to develop analytical tools unique to various jazz styles.[35] Yet, despite the importance of refining analytical methods, what the field most urgently needs is more articles or books discussing in musical detail either specific musicians, stylistic periods, or bodies of repertory. As for analytical studies of musicians or repertories, the field is virtually wide-open.

It is a hallmark of musical scholarship in our time that both European tonal theory and 12-tone theory have grown more sophisticated throughout the twentieth century. The development of the former is owed mostly to the work of Schenker, who, interestingly, influenced theorists far more in the second half of the century than in his own time. For the latter, the fountainhead was Schoenberg initially, thereafter Babbitt and, in Europe, Boulez. We need to start building such bodies of work in jazz theory. The candidate for the central focus of tonal jazz theory is bebop, comparable in stature in jazz to the Classical era in common-practice European music.[36] Nontonal jazz has mostly been associated with free jazz, where there is excellent opportunity to profit by earlier work on atonal concert music.[37] But again, there is much to be done in virtually all styles of jazz; what is most urgently needed is a sense of continuity in the field.

And finally, we need to have a clearer, wiser sense of jazz more broadly conceived, how its aesthetic differs from the European and African, and how we should relate to it within the broader cultures of Western music on the one hand and other world musics on the other. While these issues invite input from various intellectual disciplines, there are many questions that jazz theorists are especially well qualified to ponder. What is the nature of jazz composition? For one thing, since a jazz composition may change radically over time, unlike, say, a Brahms symphony, we may need to redefine the idea of "composition." Our concept of a composer derives from the European tradition, especially the Romantic image of the powerful Beethoven-like figure as sole creator. Does a jazz composer fit such a mold? How does the practice of solo duplication common in early jazz change our view of the necessity of improvisation in jazz performance, a concept which, perhaps, derives more from modern practice than from a larger-scale view? What has been the precise effect of recording, given that jazz is the first major branch of Western music with a virtually complete sonic representation? It has been long established that complex blends of the African and European traditions created jazz. To justify this more exactly, can we pinpoint specific examples in the music of each?

I could go on, but I think the point is made: we have accomplished much, but the field is young enough that there remains much yet to be done. It is a promising sign of the times that the study of jazz both as music and cultural phenomenon continues to flourish. I am confident we can look forward to jazz theory playing a vital role in the vigorous and welcome expansion of all areas of jazz scholarship.

NOTES

1. I would like to thank Lewis Porter and Robert Sadin for useful comments on a previous draft of this article.
2. Nor, if jazz criticism since the 1920s is examined in detail, would I suspect that most would feel it discusses the music excessively. If anything, impressionistic, biographical, and anecdotal work would seem to dominate jazz writing.
3. Chicago: Melrose Brothers.
4. New York: Concept, 2nd ed., 1959.
5. New York: Watson-Guptill.
6. Englewood Cliffs, New Jersey: Prentice-Hall.
7. Viera, Joe, et al., *Reihe Jazz.* Vol. 1: *Grundlagen der Jazzrhythmik* (1970); vol. 2: *Grundlagen der Jazzharmonik* (1970); vol. 3: *Arrangement und Improvisation* (1971); vol. 4: *Das Schlagzeug im Jazz* (1971); vol. 5: *Die Posaune im Jazz* (1972); vol. 6: *Band Clinic I* (1973); vol. 7: *Der Free Jazz—Formen und Modelle* (1974). Wien: Universal Edition.
8. Chicago: Maher, 1969.
9. Chicago: Maher, 1974.
10. I own a recording called *Evolution of the Blues* (Music Minus One MMO 1008), with no date given but probably issued around 1964. The featured musicians are Clark Terry, Bob Wilber, Dick Wellstood, George Duvivier, and Panama Francis.
11. The Aebersold series began in 1967 with *A New Approach to Jazz Improvisation,* first published by Jamey Aebersold (New Albany, Indiana).
12. Dubuque, Iowa: Wm. C. Brown.
13. Dubuque, Iowa: Wm. C. Brown.
14. The rise in interest in jazz theory parallels the increasing activity in jazz scholarship more generally. From our vantage point in the late 1990s, it is reassuring to find that the lamentable state of jazz scholarship, noted by James Patrick in the first issue of *The Journal of Jazz Studies*— "Discography as a Tool for Musical Research and Vice Versa" (October 1973): 65–81—has improved greatly during the intervening years.
15. New York: E. P. Dutton, republished and expanded in 1946. The following page citations are from the 3rd ed. (reprinted, New York: Da Capo, 1975).

16. An exception is the Waterman article noted below.
17. Originally published as *Hommes et Problèmes du Jazz* (Paris: Au Portulan, chez Flammarion, 1954); rev. ed., trans. David Noakes (New York: Grove, 1979).
18. Reprinted in a collection of essays by Schuller: *Musings* (New York and Oxford: Oxford University Press, 1986).
19. New York and Oxford: Oxford University Press.
20. New York and Oxford: Oxford University Press.
21. University of California, Los Angeles.
22. Published in *Jazzforschung* [*Jazz Research*] 6/7, 1974–75.
23. A sampling: Theodore Brown's "A History and Analysis of Jazz Drumming to 1942" (University of Michigan, 1976), Henry Martin's "Jazz Harmony," (Princeton University, 1980), Carol Heen's "Procedures for Style Analysis of Jazz: A Beginning Approach (University of Minnesota, 1981), J. Kent Williams's "Themes Composed by Jazz Musicians of the Bebop Era" (Indiana University, 1982), Gregory Smith's "Homer, Gregory, and Bill Evans?" (Harvard University, 1983), Steven Larson's "Schenkerian Analysis of Modern Jazz" (University of Michigan, 1987), and Paula Berardinelli's "Bill Evans: His Contributions as a Jazz Pianist and An Analysis of His Musical Style" (New York University, 1992).
24. Published at the Hochschule für Musik in Graz, Austria.
25. Under the auspices of the Institute of Jazz Studies at Rutgers University in Newark.
26. Specifically, Lawrence Koch's "Ornithology: A Study of Charlie Parker's Music (Part One)," *Journal of Jazz Studies* 2/1 (December 1974): 61–87.
27. Curiously, an article of jazz-theoretical interest appeared in the inaugural issue of *The Journal of the American Musicological Society,* Richard A. Waterman's "'Hot' Rhythm in Negro Music" (1/1 [Spring, 1948]: 24–37). Unfortunately, there was no follow-up work on jazz for many years to come. Perhaps the next article of a jazz-theoretical nature appearing in a prestigious scholarly music publication was Frank Tirro's "The Silent Theme Tradition in Jazz" *(Musical Quarterly,* 53/3 [July, 1967]: 313–34).
28. In addition to Gunther Schuller, discussed above, books by such jazz historians as James Patrick, Frank Tirro, Scott DeVeaux, Lawrence Gushee, Max Harrison, or Lewis Porter will often contain analytical sections of exceptional interest and insight.
29. Two possible reasons for their scarcity: first, the analytical material

is often better concentrated in an article, and, second—in marked contrast to the situation with pedagogy—there is not much of a market for analytical books.

30. London and New Haven: Yale University Press.

31. Chicago and London: University of Chicago Press. While this extensive ethnomusicological study would not normally be thought of as "analytical," it features many sections of utmost importance to jazz theorists.

32. Lanham, Maryland: Scarecrow Press. This volume is the first music-analytical work to appear in the series *Studies in Jazz,* published by The Institute of Jazz Studies, Rutgers University, Newark, New Jersey, in conjunction with Scarecrow Press.

33. Coleman, reportedly, has been preparing a book on harmolodics.

34. To clarify this further: I am not suggesting that 12-tone theory must be applied to jazz, but merely pointing out that it has increased in sophistication in the last several decades. It is this sense of *growth* in jazz theory—in any of its aspects—that would be welcome.

35. See, for example, Gary Potter's "Analyzing Improvised Jazz," *College Music Symposium* 30, no. 1 (spring 1990): 64–74.

36. See, for example, Steven Strunk's "Early Bop Harmony," *Journal of Jazz Studies* 6, no. 1 (fall/winter 1979): 4–53, Strunk's "Bebop Melodic Lines: Tonal Characteristics," *Annual Review of Jazz Studies* 3 (1985): 97–120, and J. Kent Williams's "Archetypal Schemata in Jazz Themes of the Bebop Era," *Annual Review of Jazz Studies* 4 (1988): 49–74.

37. For pitch relationships in post-tonal jazz styles, a promising start has been made by Steven Block with his articles "Pitch-Class Transformation in Free Jazz," *Music Theory Spectrum* 12, no. 2 (fall 1990): 181–202, and "Organized Sound: Pitch-Class Relations in the Music of Ornette Coleman," *Annual Review of Jazz Studies* 6 (1993): 229–52.

BLURRING THE BARLINE: METRIC DISPLACEMENT IN THE PIANO SOLOS OF HERBIE HANCOCK

Keith Waters

Traditionally, the 12-bar blues and 32-bar song form have been the standard vehicles for the jazz improviser. Since their circularity makes acute the problem of redundancy, jazz soloists have often sought techniques to camouflage the harmonic and rhythmic regularity of the formal structure. While jazz pedagogy and the critical literature normally focus upon the harmonic dimension—often harmonic substitution—perhaps equally crucial for extended improvisations are the rhythmic techniques that obscure the barline, as well as 4-bar, 8-bar, and other formal divisions.

One high point of metric sophistication and subtlety within the traditional jazz framework may be found in the piano solos of Herbie Hancock, especially during his tenure as pianist with the Miles Davis Quintet and as a leader during the 1960s. In an interview in the September 1994 issue of *Jazz Magazine,* Hancock cited rhythmic displacement and accent as the primary force in his improvisations of that period, attempting, in his words, "to displace the accents and avoid rhythmic cliche."[1]

Hancock joined the seminal Miles Davis Quintet in 1963 at the age of twenty-three and remained for five years, recording both with Davis's quintet and under his own name during this time. This period produced a number of significant recordings, including Davis's *My Funny Valentine, Four and More, ESP, Nefertiti, Miles Smiles,* and Hancock's *Maiden Voyage, Empyrean Isles,* and *Speaks Like a Child.* Within the format of the 32-bar standard tune and 12-bar blues form, Davis's rhythm section sought a freer role for itself through the use of polymeter, metric shifts, as well as through sophisticated techniques of harmonic substitution. Critic Bill Dobbins writes:

(W)orking with the double bass player Ron Carter and the drummer Tony Williams, Hancock helped revolutionize traditional jazz concepts of the rhythm section and its relation to the soloists. He built on the earlier de-velopments of such diverse groups as Bill Evans's trio and Ornette Cole-man's quartet, and established a musical rapport with an extraordinary de-gree of freedom and interaction.[2]

This study takes as a point of departure rhythmic theories and analyt-ical techniques current in music-theoretical literature. Following a sum-mary of these theories and some general observations about Hancock's rhythmic strategies, the paper examines a transcription of the piano solo in the composition "The Eye of the Hurricane," a 12-bar blues in F mi-nor. The composition is from Hancock's 1965 album *Maiden Voyage;* Hancock is accompanied by Ron Carter on bass and Tony Williams on drums. Characteristically, Hancock keeps intact the eighth-note lan-guage of bebop, yet his solo develops a variety of subtle and supple met-ric displacement techniques which mask the metric and formal circular-ity of the 12-bar form. Characteristic, too, is Hancock's consistently inventive harmonic and melodic language: while the analysis focuses primarily upon strategies of metric displacement, we will observe how pitch and harmonic events operate in tandem with these displacement techniques.

CRITICAL LITERATURE: JAZZ AND RHYTHMIC THEORY

Outside of the oral tradition, the theoretical content of jazz has until re-cently been disseminated primarily through pedagogical means. The prac-tical manuals and instruction books for improvisers are primarily pitch-oriented, often focusing on scales and principles of harmonic substitution. A number of theoretical and analytical studies of jazz have appeared within the last fifteen years, yet many of these likewise maintain a pitch orienta-tion. Several studies are indebted to established analytical techniques, and adopt a Schenkerian model to uncover and examine long-range linear con-nections in jazz solos and compositions,[3] use reductive techniques to evince linear pitch connections beneath the surface of the music,[4] or apply pitch-class set analysis to demonstrate structural coherence.[5]

Polyrhythm

One study that examines jazz solos from a rhythmic standpoint is Cyn-thia Folio's "An Analysis of Polyrhythm in Selected Improvised Jazz

Solos."[6] In solos of Thelonious Monk, Ornette Coleman, and Eric Dolphy, Folio points out a number of polymetric passages in which the soloist stratifies a conflicting meter above the primary meter of the rhythm section. The resultant rhythmic conflicts provide a device for generating musical tension and interest. Folio also raises a number of important questions regarding the perception of two or more simultaneous metric strands.

Accentual Structure

Similarly, recent literature on rhythm in tonal music of the common practice period addresses the notion of rhythmic interest articulated by conflicts with the regular meter. While the meter of a composition asserts a hierarchy of strong and weak beats within each measure,[7] the rhythmic vitality of a composition may result from the accents which do *not* coincide with the strong beats of the metric hierarchy. Thus, those accents that emphasize metrically weak beats engage in a conflict with the strong-weak metric patterning maintained by the listener.

Louder volume—dynamic accent—creates one type of accent; nevertheless, other factors may also contribute to the perception of accent. Joel Lester's *The Rhythms of Tonal Music*[8] enumerates qualities of accent that may challenge and compete with, but not necessarily override, a prevailing meter. From Lester's list of accentual types, we may cite durational accent, contour accent, pattern beginning, as well as dynamic accent. Example 1 provides examples for each. Durational accent accrues to a pitch which is longer in duration than other surrounding pitches; contour accent refers to pitches which occur at the upper or lower registral extreme of a melodic gesture. Pattern beginning attracts accent at the initiation of a repeated motivic pattern and, finally, louder volume effects dynamic accent. Note that each accent occurs on the weaker second (and, sometimes, fourth) beat of the measure, creating a conflict with the stronger metric beats.

Example 1: Types of Accent

Grouping and Meter

In addition to accentual structure, writers have described other types of conflicts with meter. Lerdahl and Jackendoff's *A Generative Theory of Tonal Music*[9] defines two constituents of rhythmic organization, metric structure and grouping structure. Metric structure refers to the regular patterning of strong and weak beats of the metric hierarchy. Grouping structure, on the other hand, is determined by the begin- and endpoints of the melodic events which are "overlaid" upon the meter.

Grouping structure may corroborate or contradict the metric structure. For example, a melody beginning on a metric downbeat aligns with the meter: the authors describe this relationship between grouping and meter as being "in phase." However, a melody which begins with an anacrusis does not align with the metric downbeat: grouping structure and metric structure are now said to be "out of phase."

Hypermeter

Lerdahl and Jackendoff and others have advanced the thesis that a metric hierarchy upholds at higher levels, and may be conceptually if not literally regular in larger parcels of four, eight, sixteen or more measures.[10] Thus the Strong-Weak-Strong-Weak metric patternings of the 4/4 measure inflate to larger levels: at a 4-measure level the downbeats of the first and third measures receive greater metric weight than downbeats of the second and fourth measures; at an 8-measure level the downbeats of the first and fifth measure are strong in relation to the downbeats of the weaker third and seventh measures.

This can be displayed through a durational reduction, which may show hypermeter at differing hierarchical levels. Example 2 shows durational reductions at two levels for the repeating 32-measure form of the AABA standard tune. In 2a, the 8-measure level is visually reduced to a single measure, called a *hypermeasure*. Therefore each two-measure group is represented in the reduction by a single beat, called a *hyperbeat*. At this level, then, the first and third hyperbeats receive a stronger metrical accent than the second and fourth. The 32-measure form is represented in the reduction by four repeating measures. In 2b, on the other hand, the *entire* 32-measure form is represented by a single repeating hypermeasure: each 8-measure segment therefore is represented by one hyperbeat. Again, the first and third hyperbeat attract a stronger accent than the second and fourth.

2a: 8 measures = one hypermeasure

2b: 32 measures = one hypermeasure

Example 2: Durational reduction for 32-bar standard

For analysis of jazz, hypermeter is an attractive construct. The notion represents clearly the larger formal divisions within the 32-bar standard tune form and the 12-bar blues. It is also a principle intuited by improvisers who articulate longer musical spans by providing a release point which gives stronger metrical weight to the larger divisions of the formal structure.[11]

The literature on rhythm provides a convenient starting point for jazz analysis, yet suggests the need to refine taxonomy and to examine more rigorously the conflicts between melodic events and regular meter. In what different ways does polymeter arise? What are the types of accentual shifts that challenge a regular meter? What are the different ways that grouping and meter may be out of phase? How high up the metric or hypermetric hierarchy can accentual displacement operate? The questions raised may be only partially answered by this discussion.

IMPROVISATIONAL AND COMPOSITIONAL STRATEGIES

Within the jazz idiom, the rhythm-section instruments (piano, bass, and drums) and the soloist often fill conventional and well-defined roles in establishing meter. Example 3 shows a typical rhythmic interplay of the instruments for a standard 4/4 context. The bass establishes quarter-note motion ("walking bass"), and the soloist, within the idiomatic norm, articulates eighth-note motion. As many writers and performers have noted, eighth notes in jazz performances are often performed unequally. One convention in medium tempos has on-the-beat eighth note lasting approximately twice as long as off-the-beat eighth notes, implying a

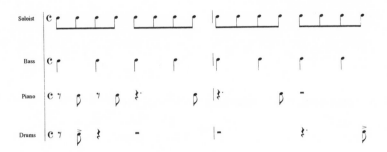

Example 3: Rhythm section and soloist

background metric grid of 12/8.[12] The piano accompaniment normally articulates the eighth-note level off the beat; the example here provides one possibility among many. Finally, the drums not only integrate all these previous levels but will often articulate (4-, 8-, 16-bar, and formal) hypermetric divisions through accenting the eighth note directly before or directly after that division, helping listeners orient themselves in the structure.

Soloists often seek ways to obscure the regularity of this metric grid, employing techniques such as playing over the barline or delayed resolution. A characteristic move of Hancock's involves the stratification of 3/4 over 4/4 through motivic patterning. Example 4 is taken from the solo in the composition "Oliloqui Valley" from Hancock's album *Empyrean Isles*. Note that the polymeter arises through four-note patterns cast in eighth-note triplets. In the example, the accents point out the repeated occurrences of the four-note motive. Interestingly, too, the 3/4 pattern is displaced from the metric downbeat, beginning on the second beat of the measure.

It may be useful to distinguish between two types of polymeter. The type given in Example 4 involves conflicting subdivisions of the notated measure. An abstract realization is given in Example 5a. We can refer to

Example 4: Polymeter in Oliloqui Valley

Example 5a: "Measure-preserving" polymeter

Example 5b: "Tactus-preserving" polymeter

this type of polymeter as "measure-preserving." Example 5b, in contrast, shows "tactus-preserving" polymeter which is brought about by conflicting groupings of the notated beat. While these two types of polymeter are related abstractly—the accentual patterns of Example 5b compose out in augmentation those of 5a—they are distinguished by their orientation in relation to the tactus and to the barline, composing out the rhythmic conflict at different levels of rhythmic/metric structure.[13]

At a higher metric level, some of Hancock's compositions from the mid-1960s exhibit hypermetric structure at odds with the traditional 8-bar patterning which underlies the 32-bar standard form. For example, the composition "One Finger Snap" from *Empyrean Isles* is a 20-measure composition, made up of *five* units of four bars each. During the statement of the melody, the rhythm section does not keep time until m. 5, imparting to the first four measures the sense of an extended upbeat, as represented in the durational reduction of Example 6a. The quadruple

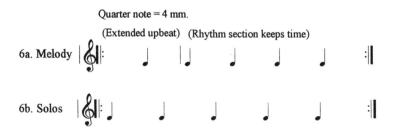

Example 6: Durational reduction of One Finger Snap

regularity of 6a is lost once the solos begin and the rhythm section keeps time throughout. As the durational reduction in Example 6b might imply, the "extra" hyperbeat during the solos often causes the listener or performer to perceive a formal return after the sixteenth bar, not after the twentieth. Thus, although a 4-bar regularity is preserved, its higher-level organization departs from the norm of the traditional jazz standard.

"THE EYE OF THE HURRICANE"

In contrast to the 8-measure units which make up the AABA 32-bar standard tune form, the 12-bar blues form is constructed from three units of four measures. The lyrics are normally distributed over the three 4-bar units in an AAB form. This 12-bar blues structure remains one of the most persevering and prevalent frameworks in the jazz tradition, and the solidity and regularity of the 12-bar form often allow the improviser to take a number of harmonic and metric liberties.

Hancock's solo in his 12-bar blues in F minor "The Eye of the Hurricane"[14] reveals a number of subtle and complex examples of metric displacement superimposed upon the metric regularity. Metric displacement occurs against the established meter on several levels. On the surface, there are three types of displacement: (1) shift of accent, (2) displaced motivic repetition, and (3) metric superimposition. As the solo develops in complexity, grouping and motivic correspondences generate displacement at higher hypermetric levels, even obscuring the hypermetric divisions at the level of the 12-bar form. Despite these displacements, however, the integrity of the 12-bar structure remains intact.

Accentual Shift

On one level, accentual shift is built into the jazz language: accents given to off-the-beat eighth notes do not disorient the listener familiar with the idiom. While this may often be the only level of displacement explored by jazz musicians, the potential for accentual displacement at higher levels is realized in Hancock's solo. These displacements often serve to obscure the perceived downbeat. Example 7 shows two abstract realizations of the first type of surface displacement, with arrows showing how accents might create this shift. Ex. 7a shows the emphasis shifted away from the downbeat to the third beat in 4/4 meter, hereafter called a "3-

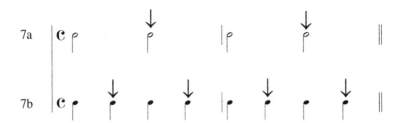

Example 7: Accentual shift
   7a: "3-Shift"
   7b: "2- and 4-Shift"

shift." Analogously, a shift of emphasis to the second and the fourth beat (Ex. 7b) will be referred to as a "2- and 4-shift."

In Hancock's solo, occurrences of these accentual shifts are not protracted. They often appear in consecutive pairs, allowing the soloist to shift in and out of metric focus.[15] The transcription shows how these displacements are realized at the beginning of the solo. The solo opens with 3-shift displacement in mm. 2 and 3, generated first by durational accent in m. 2 and then dynamic accent in m.3. The motive is then realigned with the meter in mm. 5 and 7. Durational accents subsequently create a 2- and 4-shift in m. 11.

These surface accentual shifts are prevalent throughout the solo. Measures 61–63, beginning the sixth chorus, provide another example of a 3-shift, effected through dynamic accent. These three consecutive accents serve to displace the perceived downbeat for the first three measures of the chorus. At m. 122, the transcription shows a 2- and 4-shift brought about by pattern repetition and contour accent, lasting for five consecutive accents between m. 122–124. The four-note pattern is then squared with the meter beginning in m. 125.

Displaced Motivic Repetition

The second type of surface displacement is displaced motivic repetition. Example 8 contains a rhythmically normalized version of the two motives at mm. 17–24. The example begins with a motive which recurs one bar later, transposed to reflect the change in harmony: first outlining the subdominant harmony, B♭ minor, then the tonic F minor. This is followed by

Example 8: Rhythmically normalized version of mm. 17–24

an octatonic-based motive which likewise recurs one bar later, transposed to reflect the change in harmony, progressing from V/V, G7, to V, C7. In comparing the sanitized Example 8 to the solo itself, which begins at m. 17 of the transcription, we see that the first motive and its transposition appear between mm. 17–19, beneath the dotted slurs. In contrast to Example 8, the transposed version at mm. 18–19 occurs five beats later. This rhythmic elasticity continues with the phrase immediately following in mm. 21–24. The dotted slurs show how the octatonic-based motive at the beginning of this phrase now returns six beats later, transposed.

In addition, the tail of the motive at m. 24 displays a double level of displacement of both harmony and meter. Example 9a–c shows the two levels of displacement. The first transformation, from 9a to 9b, involves the tritone transposition of a typical bebop formula which outlines the ii-V turnaround progression of Gmin7(♭5) to C7. The second transformation from 9b to 9c shifts the motive over one beat: 9c now corresponds to m. 24.

9a: ii-V Turnaround figure

9b: Tritone substitution

9c: Rhythmic shift (= m. 24)

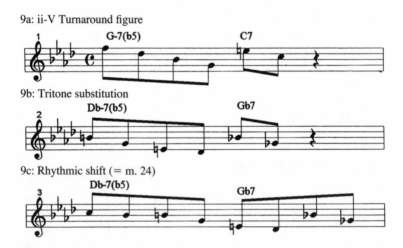

Example 9a–c: Double displacement at m. 24

Polymeter

Similarly, the metric superimpositions in the polymetric passages occur in tandem with rather sophisticated harmonic superimpositions. The fifth chorus, beginning at m. 49, primarily develops the <027> (perfect fourth) set-class: note that the ascending forms of <027> in mm. 49–50 are balanced by the descending forms in mm. 51–52. Measures 53 and 54 continue to develop the motive, now registrally expanded.

Beginning with the arrows in m. 55, pattern repetition occurs over every three beats, stratifying 3/4 over 4/4, indicated by the arrows between mm. 55–57. The pattern is initiated with the C in mm. 55 and followed by the B in m. 56. In these two instances, too, the slurs indicate how pattern repetition is out of alignment with the "harmonic rhythm": note that the shift of the <027> set-classes, indicated by the slurs, precedes by one beat the pattern change denoted by the arrows. On the third repetition, the pattern is altered; the accent is implied rather than overt at the beginning of m. 57, and the contour of the original pattern returns again with the G♭ three beats later in m. 57. Hancock ends the fifth chorus by realigning the motivic structure with the meter at mm. 59–60.

Another example of polymeter occurs later in the solo, beginning at m. 117. Here 6/8 is superimposed over 4/4. Notice that the rhythmic pattern occurs every three beats, stratifying 6/8 above the 4/4 meter for these bars. Again, metric superimposition coincides with harmonic substitution: these four measures outline the harmony of D♭ Maj. 9. Interestingly, too, the 2:1 proportion of the quarter-note/eighth-note pattern yields in augmentation the characteristic 2:1 proportion of the swing eighth note.

Accentual Shift at the Level of Hypermeter

The three surface displacement techniques of accentual shift, displaced motivic repetition, and metric superimposition recur throughout the solo. Additionally, through motivic overlay, displacement takes place at higher levels of metric structure as the solo progresses. Within the fourth chorus, the downbeat of m. 38 is articulated strongly through contour accent and through pattern beginning of the four-note motive which repeats a half-step lower. Yet the *absence* of motivic events in m. 37 and again in m. 41 shifts the focus away from the first measure of the 4-measure units, inflecting instead the second measures.

This, then, engenders a 2-shift at this level of hypermetric structure for the pair of 4-measure units. The shift is modeled in Example 10. Thus, in the same way that accentual shift on the surface displaces the metric downbeat, this accentual shift at the level of hypermeter creates a conflict with the hypermetric downbeats of mm. 37 and 41, displacing the larger 4-bar units.

Finally, pitch and motivic connections cut across the 12-bar formal divisions and serve to blur the largest hypermetric divisions for two successive 12-bar choruses. The motivic fragment which ends the sixth 12-bar chorus, designated by the dotted slurs in m. 71, is repeated two measures later on the hypermetric downbeat. The dotted slurs in m. 73 show its connection to m. 71.[16] Subsequently a motive appears twice within the last four measures of the seventh chorus, designated by the dotted slurs in m. 81 and 83. This motive, beginning with the pitches F, E, E♭, and B, is then continued and developed across the next hypermetric division into the eighth chorus. Again, dotted slurs point out the three subsequent occurrences of the motive in mm. 85, 87, and 89.

Therefore, for these two consecutive choruses, motivic events bridge the 12-measure hypermetric divisions. Additionally, while the pitch content of the repeated motive in mm. 81–89 makes ambiguous the harmonic structure of the blues form, more significant is its placement in relation to the 12-bar structure. The durational reduction in Example 11 represents the 12-measure form as single 3/4 hypermeasures whose three hyperbeats each represent the notated four measures. Motivic events initiated within the third hyperbeat and repeated across the hypermetric divisions are now profoundly out of phase with the hypermeter, masking the 12-bar divisions. This inflects the third hyperbeat, engendering a 3-shift at this hypermetric level, and displacement now occurs *at the level of the 12-bar form.*

The question arises, however, whether this last is a metric phenomenon. If, as a number of writers have asserted, accents accrue to time-points and not time-spans, can we speak of the lack of alignment of motivic and formal structure here as a form of metric displacement? Or has meter yielded, in Edward Cone's words, to a "more organic rhythmic principle?"[17] Yet the motivic events cut across the grain of the 12-bar

Example 10: 2-Shift at the hypermetric level

Example 11: 3-Shift at the hypermetric level

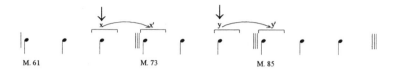

structure, clouding the formal divisions and the perception of the 12-bar form. As Example 11 suggests, Hancock has motivically, if not metrically, syncopated the 12-bar form.

Within the final chorus the motivic structure is brought back into phase with the 12-bar form. Beginning in m. 145, an <027> set-class beginning on G dominates the first four measures. The motive recurs within the second four measures (between mm. 149–152), and is heard transposed within the last four measures of the solo. Within the final 12-bar chorus, this loose AAB structure provides a distant echo of the call-and-response AAB vocal form of the traditional blues.

As noted earlier, individual occurrences of the displacement techniques are not protracted; rather than pursuing a single level of displacement, the soloist establishes and explores a variety of displacement techniques. Surface displacement techniques—accentual shift, displaced motivic repetition, and polymeter—frequently make opaque the metric downbeats, while on higher metric levels motivic events displaced from or straddling the hypermetric downbeats blur the larger 4-bar and 12-bar divisions. Throughout, Hancock is able to graft onto the periodic 12-bar formal structure another structure whose rhythmic elasticity and sophistication surpasses that achieved by most jazz artists.

NOTES

1. "Déplacer les accents, éviter les lieux communs." Quoted from Laurent de Wilde, "Quand Herbie écoute Hancock," *Jazz Magazine* (September 1994): 19. For one of the more substantive interviews with Hancock, see *The Black Composer Speaks,* ed. David Baker, Lida Belt, and Herman Hudson (Metuchen, N.J. and London: Scarecrow Press, 1978): 108–138.

2. Bill Dobbins, "Hancock, Herbie," *The New Grove Dictionary of American Music,* ed. H. Wiley Hitchcock and Stanley Sadie (London: Macmillan, 1986), vol. 2, 317.

3. Steven Strunk, "The Harmony of Early Bop: A Layered Approach," *Journal of Jazz Studies* 6 (1975): 4–53; Strunk, "Bebop Melodic Lines: Tonal Characteristics," *Annual Review of Jazz Studies* 3 (1985): 97–120; Steven Larson, "Schenkerian Analysis of Modern Jazz" (Ph.D. diss., University of Michigan, 1987); Milton Stewart, "Structural Development in the Jazz Improvisational Technique of Clifford Brown," *Jazzforschung/Jazz Research* 6/7 (1974/1975): 141–273.

4. J. Kent Williams, "Themes Composed by Jazz Musicians of the Bebop Era: A Study of Harmony, Rhythm, and Melody" (Ph.D. diss., Indiana University, 1982); Gary Potter, "Analyzing Improvised Jazz," *College Music Symposium* 30/1 (Spring 1990): 67–74.

5. Jeff Pressing, "Pitch Class Set Structures in Contemporary Jazz," *Jazzforschung/Jazz Research* 14 (1982): 133–172; Steven Block, "Pitch-Class Transformations in Free Jazz," *Music Theory Spectrum* 12/2 (1990): 181–202.

6. Cynthia Folio, "An Analysis of Polyrhythm in Selected Improvised Jazz Solos," in *Concert Music, Rock, and Jazz since 1945*, ed. Elizabeth Marvin and Richard Hermann (Rochester, New York: University of Rochester Press, 1995).

7. For example, the four beats of a 4/4 measure assert the pattern of Strong-Weak-Strong-Weak.

8. Joel Lester, *The Rhythms of Tonal Music* (Carbondale and Edwardsville: Southern Illinois University Press, 1986), especially chapters 2–4.

9. Fred Lerdahl and Ray Jackendoff, *A Generative Theory of Tonal Music* (Cambridge: MIT Press, 1983).

10. See, especially, William Rothstein, "Rhythm and the Theory of Structural Levels" (Ph.D. diss., Yale University, 1981), and *Phrase Rhythm in Tonal Music* (New York: Schirmer Books, 1989); Carl Schachter, "Rhythm and Linear Analysis: A Preliminary Study," in *The Music Forum, Vol. 4,* edited by Felix Salzer and Carl Schachter (New York: Columbia University Press, 1976), 281–334, "Rhythm and Linear Analysis: Durational Reduction," in *The Music Forum, Vol. 5,* edited by Salzer and Schachter (New York: Columbia University Press, 1980), 197–232, and "Rhythm and Linear Analysis: Aspects of Meter," in *The Music Forum, Vol. 6, Part 1,* edited by Salzer, Schachter, and Hedi Siegel (New York: Columbia University Press, 1987), 1–59.

11. This point was made clear to me during a piano lesson with Richie

Beirach. Despite the metric ambiguity and a number of sophisticated harmonic substitutions during a solo piano version of "Stella by Starlight," he would always follow the eighth or sixteenth bar with a point of harmonic and metric resolution.

12. In the liner notes for his album *The Prisoner* (Blue Note 84321), Hancock refers this as the "triple meter" feeling of jazz.

13. I would like to acknowledge Steve Larson for helping me fashion the terminology for these two types of polymeter.

14. Transcription of the solo follows these notes. Due to space considerations and the analytical emphasis here on the melodic events, I have included here only the transcription of the right hand part.

15. The fact that the bass and drums do *not* strongly articulate the metric hierarchy above the level of the beat contributes to the metric ambiguity within the piano solo.

16. The contour of the first four notes of the motive is maintained on successive downbeats at m. 74 and 75.

17. Edward T. Cone, *Musical Form and Performance* (New York: W.W. Norton, 1968), 40.

Piano solo: "The Eye of the Hurricane," from Herbie Hancock, *Maiden Voyage* (1965, Blue Note LP 84195); reissued on Blue Note CD B21Y-46339

BLUES FOR YOU, JOHNNY: JOHNNY DODDS AND HIS "WILD MAN BLUES" RECORDINGS OF 1927 AND 1938

Gene Anderson

I

Shortly after Johnny Dodd's death Sidney Bechet invited Johnny's brother to join his New Orleans Feetwarmers in a recording honoring Bechet's hometown musical colleague and lifelong friend. Although Baby Dodds pronounced "Blues for You, Johnny," recorded in Chicago on September 6, 1940, a "fine tribute," *Down Beat* found vocalist Herb Jeffries "from hunger on blues."[1] A more fitting memorial would have been "Wild Man Blues" cut by Bechet a few months previously. Said to be his favorite number,[2] "Wild Man Blues" was recorded by Dodds three times in 1927 and once again in 1938. This study examines Johnny Dodds's style of performance and methods of improvisation by comparing the extant recordings, of which, counting alternate takes, there are six (Table 1).

Table 1: Publication and Recording Chronology of "Wild Man Blues"

February 5, 1927: Copyright deposit of a lead sheet for "Ted Lewis Blues" by Jelly Roll Morton, sent in by Melrose Brothers Music Company of Chicago (see Example 1).

April 22, 1927: Recording of "Ted Lewis Blues" as "Wild Man Blues" for Brunswick (two takes) in Chicago by Johnny Dodds's Black Bottom Stompers (Louis Armstrong, trumpet; Roy Palmer, trombone; Dodds, clarinet; Barney Bigard, tenor saxophone; Earl Hines, piano; Bud Scott, banjo; Baby Dodds, drums).[3] Morton and Armstrong are listed as joint composers, the verse is omitted, and the chorus (in concert F minor) is repeated with back-to-back solos by trumpet and clarinet.

39

May 7, 1927: Recording of "Wild Man Blues" for OKeh in Chicago by Louis Armstrong's Hot Seven (Armstrong, trumpet; Fred Robinson?, trombone;[4] Dodds, clarinet; Lil Armstrong, piano; Johnny St. Cyr, banjo/guitar; Pete Briggs, tuba; Baby Dodds, drums).[5] Morton and Armstrong are listed as joint composers; the form and key duplicate the Stompers' recording.

June 4, 1927: Recording of "Wild Man Blues" for Bluebird (two takes) in Chicago by Jelly Roll Morton's Red Hot Peppers (George Mitchell, cornet; Gerald Reeves, trombone; Dodds, clarinet; Paul "Stump" Evans, alto saxophone; Morton, piano; Bud Scott, guitar; Quinn Wilson, tuba; Baby Dodds, drums).[6] Armstrong and Morton share composer credit on the label; the form follows the lead sheet, except that a chorus (in concert F minor) precedes the verse (in concert A♭ major), which is succeeded in turn by two more choruses.

June 8, 1927: Copyright of a piano solo in A♭ major/F minor of "Wild Man Blues" by Melrose Brothers Music Company. On the front cover Morton is listed as the composer, but on the first page of music Armstrong and Morton are both credited; the form follows the lead sheet except for a repeat of the chorus.

July?, 1927: Orchestration of "Wild Man Blues" published by Melrose. Other than a modulation into concert C minor for the first chorus after the verse, the form and keys duplicate the Peppers recording. The arrangement by Tiny Parham includes a rough transcription of Armstrong's introduction and opening chorus from take 1 of the Stompers recording. Morton is credited as the composer on the cover but the parts list both Morton and Armstrong.

January 21, 1938: Recording of "Wild Man Blues" for Decca in New York City by Johnny Dodds and His Chicago Boys (Charlie Shavers, trumpet; Dodds, clarinet; Lil Armstrong, piano; Teddy Bunn, guitar; John Kirby, bass; O'Neill Spencer, washboard). Although in concert G minor, the form follows the Stompers recording with the addition of a chorus each for guitar solo and ensemble (clarinet-trumpet duet).[7]

Example 1 is an edited lead sheet of Jelly Roll Morton's "Ted Lewis Blues."[8] The copyright deposit reveals that the composer had a band piece in mind from the start, and the specific indication of a break for clarinet (Ted Lewis's nominal instrument) may explain the title. The dedication could have occurred to Morton after catching Lewis's act at Billy Bottoms's Dreamland Café, where the famous "jazz king" appeared as a guest of the black musicians' union the previous October.[9]

(1) No E-natural in original
(2) No triplet sign in original
(3) C-sharp in original
(4) F-sharp in original
(5) G-flat in original
(6) C-flat in original
(7) No dot in original
(8) F-flat in original

Example 1: "Ted Lewis Blues"

Like many tunes from the 1920s whose titles include the word "blues," the composition lacks the 12-bar blues chord progression, but in this case the presence of blue or minor thirds and multiple breaks in the chorus evoke a pervasive blues character.

Marketability was the probable motivation for including Louis Armstrong, already billed "The World's Greatest Jazz Cornetist" in the *Chicago Defender*,[10] as co-composer of "Wild Man Blues." In her bio-discography of Morton, Laurie Wright cites Lil Armstrong's insistence that the tune was her husband's, but in a c. 1970 phone interview with Bill Russell, Armstrong said he played the piece but didn't write it.[11]

II

1927 was the pinnacle of Johnny Dodds's career. Born in New Orleans in 1892, he began playing professionally around 1912 with Kid Ory, with whom he continued off and on until Ory moved to California in 1919.[12] Except for a tour through the South and Midwest with Mack's Merry Makers vaudeville troupe in the latter half of 1918, Dodds remained in the Crescent City until summoned to Chicago by King Oliver to join his Creole Jazz Band at the Dreamland Café in early 1921.[13]

Dodds stayed with the Creole Band until falling out with Oliver in autumn 1923, after which, in apparent retaliation, Oliver replaced him with Jimmie Noone on the Columbia recordings of mid-October. Oliver's emerging egotism had generated friction—Baby Dodds charged that after the recordings for Gennett in April 1923 "our band" became "his band"—and recording royalties sent to Oliver for distribution to band members began suspiciously to diminish. When after an argument Oliver refused to produce the royalty checks, the band broke up.[14] Johnny Dodds then began a residency at Burt Kelly's Stables on Chicago's North Side that lasted until its closure for alleged Prohibition violations on New Year's Day, 1930.[15]

With over one hundred titles already to his credit as sideman with Oliver, Armstrong, and dozens of lesser luminaries since 1923, the session producing "Wild Man Blues" on April 22, 1927, was Dodds's premiere as leader. Possibly he learned about the tune from Frank Melrose, one of the music-publishing brothers who sent in the copyright deposit for "Ted Lewis Blues" and with whose Dixieland Thumpers Dodds recorded some rejected sides for Gennett in late February. Other than the title change, probably an impulsive decision made at the studio,[16] the

Example 2: Trumpet motive from Take 1 of "Wild Man Blues" by Dodd's Black Bottom Stompers[17]

most obvious differences between the recording and the version of the piece submitted as a copyright deposit involve form. Stripped down to its chorus, the work is a showpiece for Armstrong and Dodds, whose almost-equal-length solos dominate the proceedings (see Table 2). The rhythm plays continuously for the first ten bars of Armstrong's solo and the first fourteen bars of Dodds's solo, making into fills the breaks implied on the leadsheet. Armstrong, as later with the Hot Seven, opens the relatively elaborate introduction with breaks, the most prominent structural feature of the piece, and concludes the introduction with a motive recalled at the end his solo and again in the coda (see Example 2).

The Black Bottom Stompers' take 1 presents a typical Dodds solo. Almost entirely in the low or chalumeau register, he plays with a full, rich, and dark tone quality characterized by an intense below-the-center-of-pitch vibrato.[18] Adhering closely to the melody, Dodds provides few surprises within the fills and breaks, which tend to be arpeggiations of the prevailing harmony spiced by an occasional blue note (e.g., the $G\flat$ in bar 56). He maintains the listener's interest within these narrow melodic and harmonic parameters by a judicious variety of rhythms, articulations, and dynamics.

Dodds's articulation of choice is the slur or legato tongue, reserving regular tonguing or staccato for emphasis, as in the break at bars 55–56. Blue notes in particular are distinguished by glissandi and lipped pitch inflections, used either separately (bars 42, 46, 56) or together (bars 65–66). Besides these embellishments Dodds could produce broader effects like prolonged descending smears over wide intervals and an exaggerated vibrato in the high register resembling a horse whinny, both audible, for example, on "Oh Lizzie" recorded the day before "Wild Man Blues." The "horse whinny" (intimated in bars 65 and 67 of the Hot Seven recording) is the closest approach to what Dodds called "clown playing," for he eschewed the whines, squawks, and squeaks of Wilber Sweatman, Ted Lewis, and others so popular in his day.[19]

Although generally superior to take 1, take 2 of the Stompers' recording was kept from commercial release in 1927 by Armstrong's fluffed note

Example 3: Dodds's solos in Takes 1 and 2 of "Wild Man Blues" by his Black Bottom
Stompers

in the first bar of the introduction. Dodds's solo is essentially the same, but
his alterations, made presumably without reflection and within minutes of
the previous take, are improvements—intensifying the structure and in-
jecting additional variety to modify more favorably the balance of fulfilled

Example 3: continued

and thwarted expectations. The third of the harmony (A♭), for example, makes an unsatisfactory cadence in bar 48 of take 1, which Dodds seems to realize almost too late by barely sounding the root (F) before beginning the next phrase. Consequently he gives the root greater emphasis in take 2. In addition, Dodds replaces the repetitious B♮-C pattern in bars 48–49 of take 1 with a dramatic octave leap (shifted from bar 50 of take 1), and shapes more effectively bars 49–54 by making a single downward arc from F to D♮ (climaxing on the downbeat of measure 52) and back to F in measure 54 (isolated by rests, embellished by a glissando, and intensified by a pronounced vibrato), which sets up superbly the double-time break in bars 55–56.[20] Other felicitous adjustments include the elimination of the disruptive leap of a tenth between bars 60–61, the combination of gut-bucket timbre (Dodds's nickname in the Ory Band was "Toilet") with hemiola rhythm for the break in bars 65–66, and the interpolation of a blue fifth (C♭) in bar 68. (See Example 3 for a comparison of Dodds's solos in Takes 1 and 2 of "Wild Man Blues" by his Black Bottom Stompers.

The Hot Seven "Wild Man Blues" of two weeks later is leaner and rougher than its predecessor but the style more homogeneous. The elegant and refined accompaniment by Hines and Scott on the Stompers' recordings seemed to contradict the passionate playing of Armstrong and Dodds, who are supported on the Hot Seven session by the heavier and simpler background of Lil Armstrong, Briggs, and St. Cyr, and whose discontinuous accompaniment transforms the chorus into a series of two-bar segments alternating between accompanied melody and solo breaks. The opportunity to play several breaks—and at a tempo slower than the

Table 2

Black Bottom Stompers Recording of "Wild Man Blues": Formal Scheme

Section	Intro		Chorus 1					
Subsection			A1			B1		
Instrumentation	Trp Brk	Ens	Trumpet Solo	Brk	Solo/Brk	Trumpet Solo	Break	Solo/Brk
Measures	2+2	4	10	2	2/2	8	2+2	2/2
Keys	Ab Major		F Minor					

Chorus 2					Coda
A2		B2			
Clarinet Solo	Brk	Clarinet Solo	Break		Ens
14	2	8	2+2		4
F Minor					Ab Major

Hot Seven Recording of "Wild Man Blues": Formal Scheme

Section	Intro		Chorus 1				
Subsection			A1		B1		
Instrumentation	Trp Brk	Ens	Trumpet Solo/Break		Trp Solo/Break	Break	Solo/Brk
Measures	2+2	4	2/2/2/2/2/2/2		2/2/2/2	2+2	2/2
Keys	Ab Major		F Minor				

Chorus 2				Coda
A2		B2		
Clarinet Solo/Break		Clarinet Solo/Break	Break	Ens
2/2/2/2/2/2/2		2/2/2/2	2+2	4
F Minor				Ab Major

Black Bottom Stompers recording—may have further stimulated and liberated the soloists' imaginations, for the performances of Armstrong and, especially, Dodds surpass their previous efforts.

Table 2 presents the formal scheme of "Wild Man Blues" as recorded by Dodds's Black Bottom Stompers and Armstrong's Hot Seven.

The Hot Seven session represents Dodds at his best. Sounding more comfortable and confident with a slower tempo, his performance is an effective foil for Armstrong's bravura playing (see Example 8).[21] Rather than restricting himself to a single register, Dodds explores the full compass of the instrument from low F to high C, retaining hardly a pitch or rhythm from his earlier improvisations, although Gunther Schuller's discernment of Dodds's difficulty with the register change on the clarinet is supported by the squawk on D♮ in bar 53.[22] Dodds exhibits flashes of virtuosity in bars 52 and 64 and employs a wider variety of rhythms than before. The "Scotch snap" or sixteenth note–eighth note figure, a feature of Armstrong's Stompers solos unexploited by Dodds at the time, is now appropriated (bar 41), developed into a rhythmic motive (bars 43, 45, 46), and made the basis of a break (bars 47–48). Straight eighth and sixteenth notes in the breaks, inconsistently applied in the Stompers solos, are here the rule. Dodds also finds a new use for the E♮-F neighbor pattern by balancing it with the B♮-C pattern in bar 44 or using the figure independently in bars 49 and 50. In general, Dodds is less confined to the melody than with the Stompers; after the first few measures and with the exception of bars 57–58, the tune is barely discernable or avoided completely. Likewise, the first two breaks (bars 43–44 and 47–48) bear some semblance to their counterparts on the Stompers recordings, but subsequent ones diverge increasingly from their former shape and content (see Example 4).

Example 4: Dodds's solo in "Wild Man Blues" by Armstrong's Hot Seven

Morton's "Wild Man" a month after the Hot Seven's differs radically from its predecessors, the change effected largely by a relatively fast two-beat tempo which suppresses, or at least minimizes, the blues character. No doubt asked to limit his playing to the low register as Morton requested him to do a few days later for the Morton Trio sides of "Wolverine Blues" and "Mr. Jelly Lord,"[23] Dodds nevertheless seems to adapt comfortably to the composition's arrangement, one of Morton's most intricate. In less than three minutes Morton compresses five textural and timbral combinations—muted cornet solo with rhythm (guitar, tuba, drums) and trombone; alto saxophone solo with rhythm, trombone, and piano; piano solo with drums; clarinet solo with rhythm; full ensemble (itself varying between unison rhythm and collective improvisation)—and sixteen breaks for five instruments. Melody-break combinations utilized by the Stompers and Hot Seven are incorporated, and a sequence of one-bar breaks for ensemble and drums (cymbal) is introduced.[24] Morton imposes order on the surfeit of contrast by employing the B section of the chorus as a refrain while reserving the subtle change of a full ensemble accompaniment for the clarinet soloist and the surprise of a trombone break for its final statement.[25]

Despite the arrangement's ingenuity, flaws of performance prevent "Wild Man Blues" from ranking among Morton's best recordings. The cornet and piano are apparently to open the piece, followed by the rest of the ensemble a bar later. Both takes get off to a bad start. On the first the cornet and piano fail to come in together; on the third the saxophone enters before the rest of the ensemble and the cornet fluffs a note. The cornetist's solo entrance obscures the intended drum break at bar 24 in B1 and the ensemble accompaniment covers the clarinet solo in B3 on both takes as well. See Table 3 for the formal scheme of "Wild Man Blues" by Morton's Red Hot Peppers.

Dodds's alternating breaks with the piano solo form a study in obtaining heightened complexity from a minimum of materials. In the series of four breaks from both takes, each is an amplification of the preceding—either in rhythmic intricacy, extent of range, pitch-content, or combinations thereof. Especially instructive is the progression in take 3, beginning in bars 51–52 with a syncopated F diminished triad. The next break (bars 55–56) adds a new pitch (B♭), expands the range downward a minor second to E♮, and eliminates syncopation. The third break (bars 59–60) reintroduces syncopation, introduces triplets along with another new pitch (A♭), and expands the range upward a major second to D♭. The series climaxes with the final break (bars 63–64) in double time over a

Table 3

Red Hot Peppers Recording of "Wild Man Blues": Formal Scheme

(drum roll) Spoken: "Git away from there boy 'fore the wild man gits 'ya" (roar)

Section	Intro	Chorus 1								
Subsection		A1				B1				
Instrumentation	Ens	Cornet Solo	Brk	(Dr)	Ens	Cor	Cor	Ens	Cornet	Ens
Measures	4	14	2	2	1	1	2	2	2+2	4
Keys	A♭	F Minor								A♭

Verse	Chorus 2							
C	A2		B2					
Saxophone Solo	Piano Solo/Clarinet Break	Pno	Ens	Dr	Pno	Ens	Sax	Ens
12	2/2/2/2/2/2/2	2	1	1	2	2	2+2	4
A♭	F Minor							A♭

Chorus 3									Coda
A3		B3							
Clarinet Solo/Saxophone Break	Clar	Ens	Dr	Clar	Ens	Sax	Trom	Ens	Ens
2/2/2/2/2/2/2	2	1	1	2	2	2	2	2	2
F Minor									A♭

complete octave. Dodds's spare melodic statements, cast into sharp relief by the florid saxophone breaks, are occupied with filling in the tritone: C♭-F (bars 81–82, 85–86), B♭-F (bars 89–90, 93–94 of take 1), and
A♭-D♮ (bars 93–94 of take 3).

Example 5 compares Dodds's solos in Takes 1 and 3 by Morton's Red
Hot Peppers.

When Lil Armstrong convinced Decca to bring Johnny Dodds to New
York to record "Wild Man Blues" among other old titles in 1938, it was
his first venture outside Chicago since a trip to the West Coast with
Oliver in 1921–22 and almost nine years since he had entered a studio.
The Depression, the public's changing taste in jazz, and the death of his
wife in 1931 had taken their musical and personal toll. But a renewed interest in traditional jazz, reflected by the publication of *Jazzmen* in 1939
and known as the New Orleans Revival, stimulated the rediscovery of
early players who, like Dodds, were working in obscurity or who, like
Bunk Johnson, had given up music entirely.

Johnny's Chicago Boys were actually members of the John Kirby
Sextet whom Decca used as a house band for recordings with visiting

Example 5: Dodds's solos in Takes 1 and 3 by Jelly Roll Morton's Red Hot Peppers

artists. Only half a generation younger than Dodds but several generations removed musically, Kirby's group provided a collaboration that resulted in a paragon of stylistic incongruity. Even Lil Armstrong, who tried to adapt her playing to the light, sophisticated swing of the

Example 5: continued

Kirby musicians, provided scant support for her old friend. As a New Yorker Dodds proved himself an unrepentant and unmitigated New Orleanian.

The tempo—even faster than Morton's—appears to be Dodds's chief disadvantage. Although up to its technical demands, Dodds is constrained by the speed, which prevents him from effectively exhibiting the kaleidoscopic nuances of pitch, articulation, and timbre that comprise his special strengths. The quick tempo, too, transforms the character of the piece by infringing on the time allowed to create interesting breaks or fills, the musical point of the original, and precludes its most exciting feature, the double-time break. The rhythm section in fact allows no actual breaks in the solos and only two in the final chorus. Thus Dodd follows the melody more closely than in previous recordings and keeps rhythmic complexity to a minimum.

Table 4 presents the formal scheme of "Wild Man Blues" by Johnny Dodds's Chicago Boys. After rushing through a parody of his earlier recorded breaks in bars 11–12, Dodds comes up empty at opportunities for improvised fills in bars 15–16, 19–20, 27–28, 31–32, and 35–36.

Table 4

Chicago Boys Recording of "Wild Man Blues": Formal Scheme

Section	Intro		Chorus 1		Chorus 2	
Subsection			A1	B1	A2	B2
Instrumentation	Trp	Ens	Clarinet Solo	Clarinet Solo	Trumpet Solo	Trumpet Solo
Measures	2+2	4	16	16	16	16
Keys	B♭		G Minor			

Chorus 3		Chorus 4				Coda
A3	B3	A4		B4		
Guitar Solo	Guitar Solo	Ensemble	Clr	Ensemble	Clar	Ens
16	16	14	2	8	2+2	4
G Minor						B♭

Only in the fill of bars 23–24 is there a flash of technical brilliance (see Example 6).

Dodds shines, however, in the concluding ensemble chorus with Shavers, in which he demonstrates his fine ear for counterpoint; the duet is marred solely by the corny break in bars 119–20, a hackneyed version of the fill from bars 23–24 (see Example 7).

III

Dodds's final two years were ones of decline. A precipitative second marriage to Georgia Green in April 1938 alienated his children, who found their stepmother overly critical, distant, and demanding.[26] That October Dodds moved from the Three Deuces on 222 North State to a steady job at Rocky Gallo's 29 Club on 47th and Dearborn,[27] but within a few months wrote a friend in Cleveland that the 29 Club had closed, work was scarce, and he was thinking of leaving Chicago for New York City.[28] A nearly fatal stroke in July 1939 interrupted any travel plans, and, after a six-month recovery, Dodds had to have all his teeth removed.[29] Dental problems and poor health, however, could not prevent him from playing weekends with Baby's band at a club on the outskirts of Chicago in early 1940,[30] and from recording again with Decca as part of their New Orleans series in June. He had been out of work almost five months[31] when stricken at his home by a second and fatal stroke the morning of August 8.

Example 6: Dodds's solo with his Chicago Boys

Dodds's premature death prevented him from sharing in many benefits of the New Orleans Revival, but his historic importance was by this time secure. Named one of the "Immortals of Jazz" by *Down Beat* in April 1940, his influence was recalled by Benny Goodman the following year[32] and eulogized by John Lucas two years later.[33] Gunther Schuller's subsequent classification of Dodds with Bechet and Noone as one of the three greatest representatives of the New Orleans clarinet tradition has since become standard.[34]

Historical importance aside, Dodds criticism has been beset by hyperbole. Two examples should suffice to make the point:

Johnny Dodds is a musician idolized by most "experts"—yet his talents were pitifully meager. Anyone who denies that he was frequently out of

Example 7: Dodds-Shavers duet-chorus with Dodds's Chicago Boys

tune proves himself tone-deaf. Without juggling the obvious truth, no one can deny that his tone was thin and screaming. And most authorities who deny that he was a crude technician, that his ideas were simple, repetitive and un-beautiful do not really believe their own assertions. . . .[35]

Example 7: continued

Johnny's was the highest and most genuine expression of hot jazz ever known. . . . His attacks could not be stopped, his vigor was inexhaustible, surpassing men the stature of Armstrong. . . . His presence in small groups singled him out as the master of masters. . . . Besides being the best and greatest clarinetist known he was a creative genius.[36]

Though the invective of the first can be refuted by a moment's listening, the plaudits of the second are tainted by the mention of Armstrong, with whom Dodds has long been invidiously compared and by whose presence on recordings he has been said to be intimidated.[37] While this may be arguably so for some of the Hot Fives, it is less true for the Hot Sevens in general, and decidedly not the case with "Wild Man Blues." Armstrong's "Wild Man" solo is indeed a masterful incorporation of his advanced rhythmic, harmonic, and formal ideas: the escalating progression of note values in the breaks of bars 11–12, 15–16, 19–20, 23–24; the juxtaposition of minor and major of bar 25; the dominant minor fifteenth (diminished tonic over a dominant seventh) of bars 14 and 26; the applied leading tone seventh chords of bars 36–37; and the climax of bar

Example 8: Armstrong's solo in "Wild Man Blues" by his Hot Seven

28 reached exactly at its golden section on an accented high C approached from a high A♭ (see note 24), a combination of pitches to which
Armstrong returns to conclude his declamation (see Example 8).

But Dodds's more conservative and less complex Hot Seven solo has
its own merits, as noted above. Neither dominated nor intimidated,
Dodds's playing complements Armstrong's by being different without
being inferior. He facilitates coherence by adopting Armstrong's Scotch
snap rhythmic motive and his regular use of even note-values in the
breaks. The most noticeable disparity is Dodds's relative lack of swing,
or rhythmic phrasing in the lilting triplet subdivisions made definitive by

Example 9: George Mitchell's solo in Take 1 of "Wild Man Blues" by Morton's Red
Hot Peppers

Armstrong.[38] Measured against Armstrong's standard, Dodds's rhythm
at times sounds square and old-fashioned but rarely if ever poor, weak,
or bad.[39] Dodds's rhythmic phrasing is in fact more adventurous than
many of his colleagues, of which George Mitchell's relentlessly and pre-
dictably syncopated "Wild Man Blues" solo from the Red Hot Peppers
recording might serve as a typical example (see Example 9).

The depiction of Dodds emerging from this study, corroborated by those
of others[40] as well as by the opinions of his contemporaries,[41] is that of a
largely conventional and somewhat limited player. Within his limitations,
however, Dodds reveals an immense capacity for invention. Evident
enough in the alternate takes of "Wild Man Blues," this facility abounds
in the two takes of "Wolverine Blues" referred to above. Within a total of
six 32-bar choruses—all confined to the chalumeau register and comprised
almost exclusively of diatonic arpeggios—Dodds creates two exuberant
and motivically organized solos containing virtually no literal duplication.

As an ensemble player, Dodds understands well the clarinetist's des-
cant function within the band, fulfilling it always competently and often
consummately; his handling of the harmonic third at the end of phrases,
played frequently with little emphasis or as a "throwaway," has been
noted as an innovative trademark.[42] Not an improviser in the extroverted
and intuitive manner of Armstrong or Bechet, Dodds evinces in his
earliest recorded solos formative devices common to players of his
time—constructive techniques he would rely upon in varying degrees

throughout his career; memorization, working-out in advance, and reshuffling of stock phrases.[43] Alternate takes of his solos suggest Dodds entered the studio with a rather clear notion of an intended performance to be deviated from minimally. Able to comprehensively revise his conception of a piece over time, he had not the will or imagination to do so instantaneously like, for example, Louis Armstrong, whose breaks and fills in the successive takes of the Stompers' "Wild Man Blues" are equally inventive but totally dissimilar. Finally, his recordings display almost no perceptible musical development or change of style.

Wherein lies Dodds's greatness? Even his harshest critics acclaim his preeminence as a purveyor of the slow blues. No one can make the clarinet cry and moan like Dodds, whose wailing interpretations of the blues have been rightfully hailed as peerless and powerful expressions of emotion and personality.[44] Nearly impossible to duplicate, his shadings of pitch and tone color resist if not defy imitation. In short, his greatness can be heard but not notated. A propitious balance of technical nuance with structural understanding, Dodds's Hot Seven "Wild Man Blues" solo represents a culmination of his musical virtues, tempting one to concur with a reviewer of that performance: "If Johnny Dodds had never made another recording, 'Wild Man Blues' would be enough to ensure his place as a major artist in the history of jazz."[45]

NOTES

1. Warren Dodds, *The Baby Dodds Story as Told To Larry Gara,* rev. ed. (Baton Rouge: Louisiana State University, 1992), 76. "For some unknown reason . . . Herb Jeffries sings the vocal to 'Blue [sic] For You, Johnny'. . . . Jeffries, billed as the 'bronze buckaroo' and ordinarily singer with the Ellington band, is from hunger on blues. He has no feeling. . . . And his vocal, stiff and insincere, makes poor Sidney and the others sound bad" (Barrelhouse Dan, *Down Beat* 7/, no. 20, October 14, 1940). "Blues for You Johnny" is available on *Sidney Bechet, The Victor Sessions Master Takes 1932–43,* 2402-2-RB (BMG Music, 1990).
2. G.E. Lambert, *Johnny Dodds* (New York: A. S. Barnes, 1961), 40.
3. Transcriptions for this study were made from Classics 603, *Johnny Dodds 1927* (Classics Records, 1991) for take 1 (C-796) and Decca MCAD-42326, *Johnny Dodds: South Side Chicago Jazz* (MCA Records, 1990) for take 2 (C-797).
4. Since Kid Ory, Armstrong's regular trombonist, was in New York

with King Oliver at this time (Walter C. Allen and Brian A.L. Rust, *"King" Oliver,* rev. Laurie Wright [Chigwell, Essex: Storyville, 1987], 76–79) his substitute has been a source of speculation. Although Gunther Schuller (*Early Jazz, Its Roots and Musical Development* [New York: Oxford University, 1968], 108) suggests Honoré Dutrey, most other writers have favored John Thomas, then a member of Tate's Vendome Theater Orchestra, for all the Hot Seven dates. When interviewed forty years later, Thomas, however, could recall making only "12th Street Rag" and "Weary Blues," both cut on May 11, while being certain of Fred Robinson, a regular member of the later Hot Five, as the trombonist on "Alligator Crawl" and "Keyhole Blues," recorded respectively on May 10 and May 13 (Bertrand Demeusy, "The Musical Career of John Thomas," *Jazz Journal* 20, no. 1 [1967]:23). The trombone barely plays on "Wild Man Blues," but the solo on "Willie the Weeper," recorded the same day and presumably by the same trombonist, sounds to this author more like Robinson than Thomas or Dutrey.

5. Transcriptions for this study were made from Columbia CK 44253, *Louis Armstrong: The Hot Fives & Hot Sevens,* Volume II (CBS Records, 1988).

6. Three takes were made but the second was destroyed and the third was unknown until reissued in 1979 by Meritt Records; see Laurie Wright, *Mr. Jelly Lord* (Chigwell, Essex: Storyville, 1980), 45. Transcriptions for this study were made from Bluebird 2361-2-RB, *The Jelly Roll Morton Complete Victor Recordings* (BMG Music, 1990).

7. Transcriptions for this study were made from Classics 635, *Johnny Dodds 1928–1940* (Classics Records, 1992).

8. Copyright deposits of the lead sheet, piano solo, and orchestration are on microfilm in the Music Division of the Library of Congress. An edited version of the piano solo appears in James Dupagny, *Ferdinand "Jelly Roll" Morton: The Collected Piano Music* (Washington, D.C.: Smithsonian Institution, 1982).

9. *Chicago Defender* October 9, 1926.

10. November 14, 1925.

11. *Mr. Jelly Lord,* 45; author's interview of Bill Russell in New Orleans, March 27, 1989.

12. See Gene Anderson, "Johnny Dodds in New Orleans," *American Music* 8, no. 4 (winter 1990); 403–40.

13. For questions about the date, see Gene Anderson, "The Genesis of King Oliver's Creole Jazz Band," *American Music* 12, no. 3 (fall 1994):283–303.

14. *"King" Oliver,* Wright rev., 33; *The Baby Dodds Story,* rev. ed., 48; Bill Russell interview of Baby Dodds, May 31, 1958 (Tulane Jazz Archive). John Dodds Jr. said his father broke with Oliver over money (author's interview of John Dodds Jr., Chicago, March 4, 1989). Financial disputes were not unprecedented for Oliver, who had attempted to embezzle funds collected for band uniforms in New Orleans before coming to Chicago (Bill Russell interview of Lewis Keppard, January 19, 1961, Tulane Jazz Archive). For more on the demise of the Creole Band, see Frederick Ramsey and Charles Edward Smith, *Jazzmen* (New York: Harcourt Brace Jovanovich, 1939), 74–5; Onah Spencer, "Preston Jackson Recalls First Gig," *Down Beat* 9, no. 21 (November 1, 1942), 23; and Bill Russell interview of Preston Jackson, June 1, 1958, (Tulane Jazz Archive).

15. *The Baby Dodds Story,* rev. ed., 52. Although back with the Creole Band for their final recordings of October 25, 1923, Dodds was possibly no longer a regular member (*"King" Oliver,* Wright rev., 38). On August 24, 1929, the *Chicago Defender* reported that "Johnny Dodds, the clarinet wizard, and his orchestra are still holding down the job at Kelly's Stables and are a big attraction. These boys have been on this one job seven [*sic*] years."

16. "Jungle music" was popular; "Jungle Blues" was "Wild Man's" companion piece at the Peppers' session.

17. All musical examples are in concert pitch and have been transcribed by the author.

18. Schuller (*Early Jazz,* 202) was the first to call attention to Dodds's unique vibrato; his brief discussion of Dodds's playing remains the most balanced and perceptive in the literature.

19. John Steiner interview of John Dodds Jr. from liner notes to "Johnny Dodds, Chicago Mess Around," Milestone Records, MLP 2011 (1969). The flutter-tonguing Gunther Schuller heard on a 1925 Lovie Austin recording (*Early Jazz,* 200) was undoubtedly that of Jimmie O'Bryant and not Dodds.

20 This double-time break is a favorite of Dodds. Besides the recordings of "Wild Man" with Morton (Example 5, bars 63–64), a version of it appears in "After You've Gone" recorded with his Black Bottom Stompers on October 8, 1927.

21. Armstrong's relatively subdued Stompers solos were an attempt to disguise his playing on Brunswick from OKeh with whom he was under contract. His deception, however, was treated as a joke by an OKeh executive who purchased the Stompers recording and called

in Armstrong to identify the trumpet player (1953 Armstrong radio interview, Cassette 26, Louis Armstrong Archive, Queens College, Flushing, NY).

22. *Early Jazz,* 200. The register change on the clarinet occurs between A♭ and A♮ concert.

23. *The Baby Dodds Story,* rev. ed., 75.

24. The pianissimo cymbal break following the fortissimo entrance of the ensemble comprises the dramatic climax of the chorus and occurs at its golden section (e.g., the 20th bar or 0.618 of its length). Other instances of proportional relationships are the second of successive two-bar breaks in the chorus at the golden section of Morton's B sections and Armstrong's accented high C at the golden section of his Hot Seven solo (see Example 8). For an introduction to the golden section in music see Roy Howat, "Bartok, Lendvai and the Principles of Proportional Analysis," *Music Analysis* 2, no. 1 (1983), 69–95.

25. The trombone break is taken note-for-note from Morton's lead sheet as is the cornet's (see Example 9, bars 19–20).

26. Author's interview of John Jr. and Dorothy Dodds Davis, Chicago, June 18, 1989.

27. Dodds had Anatie "Natty" Dominique on trumpet, Fred "Tubby" Hall on drums, and Leo Montgomery on piano in his 29 Club band (*Chicago Defender,* November 11, 1938); see also weekly reviews of 29 Club in the *Chicago Defender* from October 22, 1938 through January 14, 1939. On the Three Deuces and 29 Club, see also *The Baby Dodds Story,* rev. ed., 55–58. For an incident at the 29 Club involving Dodds, see *Jazzmen,* 186–87.

28. Dodds wrote to thank jazz enthusiast Hoyte Kline about locating a replacement for his clarinet currently "on the bum." The letters, dated March 23 and April 3, 1939, were shared with the author by Bill Russell in New Orleans, March 24, 1989.

29. Notices of Dodds's stroke and recovery appear in July (6, no. 7:1), August (6, no. 8:2), and December (6, no. 14:9) 1939 issues of *Down Beat.* Dodds mentions the impending extraction of his teeth in a postcard to Bill Russell of January 29, 1940 (shared by Russell with the author in New Orleans, March 24, 1989).

30. The booking at the 9750 Club on 9750 South Western Avenue, lasted from January 20 to March 18; see notices in *Jazz Information* of January 26, February 2, February 16, and March 8, 1940. See also *The Baby Dodds Story,* rev. ed. 67–8.

31. *Jazz Information* (April 26, 1940):6; "What's the Beat?" *Down Beat* 7, no. 14 (July 15, 1940):5.

32. Benny Goodman, "My Ten Favorite Clarinetists," *Music and Rhythm* 2, no. 11 (October 1941):8.

33. "Jazz Clarys, Henchmen of Kings," *Down Beat* 10, no. 6 (March 15, 1943):19.

34. *Early Jazz,* 198–203.

35. D. Leon Wolff, "Bix Half-Baked, Johnny Dodds Corny, Tesch Out of Tune," *Down Beat* 8, no. 11 (June 1, 1941):8. The stylistic bias of the author is clinched by the title of a later *Down Beat* article, "Bop Nowhere, Armstrong Just a Myth," 16, no. 11 (June 17, 1949).

36. José Francisco Riesco, *El jazz clasico y Johnny Dodds, su rey sin corona* (Santiago, 1972), 195 (Riesco's translation).

37. André Hodeir, *Jazz, Its Evolution and Essence,* trans. David Noakes (New York: Grove, 1956), 60.

38. For an informative but tortuous definition of swing as the "essence of jazz," see Hodeir, 195–209.

39. On Dodds's rhythmic weaknesses, see Hodeir, 52–4, 59 and Schuller, 105, 108, 203.

40. Besides Schuller, see Humphrey Lyttleton *The Best of Jazz, Basin Street to Harlem* (New York: Taplinger, 1978), 163–77.

41. For a survey, see Anderson, "Johnny Dodds in New Orleans," 415–16.

42. Sandy Brown, "Johnny Dodds, A Clarinetist's View," *Storyville* (February 1966), 12.

43. Dodds's Dippermouth Blues" solo on the OKeh recording of June 1923 is a repetition of the Gennett "Dippermouth" solo two months earlier, his solo from the same period on "High Society Rag" is a New Orleans set piece (see William J. Schafer, "Breaking Into 'High Society': Musical Metamorphoses in Early Jazz," *Journal of Jazz Studies* 2, no. 3 [1975]:53–60), his back-to-back choruses in "Room Rent Blues" in October 1923 are almost identical, and his breaks in two versions of "Working Man Blues," recorded three weeks apart also in October 1923, are measure-for-measure redistributions of the same pitches. On the emergence of the improvised solo in jazz, see James Lincoln Collier, *Jazz, the American Theme Song* (New York: Oxford University, 1993), 25–47.

44. E.g., Hodeir, 60–1, and Lyttleton, 172.

45. Bob Dawbarn, "Great Jazz Solos," *Melody Maker* 42, no. 8 (February 25, 1967).

LINEAR INTERVALLIC PATTERNS
IN JAZZ REPERTORY

Steven Strunk

INTRODUCTION

Linear intervallic patterns are usually defined as voice-leading patterns made up of streams of repeated intervals or pairs of intervals between the outer voices of a musical texture. The concept was discussed by Allen Forte in his *Tonal Harmony in Concept and Practice* (1979) and further developed in Forte and Gilbert, *Introduction to Schenkerian Analysis* (1983). David Neumeyer and Susan Tepping also discuss the concept in *A Guide to Schenkerian Analysis* (1992), referring to Forte's earlier work.[1]

Like Schenker, these authors focus on eighteenth- and nineteenth-century music in their discussion of linear intervallic patterns. However, the patterns are present in tonal music of all types. This article will consider linear intervallic patterns in the mainstream jazz repertory, discuss their characteristics, and note unique aspects of jazz usage.

As the patterns do not conceptually precede the music in which they are found, but rather arise from study of that music, it is advisable to keep a flexible view of the number of potential linear intervallic patterns and the forms they may take. Indeed, the three sources mentioned above list differing numbers of patterns and illustrate them moving in different ways. Accordingly, this study will not attempt to show an example of every possible pattern, but will discuss those seen most often in the jazz repertory.

The music analyzed here consists of those original jazz compositions and standard popular songs which have been taken as vehicles for performance by jazz musicians. This study began with a consideration of the contents of *The Real Book*,[2] which is the main source of examples, although some examples were found in other sources.

The patterns are made up of chords which, as Forte puts it, do not have harmonic value.[3] They are contrapuntal connections between structural chords which do have harmonic value. Usually patterns are part of

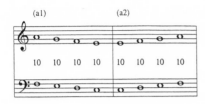

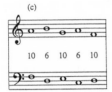

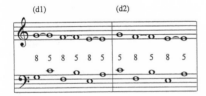

Example 1. Models for Linear Intervallic Patterns

melodic or harmonic sequences, but not always. Thus the term "linear intervallic pattern" is broader than the term "sequence." Interest in the patterns need not be entirely technical: colleagues perusing the examples to follow often commented that the passages exhibiting the patterns are among the most beautiful in the repertory.

2. THE PATTERNS

a. 10-10. Example 1(a1)[4] shows a model for the 10-10 pattern descending (after Forte-Gilbert).[5] (All examples follow the text and notes of this

Example 1 (continued)

article.) This is one of the most frequently occurring patterns in the repertory. A descending series of 10ths connect ♭III to ♭VI in "The Duke" (Example 2). The broad key context is C major, but locally the notes forming the 10ths are diatonic in A♭ major (♭VI), except for the chromatic passing tones in the B minor 7th chord in m. 6. In "Sweet Georgia Bright" (Example 3), a composition which uses only dominant seventh chords, parallel descending 10ths connect ♭III to I. The bass and soprano of "Trance" (Example 4) alternate movement as they both descend chromatically in oblique motion. The bridge of "Body and Soul" (Example 5) illustrates the possibility that the 10ths themselves may be elaborately prolonged. "Body and Soul" is a 32-bar AABA form in D♭, with its A

(h)

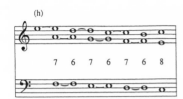

(i)

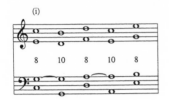

Example 1 (concluded)

Example 2: The Duke

Example 3: Sweet Georgia Bright

sections beginning on the ii chord. The bridge begins on D major, which is heard in the D♭ context as a Neapolitan key area, passes stepwise through a C major tonicization to a B♭ dominant 7th, which serves as V of the ii that begins the returning A section. The Neapolitan is prolonged by two voice exchanges, marked by X-shaped lines on the graph. The passing tone E in the bass of m. 17 supports the dominant of the surrounding D major chords, while the second approach to this temporary tonic is accomplished in m. 18 by a ♭VII7 chord that has been developed into a ii-V group. The iii7 (F♯m7) substitute for I (D) at m. 19 of the *Real Book* version quoted is replaced in the graph by the I (D), based on numerous other copies of the song as well as the variable possibilities of performance practice. The C major prolongation is accomplished by a ii-V prefix (m. 21) and an internal progression of I-ct♭7-ii-V-I.[6] C and B♭ are further connected by a chromatic passing B dominant 7th in m. 24. In "Midwestern Nights Dream" (Example 6), the 10ths first descend, then ascend, connecting C♯ minor (m. 8) to E major (m. 13) with m. 11

Example 4: Trance

as the turning point. The stemmed bass notes, interpreted as roots according to the chord symbols of the source, trace a circle-of-fifths progression.

Example 1 (a2) shows a model for the 10-10 pattern ascending. The pattern of ascending 10ths in "I'm Old Fashioned" (Example 7) helps to connect III♯ to V in a larger I-III♯-V motion. In "Lush Life" (Example 8), the ascending 10ths prolong the tonic chord, harmonizing a 3-5-♭7 ascending arpeggiation which returns to 5/I via a substitute dominant (♭II). As a final example, following the principle that, in jazz, a chordal extension a step above a consonance often replaces that consonance, "Red Clay" (Example 9) exhibits ascending parallel 11ths, replacing the usual parallel 10ths. In this case, the resolution of 11 to 10 is elided.

In *The Real Book,* many progressions are based on parallel 10ths between the bass and an inner voice, not the soprano. Although this practice differs from the definition given above, Forte and Gilbert in one case

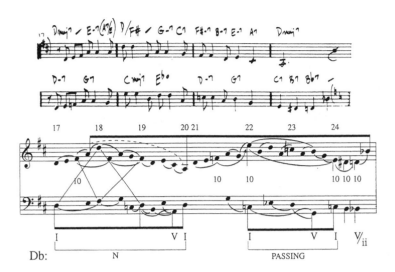

Example 5: Body and Soul

Example 6: Midwestern Night's Dream

Example 7: I'm Old Fashioned

speak of "a 10-10 pattern between alto and bass," suggesting the validity of such an extension of the definition.[7]

In the examples from *The Real Book,* the soprano behaves in three ways in relation to the 10ths. First, it may partially parallel the upper voice of the 10ths. For example, descending parallel 10ths between tenor and bass connect structural chords in "Gloria's Step" (Example 10). That the soprano remains on G while the tenor moves to F♯ in m. 2 supports interpretation of the second 10th (D-F♯) as chromatic passing tones. In mm. 3–4, while the tenor moves from F to E, the soprano moves from F to E♭. The V chord therefore includes both the major 10th (E—its third), and the minor 10th (E♭—a ♭7 blue note, enharmonically equivalent to an augmented 9th). In "Memories of Tomorrow" (Example 11) a chromatically descending bass is paired with a diatonic descent in the soprano, connecting I to IV in the local key of C. The soprano, a polyphonic melody, eventually touches upon each of the 10ths in its inner voice, but

Example 8: Lush Life

Example 9: Red Clay

Example 10: Gloria's Step

Example 11: Memories of Tomorrow

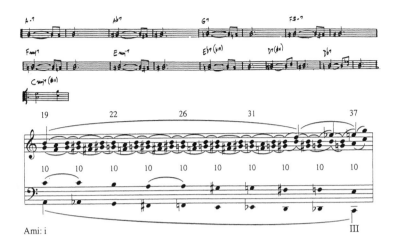

Example 12: Gary's Waltz

the expression of the 10-10 pattern falls mainly to the tenor line implied by the chord symbols.

Second, the soprano may hold steady, as a pedal point or ostinato, providing oblique motion with the 10ths. For example, the soprano of "Gary's Waltz" (Example 12) acts as an ostinato, or elaborated pedal point, as the 10ths descend below it. Ascending 10ths are the basis for the melodically nonsequential passage connecting I to III$_\sharp$ in "Chega de Saudade" (Example 13), in which only the first 10th between the alto and bass is also doubled by the soprano, which holds F$_\sharp$ elaborated by a lower neighbor. The E7 chord (m. 46) is a passing chord, however, the B minor 7th chord embellishing the tonic chord incidentally combines with it to produce a ii-V group.

Third, and more frequently, the soprano may move in contrary motion to the 10ths, producing either an expanding or a contracting wedge-shaped texture. In "Gary's Waltz" (Example 12), although the original soprano note B (mm. 19–32) is maintained as an inner voice from m. 33 through m. 36, the soprano (upward stems) ascends in contrary motion to the 10ths after m. 31. In "It Never Entered My Mind" (Example 14), the 10ths remain between soprano and bass until m. 22, when they move to a tenor-bass combination, with the soprano moving in contrary motion to the 10ths and expanding the texture. Here the pattern helps to connect I to V. The sheet music arrangement quoted also includes an inner voice 7–6 pattern (see section h, below). In the

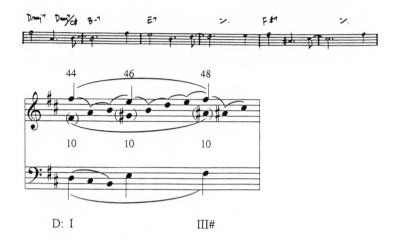

Example 13: Chega de Saudade

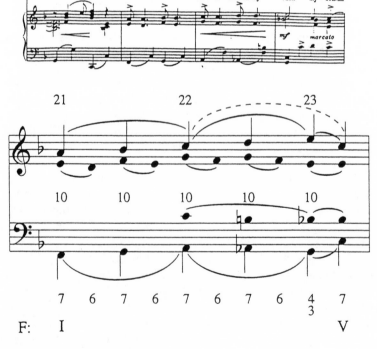

Example 14: It Never Entered My Mind

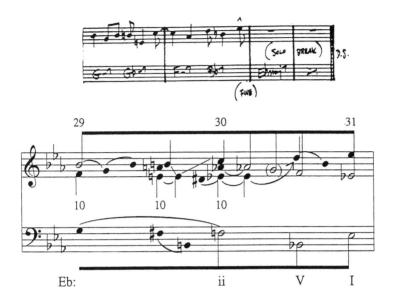

Example 15: Four

cadence of "Four" (Example 15), the alto and bass form the 10ths. The
soprano is in unison with the alto on the first 10th (m. 29), but then ascends in contrary motion to the 10ths, expanding the texture.[8] These
two examples illustrate expanding wedges of three elements (10ths). A
larger expanding wedge may be seen in "If You Never Come to Me"
(Example 16). Here four 10ths move chromatically between I and V/ii,
while three soprano pitches ascend in contrary motion to the 10ths. In
"Nefertiti" (Example 17),[9] the soprano holds through the first movement of the 10ths, which lie between the bass and its adjacent voice,
and then begins the textural expansion, with a total of five ascending
soprano pitches counterpointing the four descending 10ths. In "Little
Waltz" (Example 18), the 10ths lie between bass and alto, and once
more the soprano begins on the 10th before ascending. In "Think of
Me" (Example 19), the soprano separates from the descending 10ths at
m. 13, ascending to a higher register where it begins a 5–8 pattern with
the bass (see section d, below). Another longer passage from "The
Duke" (Example 20) shows descending 10ths above the bass which are
sometimes doubled at the unison or octave by the soprano. A crescendo
of expansions ensues: in m. 17 the texture expands from a 10th to an
octave plus a 10th; in mm. 19–20 the texture expands from an octave
plus a 9th to three octaves; (in mm. 21–22 the soprano descends in

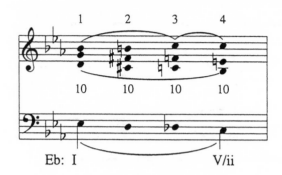

Example 16: If You Never Come To Me

Example 17: Nefertiti

Example 18: Little Waltz

Example 19: Think on Me

Example 20: The Duke

parallel with the bass); in mm. 23–25 the texture expands from an octave plus a 10th to four octaves less a half step.

In some other cases the texture contracts, as in "Crystal Silence" (Example 21 [a] and [b]). In mm. 7–8 the texture is relatively compact, so that the soprano doubles the 10th above the bass at its last pitch; in mm. 20–22 the texture is more widely spaced, but again forms a contracting wedge. In "Falling Grace" (Example 22) the basic soprano motion is elaborated by the superposition of an inner voice at m. 17. The superposed voice then descends, providing the impression of a second contracting wedge. Although these examples do not strictly fit the definition of linear intervallic pattern given above, they illustrate a closely related contrapuntal structure which jazz composers appear to favor.

b. 6-6. A model for the descending 6-6 pattern (after Forte-Gilbert)[10] is given in Example 1 (b1). The 6ths usually descend, sometimes diatonically, as in "Do I Hear A Waltz?" (Example 23). The descent in "The Folks Who Live on the Hill" (Example 24) is diatonic but for one chromatic passing chord ($E\flat°7$) in m. 3. The 6ths connect I6 to IV which then moves to I in a plagal cadence.[11] This example ends with two 7–6 suspensions, which elaborate the basic descending 6ths (see section h, below). Two chromatic passing chords ($G\flat°7$ and $B7/C\flat7$) decorate the basically diatonic descent connecting I6 to V in "You Do Something to Me" (Example 25).[12] The passage is given an original character by the rhythmic accentuation of the second chromatic chord (m. 21). Another type

(a)

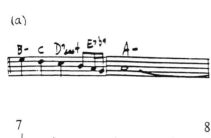

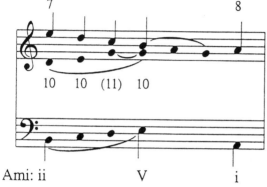

(b)

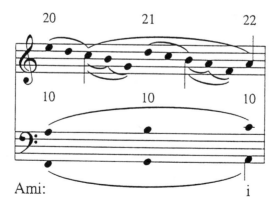

Example 21: Crystal Silence

Example 22: Falling Grace

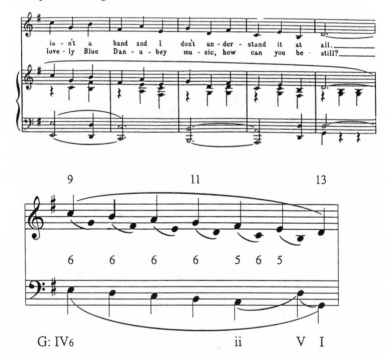

G: IV₆   ii   V I

Example 23: Do I Hear a Waltz?

Example 24: The Folks Who Live on the Hill

of descending 6th pattern involves a chromatic bass with a more slowly moving upper voice. "How Insensitive" (Example 26) has two soprano notes versus five bass notes, as the bass describes a chromatic descent from tonic to dominant (the dominant chord arrives in m. 14—not shown) in the manner of a Baroque passacaglia; "Falling Grace" (Example 27) has three versus four, in a very different, ambiguous harmonic context;[13] and "No Moon at All" (Example 28) has three versus six in another passacaglia-like descent.

A model for an ascending 6-6 pattern is given in Example 1 (b2). Ascending 6ths are rare; they may be seen in "I'm Your Pal" (Example 29), connecting vi to ii in C major by means of unexpectedly chromatic motion.[14]

c. 10–6. A model for the 10-6 pattern (after Forte-Gilbert)[15] is given in Example 1 (c). The 10-6, if considered as a chord progression, is a circle-of-fifths progression which depends on an alternation between 5/3 and 6/3 chords with a skip down a third in the bass. In jazz, "inverted" chords are usually associated with stepwise bass lines.[16] As a result, examples of this pattern are rare, despite the large number of circle-of-fifths progressions found in most tunes. One clear example occurs in "Windows" (Example 30), which, however, avoids the skip of a third by approaching the 6/3 chords stepwise through passing tones in the bass. The circle-of fifths progression here takes the form of a series of ii-Vs.

Example 25: You Do Something to Me

d. 8–5 and 5–8. A model for the 8–5 pattern (after Forte-Gilbert)[17] is given in Example 1 (d1). This pattern, if considered as a chord progression, is a circle-of-fifths progression, and occurs frequently in jazz, as the implied chords are in root position, as is usual in jazz bass lines. A simple example may be seen in "If You Never Come to Me" (Example 31), in which circle-of-fifths root position dominant sevenths approach in authentic cadence on the tonic (m. 13), which is itself a dominant seventh structure. The last chord of the example, A♭7, initiates a confirming plagal cadence back to the tonic in m. 15 (not shown). The bridge of "Jordu" (Example 32)[18] also exhibits circle-of-fifths dominant sevenths, this time directed toward D♭, a Neapolitan in the C minor context.

Melodic interest can be enhanced by the addition of suspensions to the

Example 26: How Insensitive

Example 27: Falling Grace

Example 28: No Moon at All

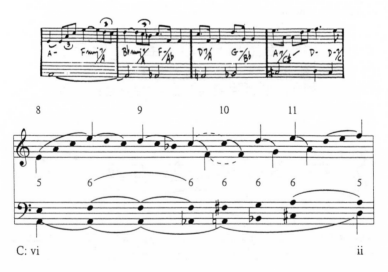

Example 29: I'm Your Pal

Example 30: Windows

Example 31: If You Never Come to Me

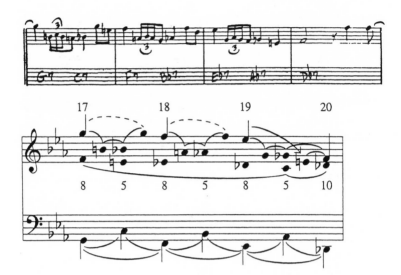

Example 32: Jordu

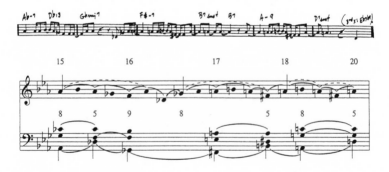

Example 33: Golden Lady

patterns. A simple 9–8 suspension may be seen at m. 16 of "Golden Lady" (Example 33), to be discussed below. The resolution of such a suspension may be delayed until the change of bass, so that the 9th effectively replaces the 8ve, as in "Grand Central" (Example 34). Here the 9ths are heard as suspensions on each of the ii chords in a sequential series of ii-Vs. Similarly a 13th may replace the 5th, as in "Minority" (Example 35), in which the ii chords have 9ths and the V chords have 13ths, so that 9–13 replaces 8–5, producing a uniquely jazz-oriented version of

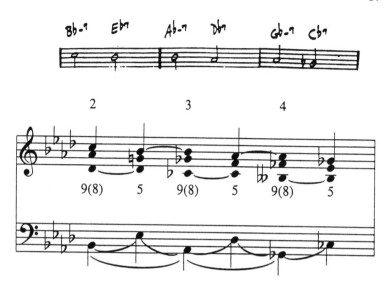

Example 34: Grand Central

Example 35: Minority

Example 36: Yesterdays

the pattern.[19] This circle-of-fifths series of ii-Vs ends with G♭m7–C♭7 (mm. 13–14) which act as a chromatic lower neighbor to the structural ii-V group in mm. 15–16. A similar example is "Yesterdays" (Example 36), in which, after m. 9, 9ths and 13ths consistently replace 8ves and 5ths.[20] In "Yesterdays" the pattern begins on 5 rather than 8; a model for this pattern is given in Example 1 (d2). The graph of "Yesterdays" makes two changes to the *Real Book* version quoted, based on the published sheet music and the variable possibilities of performance practice: The E♭maj7 of m. 14 is omitted, and the substitute dominant E♭7 of m. 16 is replaced by the diatonic V7, A7. "Golden Lady" (Example 33) shows an 8–5 pattern that is divided into two segments. First, in agreement with Example 1 (d1), there is a ii-V-I cadence on G♭ (♭III in the E♭ major context) at m. 16 with a 9–8 suspension elaborating the second 8. Second, the G♭maj7 becomes F♯mi7 and a new series of 8–5s begins, each 8–5 being a ii-V group, and disagreeing with Example 1 (d1) in that the bass interval between the 5 and the following 8 is a second rather than a fifth.[21] In "Dolphin Dance" (Example 37), this interval is a third. The use of the smaller intervals to connect 8–5 pairs produces the effect of ascent, in contrast to the descending effect of the circle-of-fifths pattern in Exam-

Example 37: Dolphin Dance

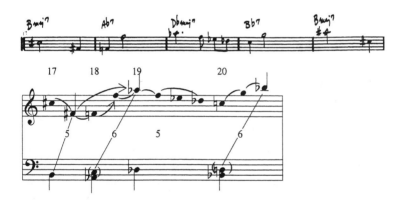

Example 38: Very Early

ple 1 (d1). "Dolphin Dance" also involves some substitution of 9 for 8 and 13 for 5. The 5 and 8 at mm. 29–30 are only implied.[22]

   e. 5–6 and 6–5 Both these patterns are voice leading strategies to avoid parallel fifths by placing a sixth between otherwise successive fifths. The sixth is connected stepwise in one voice to one or both of the surrounding fifths. Models for 5–6 and 6–5 patterns are given in Example 1 (e1–4). The Forte-Gilbert paradigm for 5–6 (Example 1 [e1])[23] ascends, suggesting a chord "progression" with root motion down a third, then up a fourth. This progression occupies mm. 17–20 of "Very Early" (Example 38); however, neither the bass nor the melody completely participate

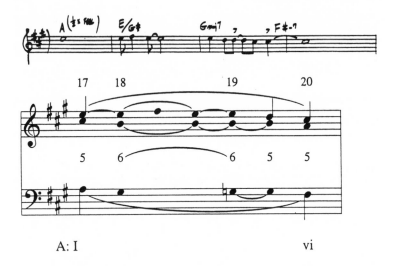

Example 39: Fortune Smiles

in forming the pattern. The Forte-Gilbert paradigm for 6–5 (Example 1 [e2])[24] descends. This pattern, but beginning with the 5th and thereby producing a descending 5–6, is shown in Example 1 (e3). This descending 5–6 pattern occurs in "Fortune Smiles" (Example 39), connecting I to vi through a chromatic bass line which, incidentally, abandons the pattern too soon to avoid parallel fifths! In the verse of "But Not for Me" (Example 40), the soprano descends diatonically from 5 to 1 while the tenor (which functions as the bass of the pattern) descends chromatically. The pattern also may be seen in more elaborate form in "Looking Back" (Example 41), again with a diatonic soprano and chromatic bass. Example 1 (e4) shows a different descending 6–5 pattern which occurs in "Wait Till You See Her." Example 42 (a) shows the harmonization given in a published edition of Richard Rodgers's songs; Example 42 (b) shows the harmonization given in *The Real Book*. Both reveal the 6–5 pattern, but in the *Real Book* version all the fifths are diminished.

   f. 5–10 and 10–5. The 5–10 pattern is presented differently by Forte-Gilbert (Example 1 [f1])[25] and Neumeyer-Tepping (Example 1 [f2]).[26] The latter version, based on a circle-of-fifths progression, appears in "Bluesette" (Example 43), with the soprano registrally displaced on each of the 10s. However, a third version, a model for which is given in Example 1 (f3), occurs in simple form in "Lollipops and Roses" (Example 44).

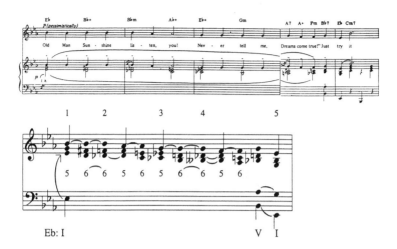

Example 40: But Not For Me

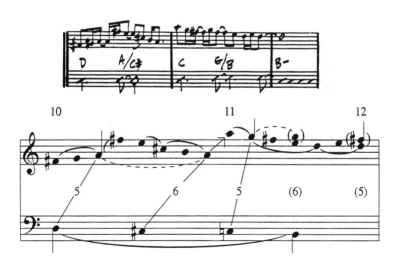

Example 41: Looking Back

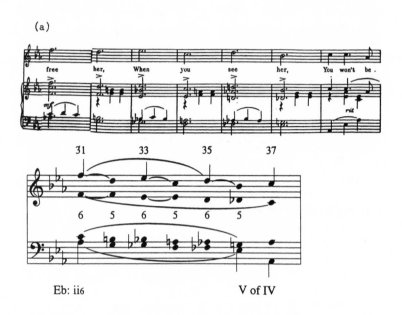

(a)

Eb: ii6   V of IV

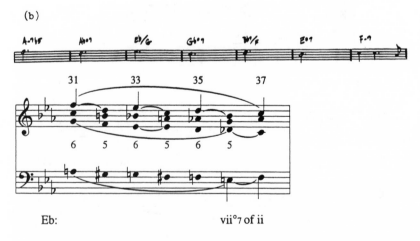

(b)

Eb: vii°7 of ii

Examples 42a and b: Wait Till You See Her

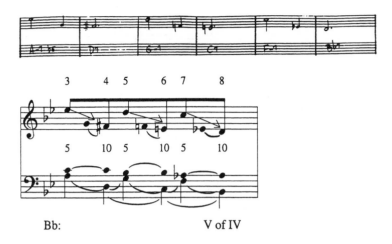

Example 43: Bluesette

Example 44: Lollipops and Roses

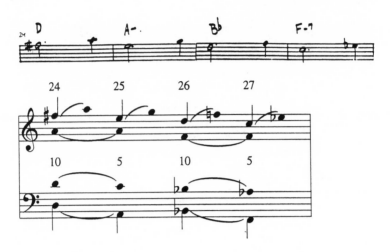

Example 45: Crystal Silence

Example 46: Gloria's Step

Models for the 10–5 pattern are given in Example 1 (f4–7). The examples in the jazz repertory do not follow the published model, given in Example 1 (f4).[27] However, they do make clear 10–5 patterns. A descending form may be found in "Crystal Silence" (Example 45), based

Example 47: Don't Blame Me

on the model given in Example 1 (f5). Here the chords emulate two Dorian plagal cadences connected by a rising step in the bass. In "Gloria's Step" (Example 46), based on the model given in Example 1 (f6), the plagal cadential effect is attenuated by the unstable half diminished structure of all the chords, and the bass connecting interval changes to a rising third. Ascending forms may also be found, based on the model given in Example 1 (f7). In "Don't Blame Me" (Example 47) a ii-V group is repeated a step higher. In "Ceora" (Example 48) the same process occurs twice, producing three iv-V groups ascending by step.[28]

    g. 10–7 and 7–10. A model for the 10–7 pattern (after Forte-Gilbert)[29] is given in Example 1 (g1). 10–7 patterns occur frequently in jazz, as, considered as chords, they show the preparation and resolution of the 7th of a 7th chord in a circle-of-fifths progression in root position. In its simplest form the pattern produces the appearance of a diatonic circle-of-fifths progression, as in "Autumn Leaves" (Example 49) and "How My Heart Sings" (Example 50). The progression may move from one diatonic area to another, as in "All the Things You Are" (Example 51), which moves from F minor (i) to C major (V). In the *Real Book* version of "Here's That Rainy Day" (Example 52 [b]), a 10–7 pattern beginning on iv approaches the tonic through an authentic cadence. The presence

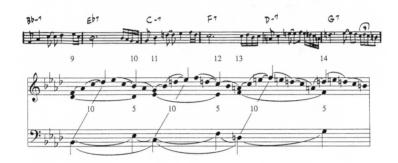

Example 48: Ceora

Example 49: Autumn Leaves

Example 50: How My Heart Sings

Example 51: All the Things You Are

Example 52: Here's That Rainy Day

Example 53: How High the Moon

Example 54: Solar

of the pattern in *The Real Book* illustrates the preference of improvisors for circle-of-fifths progressions: the sheet music version (Example 52 [a]) does not show the continuous 10–7 pattern, but cadences on ♭III (m. 11), suggesting a different interpretation.

The 10ths may be changed chromatically from major to minor by lowering the soprano, producing a series of apparent ii-V-I cadences on 10ths that descend in whole steps, as in "How High the Moon" (Example 53) and "Solar" (Example 54). "Lazy Bird" (Example 55)[30]

Example 55: Lazy Bird

Example 56: Airegin

illustrates the same procedure with an added chromatic ii-V group acting as a substitute dominant of the next dominant chord. The 10ths may
also be changed chromatically from major to minor by raising the bass,
producing a series of apparent ii-V-I cadences on 10ths that descend in
half steps, as in "Airegin" (Example 56). In "Airegin," at the point of the
change of the 10th from major to minor, an 11th replaces the 10th, as in

Example 57: What Are You Doing the Rest of Your Life?

"Red Clay" above. However, in this case the 11th resolves over the next chord. The above procedure is used in combination with the lowering of both the bass and the soprano to change the 10th from major to minor in "What Are You Doing the Rest of Your Life" (Example 57), producing apparent descending ii-V-I cadences on 10ths separated by irregular intervals. Here an 11th replaces the 10th on each of the ii chords.

A model for the 7–10 pattern (after Forte-Gilbert)[31] is given in Example 1 (g2). The 7–10 pattern is the same as the 10–7 beginning on the 7. A simple example comes from "Nostalgia in Times Square" (Example 58), a melodically nonsequential pattern consisting of a string of ii-Vs in a circle-of-fifths progression. A similar progression underlies "'Round Midnight" (Example 59),[32] a longer example with a break in the circle-of-fifths series between m. 3 and m. 4.

The 7th may be changed chromatically from major to minor, accomodating a functional change from I to ii, and producing a series of apparent ii-V-I cadences on major 7th chords that descend in whole steps, as in "The Night Has A Thousand Eyes" (Example 60). Here the pattern connects iv to ♭II (as a Neapolitan chord, not a substitute dominant). In "One Note Samba" (Example 61), the same progression is extended to the dominant chord (m. 24). The graph replaces the *Real Book* substitute dominant (B7) with the diatonic dominant (F7). This passage features a polyphonic melodic line, one voice of which reveals the 7–10 pattern (downward stems), another a simultaneous 5–8 pattern (upward stems).

Example 58: Nostalgia in Times Square

Example 59: 'Round Midnight

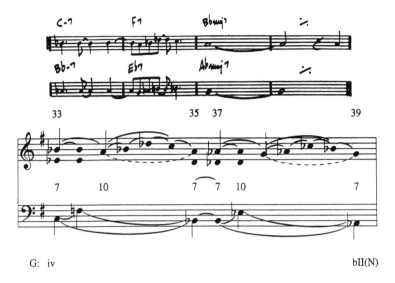

G: iv   bII(N)

Example 60: The Night Has a Thousand Eyes

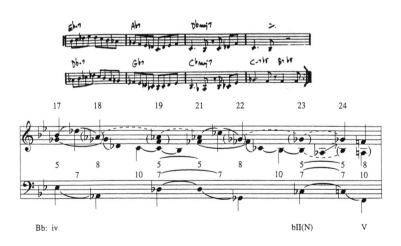

Bb: iv   bII(N)   V

Example 61: One Note Samba

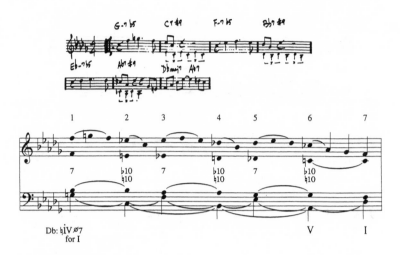

Example 62: Woody 'n You

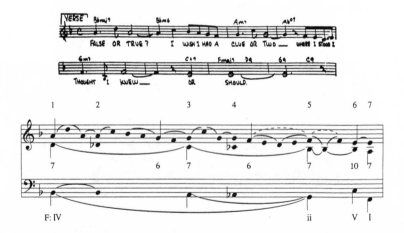

Example 63: Ev'ry Time

In "Woody'n You" (Example 62), the minor 10th (or augmented 9th) is played in the melody above the expected major 10th, which sounds in an inner voice, projecting another apparent series of circle-of-fifths ii-V groups.[33] The first chord of the passage is ♯iv°7, a common bebop substitute for the tonic.[34]

Example 64: Day Waves

h. 7–6. A model for the 7–6 pattern (after Forte-Gilbert)[35] is given in Example 1 (h). This consists of descending 6ths elaborated by delaying the movement of the upper voice to produce a chain of 7–6 suspensions. In the jazz repertory, such a chain is usually accompanied by a chromatically descending bass line. The pattern connects IV to ii in the verse of "Ev'ry Time" (Example 63). Less clearly functional is the chromatically descending pattern in "Day Waves" (Example 64). The B♭ in m. 19 is a neighbor, not a suspension, but in the context it suggests the continuation of the 7–6 pattern. In jazz harmony, the 7th of a major 7th chord can obtain a sense of resolution by moving to the added 6th of the same chord. A chain of such resolutions occurs in "Molten Glass" (Example 65). Because of the tendency in jazz to cultivate certain kinds of dissonance, the resolution of the 7th is sometimes elided, producing a series of parallel 7ths, as in "Night and Day" (Example 66) and "Spring Can Really Hang You Up the Most" (Example 67). The final 7th in the former example does resolve to a 6th in m. 12. The latter example connects two C major tonic chords by traversing the octave in three equal divisions: C-A♭-E-C. These intervening chords are each given upper neighbor chords (which approach them as if in a ii7-I relationship), producing a whole-tone scale in the bass.

Example 65: Molten Glass

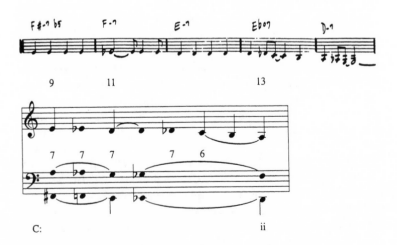

Example 66: Night and Day

Example 67: Spring Can Really Hang You Up the Most

Example 68: "Nonsequence"

i. 8–10. A model for the 8–10 pattern (after Forte-Gilbert)[36] is given
in Example 1 (i). This pattern, if considered as a chord progression, suggests a circle-of-fourths progression, a relatively rare progression in jazz.
"Nonsequence" (Example 68) presents this pattern serving to connect
G7 (V) through a series of dominant 7ths to B7, which approaches the
tonic, C in m. 7 (not shown) as a lower neighbor.[37] In "Captain Marvel"

Example 69: Captain Marvel

(Example 69), the chords are all minor triads, not in a clear tonality, as the tonic (G minor) is established considerably later in the piece. The final 10th occurs at an unexpected pitch level, as measured by the model.

3. CONCLUSION

Although the scope of this study is relatively small, a few statistical generalizations can be made on the basis of the 68 examples presented. The order of frequency of occurence of the patterns is as follows: 10–10 (21 examples), 10–7/7–10 (14 examples), 8–5/5–8 (8 examples),[38] 6–6 (7 examples), 5–10/10–5 (6 examples), 7–6 and 5–6 (5 examples each), 8–10 (2 examples), and 10–6 (1 example). The usual dominance of circle-of-fifths progressions in this music might suggest a leading role for those patterns based on them (10–7/7–10, 8–55–8, 5–10/10–5); in fact, they do lead, but not so much as one might expect. The explanation may be that most circle-of-fifths progressions in the repertory are too short to form patterns, and the other kinds of patterns (especially the 10–10 and 6–6) are desirable for the contrast they provide.

As to where in the formal structure of a piece patterns are found, in general, they may appear at any point. Although no significant preference is evident from this study, in some cases the patterns correlate with a section of the form. Some may completely occupy a section of an AABA or ABAC 32-bar form, while others simply occur within a section; in most cases, they do not bridge sectional divisions.

Linear intervallic patterns occur frequently in the jazz repertory. They take the forms long recognized in classical music, but they also take other forms and sometimes have unique characteristics. The 10–10 pattern between bass and an inner voice often moves in oblique or contrary motion with the soprano; the 10–7 pattern is inflected chromatically in numerous ways to produce chromatically related ii-V groups; and the 8–5, 5–8, and 7–6 patterns are elaborated by the addition of suspensions or extensions, both resolved and unresolved. Recognition of linear intervallic patterns can aid in the perception of the basic structures of compositions, and constitutes an important step in the understanding of their harmony.

NOTES

1. Allen Forte, *Tonal Harmony in Concept and Practice,* 3rd ed. (New York: Holt Rinehart and Winston, 1979); Allen Forte and Steven Gilbert, *Introduction to Schenkerian Analysis* (New York: W. W. Norton, 1983); David Neumeyer and Susan Tepping, *A Guide to Schenkerian Analysis* (Englewood Cliffs, New Jersey): Prentice-Hall, 1992.
2. *The Real Book,* 1978 edition. Illegal fake book, no credits. A 5th edition, dated November 16, 1988, reprints the contents of the 1978 edition unchanged, while adding a four-page list of "corrections." None of the corrections apply to the examples presented here. The aim of this book, according to the foreword, is to present the works of "major jazz composers of the last 30 years," as well as "standards and Broadway show tunes which have become part of the jazz repertoire. . . ."
3. Forte 1979, 363.
4. The reader will note that at times clefs and key signatures are missing from the excerpts taken from fake books. The clef is always treble; the key signature is furnished on the analytical graph. I wish to thank Mark Gruen for his careful computerized copying of my hand-drawn graphs.
5. Forte-Gilbert, 84.
6. The symbol "ct°7" means common-tone diminished seventh chord, also called ♯ii°7. See Steven Strunk, "The Harmony of Early Bop: A Layered Approach," *Journal of Jazz Studies 6,* no. 1, (1979):12–13.
7. Forte-Gilbert 1983, 100.
8. The expansion of the G-flat minor seventh chord (m. 29) into a ii-V group in the graph is based on numerous performances and the variations of performance practice; it has no bearing on the 10–10 pattern or the textural expansion.

9. *The Real Book* gives the composer as Miles Davis; the copyright registration correctly gives the composer as Wayne Shorter.

10. Forte-Gilbert, 86.

11. The graph may appear to indicate a ii6 rather than a IV in m. 6; however, the sheet music arrangement above reveals that the 6 of the 7–6 is an added 6th, not an inverted root. (This is also true of the 7–6 suspension at the end of Example 26, "How Insensitive.")

12. The graph ignores the bass line of the arrangement in mm. 19–20 in order to bring out the 6–6 pattern, which is usually performed.

13. In this example, the tenor and bass carry the main expression of the linear intervallic pattern, as in Examples 10 and 11 above; the soprano partially doubles the tenor.

14. Here again the tenor and bass carry the linear intervallic pattern.

15. Forte-Gilbert, 87. The example is shortened.

16. See Steven Strunk, "Harmony (i)," in *The New Grove Dictionary of Jazz,* ed. Barry Kernfeld, vol. 1 (New York: MacMillan, 1988), section 1 (iv).

17. Forte-Gilbert, 88. The example is shortened.

18. *The Real Book* gives the title as "Jordu;" the copyright registration gives it as "Jor-du."

19. The replacement of the linear intervallic pattern 8–5 by 9–13 is discussed in Steven Leroy Larson, "Schenkerian Analysis of Modern Jazz" (Ph.D. diss., University of Michigan, 1987), 43–44.

20. See also the discussion in Steven Strunk, "Bebop Melodic Lines: Tonal Characteristics," *Annual Review of Jazz Studies 3* (1985):111.

21. This might be explained as an omission of a chord with an E root between the B7 of m. 17 and the Ami7 of m. 18, were it not for the ii-V groupings. See Forte 1979, 365–69.

22. An alternate interpretation of this passage is that it elaborates ascending 10ths (shown in the graph as thirds) above the bass of the dominant seventh chords: D7–E7-F♯7. Cf. "Chega de Saudade" (Example 13).

23. Forte-Gilbert, 89. The example is shortened.

24. Ibid., 90. The example is shortened.

25. Ibid., 92. The example is shortened.

26. Neumeyer-Tepping, 20. The example is shortened.

27. Forte-Gilbert, 93. The example is shortened.

28. Although the 10–5 pattern appears obviously on the surface, a case could be made for ascending parallel 10ths in the dominant sevenths as the middleground basis of this passage. See also Note 19 above.

29. Forte-Gilbert, 93.
30. *The Real Book* gives the title as "Lazybird;" the copyright registration gives it as "Lazy Bird."
31. Forte-Gilbert, 95. The example is shortened.
32. *The Real Book* omits Cootie Williams as co-composer; the copyright registration includes him.
33. Cf. Example 10, "Gloria's Step," m. 4.
34. See Strunk 1979, 15–20.
35. Forte-Gilbert, 96. The example is shortened.
36. Ibid. The example is shortened.
37. See also Strunk 1979, 20–21.
38. Example 61 is included here and in the 10–7/7–10 count, as it exhibits both patterns.

EXAMPLES

Example 1. Models for linear intervallic patterns.

Example 2. "The Duke" by Dave Brubeck (Derry Music Co., 1956); from *The Real Book*. 1978, p. 127.

Example 3. "Sweet Georgia Bright" by Charles Lloyd; from *The Real Book*. 1978, p. 417.

Example 4. "Trance" by Steve Kuhn (Stephen L. Kuhn, 1973); from *The Real Book*. 1978, p. 435.

Example 5. "Body and Soul" by Johnny Green (Harms, Inc., 1930); from *The Real Book*. 1978, p. 59.

Example 6. "Midwestern Night's Dream" by Pat Metheny (Pat Metheny, 1976); from *The Real Book*. 1978, p. 481.

Example 7. "I'm Old Fashioned" by Jerome Kern (music) and Johnny Mercer (lyrics) (Chappell and Co., Inc., 1942); from published sheet music.

Example 8. "Lush Life" by Billy Strayhorn (Tempo Music, 1949); from published sheet music.

Example 9. "Red Clay" by Freddie Hubbard; from *The Real Book*. 1978, p. 362.

Example 10. "Gloria's Step" by Scott La Faro; from *The Real Book*. 1978, p. 172.

Example 11. "Memories of Tomorrow" by Keith Jarrett (Kundalini Music Co., 1972); from *The Real Book*. 1978, p. 289.

Example 12. "Gary's Waltz" by Gary McFarland; from *The Real Book*. 1978, p. 166.

Example 13. "Chega de Saudade" by Antonio Carlos Jobim (A. C. Jobim and Vinicius De Moraes, 1962); from *The Real Book*. 1978, p. 75.

Example 14. "It Never Entered My Mind" by Richard Rodgers (music) and Lorenz Hart (lyrics) (Chappell and Co., Inc., 1940); from published sheet music.

Example 15. "Four" by Miles Davis (Prestige Music Co., 1963); from *The Real Book*. 1978, p. 161.

Example 16. "If You Never Come to Me" by Antonio Carlos Jobim (Ipanema Music Corp., 1968); from *The Real Book*. 1978, p. 212.

Example 17. "Nefertiti" by Wayne Shorter (Wayne Shorter, 1968); from *The Real Book*. 1978, p. 317.

Example 18. "Little Waltz" by Ron Carter (Ronald L. Carter, 1966); from *The Real Book*. 1978, p. 270.

Example 19. "Think of Me" by George Cables (Contemporary Music, 1971); from *The Real Book*. 1978, p. 428.

Example 20. "The Duke" by Dave Brubeck (Derry Music Co., 1956); from *The Real Book*. 1978, p. 127.

Example 21. "Crystal Silence" by Chick Corea (Litha Music Co., 1972); from *The Real Book*. 1978, p. 100.

Example 22. "Falling Grace" by Steve Swallow (Grayfriar Music, 1969); from *The Real Book*. 1978, p. 147.

Example 23. "Do I Hear a Waltz?" by Richard Rodgers (music) and Stephen Sondheim (lyrics) (Chappell and Co., Inc., 1965); from Lee Snider, ed., *The Songs of Richard Rodgers*. Williamson Music, Inc. (n.d.), p. 305.

Example 24. "The Folks Who Live On the Hill" by Jerome Kern (music) and Oscar Hammerstein (lyrics) (T. B. Harms Co., 1937); from published sheet music.

Example 25. "You Do Something to Me" by Cole Porter (T. B. Harms Co., 1929); from Sirmay, Albert, arr., *The Cole Porter Song Book*. New York: Simon and Schuster, 1959, pp. 19–20.

Example 26. "How Insensitive" by Antonio Carlos Jobim (A. C. Jobim and Vinicius De Moraes, 1966); from *The Real Book*. 1978, p. 203.

Example 27. "Falling Grace" by Steve Swallow (Grayfriar Music, 1969); from *The Real Book*. 1978, p. 147.

Example 28. "No Moon At All" by Redd Evans and David Mann (Jefferson Music Co., 1949); from *Current Standard Songs,* Vol. 5. (illegal fake book, no credits), p. 190.

Example 29. "I'm Your Pal" by Steve Swallow (Grayfriar Music, 1969); from *The Real Book*. 1978, p. 221.

Example 30: "Windows" by Chick Corea (Litha Music, 1966); from *The Real Book*. 1978, p. 467.

Example 31. "If You Never Come to Me" by Antonio Carlos Jobim (Ipanema Music Corp., 1968); from *The Real Book*. 1978, p. 212.

Example 32. "Jordu" by Duke Jordan (Motion Music Co., 1959); from *The Real Book*. 1978, p. 245.

Example 33. "Golden Lady" by Stevie Wonder (Stein and Van Stock, Inc. and Black Bull Music, Inc., 1973); from *The Real Book*. 1978, p. 174.

Example 34. "Grand Central" by John Coltrane (Jowcol Music, 1977); from *The Real Book*. 1978, p. 178.

Example 35. "Minority" by Gigi Gryce (Jacogg Publications, Inc., 1964); from *The Real Book*. 1978, p. 295.

Example 36. "Yesterdays" by Jerome Kern (T. B. Harms, 1933); from *The Real Book*. 1978, p. 473.

Example 37. "Dolphin Dance" by Herbie Hancock (1966; Hancock Music, 1982); from *The Real Book*. 1978, p. 122.

Example 38. "Very Early" by Bill Evans (Bill Evans, 1962, Acorn Music Corp., 1965); from *The Real Book*. 1978, p. 443.

Example 39."Fortune Smiles" by Keith Jarrett (Kundalini Music Co., 1971); from *The Real Book*. 1978, p. 160.

Example 40. "But Not For Me" by George Gershwin (music) and Ira Gershwin (lyrics) (WB Music Corp., 1930); from *Gershwin on Broadway*. Warner Bros. Publications, Inc., 1987, p. 306.

Example 41. "Looking Back" by Richard Niles; from *The Real Book*. 1978, p. 275.

Example 42. "Wait Till You See Her" by Richard Rodgers (music) and Lorenz Hart (lyrics) (Chappell and Co., Inc. 1942); (a) from Lee Snider, ed., *The Songs of Richard Rodgers*. Williamson Music, Inc. (n.d.), p. 137; (b) from *The Real Book*. 1978, p. 445.

Example 43. "Bluesette" by Jean "Toots" Thielemans (Duchess Music Corp., 1963; Manitou-Duchess, 1963); from *The Real Book*. 1978, p. 56.

Example 44. "Lollipops and Roses" by Tony Velona (Leeds Music Corp., 1960); from *Current Standard Songs,* Vol. 5 (illegal fake book, no credits), p. 155.

Example 45. "Crystal Silence" by Chick Corea (Litha Music Co., 1972); from *The Real Book*. 1978, p. 100.

Example 46. "Gloria's Step" by Scott La Faro; from *The Real Book*. 1978, p. 162.

Example 47. "Don't Blame Me" by Jimmy McHugh (Robbins Music Corp., 1933); from *The Real Book*. 1978, p. 125.

Example 48. "Ceora" by Lee Morgan (Blue Horizon Music, Inc., 1965); from *The Real Book*. 1978, p. 73.

Example 49. "Autumn Leaves" by Joseph Kosma (Enoch & Cie., 1947); from *The Real Book*. 1978, p. 36.

Example 50. "How My Heart Sings" by Earl Zindars (Earl Zindars, 1963); from *The Real Book*. 1978, p. 204.

Example 51. "All the Things You Are" by Jerome Kern (T. B. Harms Co., 1939); from *The Real Book*. 1978, p. 18.

Example 52. "Here's That Rainy Day" by James Van Heusen (music) and Johnny Burke (lyrics) (Burke and Van Heusen, 1953); (a) from published sheet music; (b) from *The Real Book*. 1978, p. 191.

Example 53. "How High the Moon" by Morgan Lewis (Chappell and Co., Inc., 1940); from *The Real Book*. 1978, p. 202.

Example 54. "Solar" by Miles Davis (Prestige Music Co., Inc., 1963); from *The Real Book*. 1978, p. 386.

Example 55. "Lazy Bird" by John Coltrane (Groove Music Co., 1957); from *The Real Book*. 1978, p. 259.

Example 56. "Airegin" by Sonny Rollins (Prestige Music Co., Inc., 1963); from *The Real Book*. 1978. p. 11.

Example 57. "What Are You Doing the Rest of Your Life?" by Michel Legrand (United Artists Music Co., 1969); from *The Real Book*. 1978, p. 457.

Example 58. "Nostalgia in Times Square" by Charles Mingus (Jazz Workshop, Inc., 1976); from *The Real Book*. 1978, p. 326.

Example 59. "'Round Midnight" by Thelonious Monk and Cootie Williams (Advanced Music Corp., 1944); from *The Real Book*. 1978, p. 364.

Example 60. "The Night Has a Thousand Eyes" by Dottie Wayne, Marilyn Garrett, and Ben Weisman (Blen Music, Inc., 1962; Mabs Music Co., 1962); from *The Real Book*. 1978, p. 322.

Example 61. "One Note Samba" by Antonio Carlos Jobim (A. C. Jobim, Mrs. N. Mendonca, and Editiones Musicales Eddie Barclay, 1961); from *The Real Book*. 1978, p. 331.

Example 62. "Woody'n You" by Dizzy Gillespie (John Gillespie, 1943; Charling Music Corp., 1970); from *The Real Book*. 1978, p. 470.

Example 63. "Ev'ry Time" by Hugh Martin and Ralph Blane (Chappell and Co., Inc., 1941); from unidentified fake book, ca. 1959.

Example 64. "Day Waves" by Chick Corea (Litha Music Co., 1972); from *The Real Book*. 1978, p. 106.

Example 65. "Molten Glass" by Joe Farrell (Char-Liz Music, 1970); from *The Real Book*. 1978, p. 298.

Example 66. "Night and Day" by Cole Porter (Harms, Inc., 1932); from *The Real Book*. 1978, p. 320.

Example 67. "Spring Can Really Hang You Up the Most" by Tom Wolf (music) and Fran Landesman (lyrics) (Wolf-Mills Music, Inc., 1955); hand copied from published sheet music, 1961.

Example 68. "Nonsequence" by Michael Gibbs (Grayfriar Music, 1974); from *The Real Book*. 1978, p. 324.

Example 69. "Captain Marvel" by Chick Corea (Litha Music Co., 1972); from *The Real Book*. 1978, p. 324.

MICRORHYTHMS IN JAZZ:
A REVIEW OF PAPERS

Geoffrey L. Collier
James Lincoln Collier

Jazz people have always assumed that a mystery lies at the heart of the music. One of the most frequently repeated folk tales in the music is that when some well-known musician—usually given either as Louis Armstrong or Fats Waller—was asked what swing was, he replied, "If you gotta ask, you'll never know."

And in truth, although many knowledgeable jazz people have made attempts at defining that magical quality, nobody has yet come up with a convincing definition of swing. It all depends, so it has appeared, on many subtle nuances of time and accentuation that are beyond calculation.

But music is a physical artifact existing in time and space, and therefore can, at least theoretically, be measured. One group of people who have been particularly interested in making such measurements are perceptual motor psychologists. These scientists, who should not be confused with the clinical psychologists who deal with mental health, have long been attempting to study the way that music, acting through the human nervous system, produces its well-known emotional or mental affects. Why, in fact, do we feel stirred, uplifted, excited, by sequences of sounds we call a song, a symphony, a jazz solo? Beyond what such studies may do to help elucidate the connection between music and emotion, these experimental psychologists hope that the work will lead to a greater understanding of the brain—the real *raison d'etre* for the work.

It has been particularly since the advent of cognitive psychology in the late 1950s and 1960s that psychological studies of music have begun to yield results which have interested musicians. There now exists a burgeoning cognitive psychology of music, with its journals, meetings and seminars. The key to the new knowledge has been the development of the microcomputer, which cognitive psychologists have used as a microscope to study the microprocesses which undergird musical performance and perception: just as the biologist uses the microscope to enlarge bits of space, so the cognitive psychologist uses the computer to enlarge bits of time.

The aspect of music which the microcomputer is best suited to deal with is, thus, "time," or rhythm. Using electronic equipment, the experimenter can show how notes which are ostensibly the same, in fact vary slightly in length, begin or end a bit away from where they are expected to be, and so forth. It is assumed that these slight variations are part of the player's "interpretation" of a piece that gives it the life and emotional meaning that make it worth studying in the first place.

Until recently, however, virtually all studies in the psychology of music have involved classical, or at least "nonjazz" music. Only recently have psychologists turned their attention to jazz. This lack of interest in jazz is surprising, because if there is anything the jazz musician understands—or thinks he understands in any case—it is the almost imperceptible shadings of time that are critical to playing jazz. "Ahead of the beat," "behind the beat," "on top of the beat" are constant topics of conversation, even argument, among jazz musicians.

But finally we are beginning to see the glimmerings of a discipline of studies in the psychology of time in jazz. One obvious goal of these studies is to see if the phenomenon called "swing," which jazz people think is central to the music, can be identified and broken down into its components. However, there are many other aspects of jazz rhythm that are coming under investigation. In this paper we will look at some investigations of the psychology of time in jazz.

COGNITIVE PLANS AND INTENTIONALITY

The first question asked by any investigator into the small variations in note duration and placement that are everywhere in music of any kind is whether they are intentional or are chance effects—"mistakes," if you will. Can we show, in any given case, that the performer employs a consistent strategy in respect to these minor variations? By "intentional" we do not mean "conscious." For example, when we read ordinary prose our eyes tend to skip over functor words such as "and" and "or." We are not conscious of making these skips, but they are nonetheless intentional, as part of our strategy for reading. In the case of music, for example, one investigator (Palmer, 1989) discovered that classical pianists will say that they accent melody notes by making them louder, but in fact may be playing them earlier—slightly "ahead of the beat." The procedure is unconscious, but clearly intentional. In other instances, Palmer discovered that procedures of this kind were intentional *and* conscious—that the performers were doing what they said they were doing. Studies of this kind have forced investigators to conclude that we cannot take at face value what either performers or listeners tell us is going on in subtle aspects of a musical performance: only measurement can tell us for sure.

And we cannot read minds, how then do we infer intentionality? The approach used by music psychologists is one fundamental to much research in cognitive psychology of any kind: test the process many times, in slightly different contexts, and, if you keep getting the same sort of variation, it becomes increasingly implausible to ascribe the result to mere chance: the actor must have intended something.

Thus, if a musician varies a particular note in a certain way (say, lengthens it) only once, we cannot infer intent; but if the *same* lengthening occurs on the *same* note repeatedly, it is unlikely to be due to chance.

This raises the problem of what is meant by the "same" note, since each note in a performance is played only once. Generally, we can denote two notes as being "the same" if they have structurally similar functions. One obvious way to test for these variations is to have one or more performers play the same piece several times. However, it is often impractical to have a piece repeated sufficiently often for good results. Fortunately, there are other structural mappings that can be made. The most obvious are using repetitions of sections within a piece. At a still lower level, researchers have treated measures as repetitions, even when their contents are different, on the supposition that positions within measures may have functional similarities. In sum, one of the commonest strategies in investigating the subtleties in a musical performance is to compare how a performer treats similar notes, or groups of notes, in one or more pieces of music.

DEPENDENT AND INDEPENDENT VARIABLES

One of the major problems faced by investigators in psychology is "data collection"—that is, finding a lot of subjects and running enough tests on them to make sure that chance or coincidence is ruled out. In music, however, the problem is the reverse. Modern technology makes it possible for the researcher to collect a flood of data on the fine details of a musical performance in a relatively few hours, and the problem becomes winnowing it to manageable size. The question then becomes: What variables should the investigator look at? What are the effects of X (independent variable) on the behavior of Y (dependent variable)? Suppose, for example, we discover that a performer tends to regularly vary slightly the tempo of a piece, as we have discovered jazz groups to do (Collier and Collier, 1994). We would like to know if they are doing this systematically, and we therefore test several independent variables to see if they are having an effect on tempo. We might look to see if these tempo shifts occur at particular points of a piece, such as the bridge of a song; when certain soloists enter and exit; at specific points in a performance, such as the beginning or end, and so forth. Through a process of elimination we eventually—we hope—pin down the ways in which performers use, as in this example, tempo changes for expressive purposes.

APPROACHES TO CLASSICAL MUSIC

Psychologists have been working with classical music back to the seminal work of Carl Seashore in the 1930s, and even earlier. They have developed a considerable body of information, and the jazz researchers are presently building on their methods. It is worth looking briefly at some of these studies of classical music.

There have been two approaches. At the beginning, these studies tended to be exploratory; that is, the performer would be asked to play a piece one or more times and the researcher would then look for regularities in the performance(s). Exploratory work of this kind remains fruitful. For example, Repp (1990) obtained note onset times from a digitization of the performances of nineteen famous pianists on a single piece of music and then decomposed the similarities, using the statistical technique of principle components analysis. Poval (1977) looked at note durations for a brief segment of a Bach piece and discovered that notes of equal length in the written score were played longer or shorter, depending on their position in the bar. Shaffer (1980) extended this approach from notes to measure and found that the duration of a measure varied subtly, depending on its position within a phrase.

The second common approach to the study of music psychology is an experimental one, in which subjects are set specific tasks to prove—or disprove—a hypothesis, a procedure at the heart of scientific methodology. One common experiment is to compare an ordinary performance of a piece with a "deadpan" version, created either by electronic devices or simply by asking the performer to play a piece "as written." Palmer (1989) asked pianists to perform pieces both musically and deadpan, and looked at the differences. She found that in the musical performances, onset asynchronies between notes of a chord were greater than in the deadpan performances, with the melody notes tending to lead. That is, in the more expressive performances, the chords were arpeggiated to a greater extent than in the deadpan versions. Palmer (1989) also compared the work of experts to novice pianists on the same effect and discovered that the experts arpeggiated the chords more than the novices, indicating a greater skill at bringing out the melody.

Experiments like the above deal with performance characteristics, but there is the mirror to performance: how the auditor is perceiving the work. Repp (1992) played computer-generated deadpan pieces of music in which one note had been slightly "perturbed"—that is, its duration varied from the expected. He discovered that people's ability to detect which note was perturbed depended on the note's structural role in the musical piece.

Another widely used procedure is to compare systematically altered versions of a given piece. In a clever manipulation, Sloboda (1983) wrote pieces which contained the same melody repeated at several points, but phase-shifted in respect to the bar lines. He found that when pianists played these pieces, timing patterns differed systematically as a function of the phase shift. Clarke (1993) computer-recorded performances and systematically perturbed some of the natural rhythm patterns. When other pianists had to imitate these performances they had more difficulty with the ones that were rhythmically perturbed.

Much more research in this area has been done, and the foregoing brief review serves only to introduce some of the general ideas, as a preamble to the discussion of jazz rhythm. The interested reader will find overviews in the first few pages of both Palmer (1989) and Repp (1990), and more detailed information in some of the papers discussed herein. The journals *Music Perception* and *The Psychology of Music* carry a large share of the important research in this domain.

STUDIES IN THE PSYCHOLOGY OF JAZZ RHYTHM

Interest on the part of psychologists in jazz as a basis for study of time has developed only in the last ten years, as the dates on the foregoing papers indicate, and there are inevitably far fewer of them than ones dealing with classical music.

Pressing, 1987

A trained pianist, Pressing improvised a number of brief, unstructured, "free" jazz pieces, some of them against a click track at 60 beats per minute, some of them unaccompanied. From these he selected two for analysis, which he transcribed by hand into standard musical notation. He then subjected them to scrutiny by electronic equipment, which allowed him to measure the durations of notes, and the distance between them, down to a millisecond—that is, a thousandth of a second. He analyzed the results in several ways. Here we will concern ourselves only with the rhythmic effects of the piece which used the click track, as that allows us to see deviations of the notes from a metronomically strict performance.

Probably the most important aspect of this study has to do with where the notes fell in relationship to the mechanically performed click track beat. Pressing singled out for mathematical analysis (1) "interonset time," that is, the amount of time elapsing between successive notes; (2) duration, that is, the length of each note from the time a key was struck until it was released; and (3) the time between the ending of one note and the beginning of the next one, which would suggest degrees of staccato and legato.

One result showed many subdivisions of the beat into quarter-eighth triplets.

This result is in accord with the widespread belief among jazz theorists that the "swing" beat is based on this triplet division of the beat. Nonetheless, many onset intervals fell at other points between the beats, showing great flexibility in jazz performance, even when improvised to a metronomically exact beat; and, as we shall see, several studies indicated that this swing beat is not quite this quarter-eighth triplet.

A second of Pressing's results of interest was the duration of notes: a substantial number of them were either longer or shorter than they would have been had they been played mechanically accurately. Once again, this finding suggests that rhythmic flexibility players bring to jazz performance.

Finally, Pressing discovered that in playing chords, the notes were not struck simultaneously, but some of them earlier than others, like very subtle arpeggios. This is a common phenomenon which, as we have seen, has often been observed in classical performance. This is most often done to bring out a melody, but it may have other purposes. In his samples, Pressing found that this asynchrony depended upon the number of notes in a chord. When the chord consisted to two notes, the highest note was early; with three notes the highest note came first only half the time; and with four or five notes the highest note was always last. It is possible that these effects arose from mechanical factors having to do with the mechanics of the hand; but it may well be that these were deliberate, if unconscious, attempts to add expressiveness to the music. In this view, the top note may have a crucial melodic function when accompanied by only one note, but not as part of a larger chord.

Rose, 1989

For his doctoral dissertation, Richard Rose (1989) made use of a widely used training record made by Jamey Aebersold and called *A New Approach to Jazz Improvisation*. This record was made by "professional jazz musicians" and was "engineered so that adjusting the stereo balance of the playback device eliminates one or more rhythm section instrument(s) from the stereo mix." Rose was thus able to isolate bass, drums, etc., lines for study.

He chose three tunes presumed to represent three styles of music: a ballad, "Polka Dots and Moonbeams" (MM 60); a "swing" selection, "September Song" (MM 132); and a Latin selection, "Song for My Father" (MM 138). Rose then analyzed the results in a variety of ways.

One significant result showed in the two purely jazz tunes, "Polka Dots and Moonbeams" and "September Song," where beats one and three were shortened slightly, and beats two and four lengthened. Drums, bass, and piano all showed this tendency. This effect might have arisen from the fact that the ride beat, played explicitly by the drummer and frequently implied by the others, calls for one note on beats one and three, two notes on beats two and four; and that for purely mechanical reasons it takes more time to play two notes than one. However, the difference between the long and short beats was more pronounced in the *slower* song, "Polka Dots and Moonbeams," where the musicians had sufficient time to play the beats evenly if they had so chosen. This suggests that the difference was deliberate, if unconscious, and accords with what has been found in classical music, that when pianists wish to emphasize notes, they play them slightly longer than others.

The pattern in the Latin piece, "Song for My Father," was different.

Here the notes on the first two beats were equal in length, the note on the third beat slightly shorter, the fourth beat a little longer, suggesting a trade-off between beats three and four.

A second of Rose's results involves the subdivision of beats, a subject of intense interest to people attempting to find the roots of the swing effect. "September Song" showed the classic swing pattern, the quarter-eighth triplet division—that is, a division of two parts to one. However, the ratio was not exactly this classic two to one, but 2.38 to 1, a division somewhat more uneven than the triplet one, but not as uneven as the dotted eighth-sixteenth (3 to 1) pattern common to Western music.

For the ballad, "Polka Dots and Moonbeams," beat subdivisions were nearly equal, "as written," as would usually be the case in the performance of a popular song. In the Latin piece there was a slight tendency for the first three notes in an eighth note grouping to be slightly faster than the final one.

It is clear from the work of Rose and others that jazz players tend markedly to depart from metronomic accuracy, both within beats and within measures. But in respect to longer elements, such as phrases, Rose found the reverse: groups of measures—say the eight bars of a standard AABA pattern so common in the popular tunes jazz musicians frequently work from—are generally strikingly similar in length. That is to say, however much jazz musicians shade beats within measures, over longer stretches the beats come out very close to where a metronomically accurate performance would place them. This suggests that jazz musicians follow the principle of "borrowing from Peter to pay Paul," by compensating for a short note with a longer one, and vice versa. This result is consistent with results from studies of rhythm in classical music.

Finally, Rose observed some asynchronization of nominally simultaneous tones by different instruments. In the Aebersold record there was a rough tendency for the drums to hit first, the piano second, and the bass last. It is possible that this result is simply a consequence of the differing acoustical properties of each instrument, which gives them differing "rise" times. Nonetheless, this result does argue against the common view that the bass plays ahead of the beat in order to impart a swing feel.

Reinholdsson (1987)

Reinholdsson's approach is, like Rose's, exploratory, in that he worked from a previously recorded piece of music rather than having performers play into the computer. In this case he avoided the problem of isolating a line of music for study by working from an eight-bar drum solo by Roy Haynes. He first transcribed the solo into ordinary musical notation, and the digitized the solo, as Rose had done. Finally, he compared what Haynes actually played to the notated score of the solo. The drawback to this method is reliance on the investigator's ear in making the transcription: if there is anything that computer investigations of music have shown, it is that the ear is an extremely fallible guide to what is actually happening. Furthermore, there is the complex problem, especially in jazz, of what relationship the notated score bears, or is supposed to bear, to the actual music. As is well known, jazz arrangements are not meant to be taken literally by performers but are to be inflected in various ways according to well-understood conventions of given styles. Nonetheless, it is probably fair to assume that Reinholdsson's transcription is reasonably accurate and that something can be learned from comparing it to the actual performance as captured in minute detail on the electronic device.

Reinholdsson plotted his results on a graph, which showed how notes varied from the transcription as it might have been played by a mechanically exact drum machine. Unfortunately, his discussion of his results is brief, informal, and not as revealing as we might have wished, but some results of this interesting approach are worth noting. Deviations from the mechanical norm tended to be only on the order of five to thirty milliseconds, suggesting that Haynes was able to strike notes with great precision, but that even very small deviations have expressive importance. This is shown by a recording accompanying the book in which the paper appeared, which contains both the Haynes solo and a drum machine version of it; the differences between the two are striking, with the drum machine version almost a cartoon of the original.

A second important result of this study was that Haynes's "swing triplets" in fact ranged from 1.48 to 1, up to 1.82 to 1; that is, somewhere between the 1 to 1 ratios of even eighth notes and the 2 to 1 ratio of the supposed swing triplets.

Finally, in his paper Reinholdsson offered the results of some earlier informal experiments on bass lines. A bass player was told to play ahead or behind a beat laid down by a metronome. Examination of the electronically created graph of the bass line showed that the player was, indeed, playing ahead or behind the beat as instructed. The experimenter then asked the bassist to play a metronomically exact beat. He did not do so, although regrettably Reinholdsson does not tell us if he drifted from the beat in any systematic fashion.

Ellis (1991)

Ellis (1991) performed a study similar to the one made by Rose, except that he employed an experimental method more traditional in the field of cognitive psychology. First he created a rhythm line on a standard twelve-bar blues, using a synthesized bass line and piano chords played in real time by a competent jazz player. He then asked three saxophone players to play notated jazz riffs over the rhythm line into a MIDI-wired synthesizer. The saxophonists were in their twenties, forties, and sixties, and were chosen to represent three different styles of jazz—"swing," "traditional," and "modern," although he does not make clear what he means by the terms. (For example, "traditional," sometimes used to refer to New Orleans or dixieland jazz, is today often used to mean "bop" of the Parker-Gillespie period.) Each musician played three performances at five different tempos: MM 90, 120, 150, 180, and 210, for a total of fifteen performances.

Ellis then analyzed the results for two main properties. First he looked at asynchronies, relative to the beat defined by piano and bass. He found a strong tendency to play "behind the beat." However, this effect depended upon the tempo of the piece: for all three players the distance they played behind the beat was not proportional to the distance between beats but increased as the tempo rose.

In order to better understand this phenomenon, we have replotted Ellis's date in Figure 1. The upper figure reproduces Ellis's graph, showing delay as a proportion of the beat on the vertical axis and the metronome tempos on the horizontal axis. The data are replotted in the lower figure, in which absolute rather the proportional delay is represented on the vertical axis.

Consideration of these data helps to eliminate possible models explained in the observed patterns:

(1) If the musicians were trying to keep the delay as a constant proportion of the beat, the upper figure would be flat; but it is not.

(2) If the delay were a constant, due purely to, say, the mechanics of creating the sound, the lower graph would be flat; but it is not, as we verified using conventional statistical tests.

(3) If the delay were due to a mixture of constant time and a constant proportion, then the lower figure would be descending (i.e., delay would decrease as tempi increased); but it is ascending.

(4) Finally, consider the effects of the preparatory processes that lead up to the initiation of the first note of a sequence. These would include both mental processes and physical motions, all of which take time. It is reasonable to suppose that at least some part of these processes do not

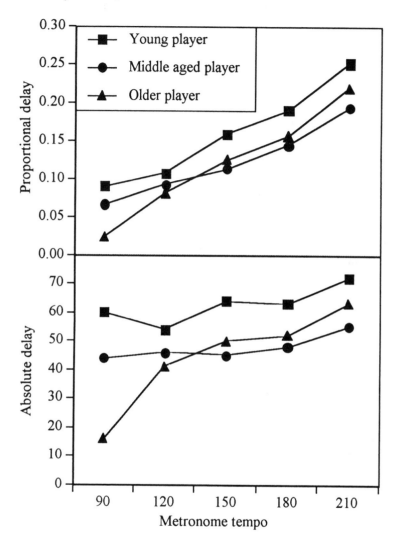

Figure 1. Ellis's data: Delay to initiate a note after the beat starts. Upper figure gives the delay as a proportion of the beat, lower figure gives the delay in absolute time.

speed up as tempo increases, but rather are fixed constants. Therefore, as the tempo speeds up, the player would have to initiate these processes earlier in order for the note to start at the same time relative to beat. But if the musician could not do this, the notes would start later and later as the tempo sped up, which is precisely the pattern observed in the data.

Further evidence would certainly be required to buttress this hypothesis, but it is the only one of the four listed above that is consistent with the data.

Turning to the beat subdivision which has interested most of these investigators, we find that Ellis has a grand average ratio of 1.7 to 1, with ranges from 1.47 to 1.87, which is more even than would be the case with true triplets. However, with Ellis's subjects this ratio tended to decrease as the tempo increased—that is, the faster the saxophonists were asked to play, the more evenly they divided the beat. To some extent, this result would be expected: at faster speeds, the shorter of the note pairs would become briefer and briefer, and thus more difficult to execute; the performer would tend to lengthen it, thus making it closer in duration to the longer note of the pair.

However, this tendency to even out the putative eighth notes in Ellis's saxophonists was not universal: one player showed the effect strongly, the other not at all. Undoubtedly, individual differences in skill entered into the equation.

We reanalyzed the data by converting metronome units into time units in milliseconds (that is, instead of calculating beats per measure, we calculated the lengths of beats). Then we divided by three as if the beat were divided into exact triplets. These were plotted with some other data (Collier, 1995), in which subjects, mostly not jazz musicians, attempted to tap out the 2-to-1 triplet ratio. In this tapping experiment, the tempo was much slower, as the subjects were supposed to be tapping beats, rather than subdivisions of the beat. Figure 2 adds the faster division of the beat played by jazz musicians with the slower subdivision of the classical musicians. The two data sets would almost fit a single curve, except that the curve for the jazz musicians is about .10 ratio unit too low. The lower portion of Figure 2 adjusts for this, to show the smooth curve. As the musicians and the circumstances of the two experiments were quite different, we can only speculate about why this .10 ratio unit difference exists. However, the important fact is that both experiments showed ratios that were less than the expected 2-to-1 triplet division, and that both could be fitted to the same curve, given suitable adjustments.

This fact is surprising, given the differences in the experiments and the musical backgrounds of the participants and suggests the possibility that these ratios are due more to mechanical than interpretive process. Perhaps the famous "swing eighth" is nothing more than a triplet, as distorted by this ubiquitous mechanical process.

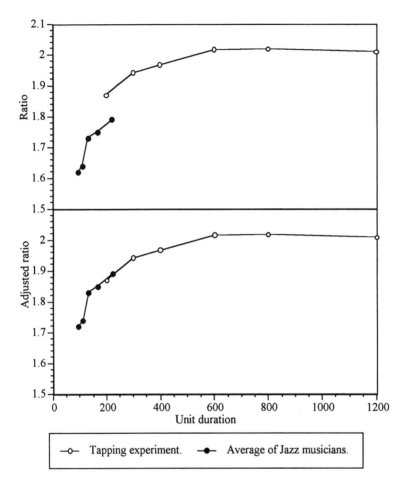

Figure 2. Ellis's data: The Y axis gives performed ratios as a function of the duration of the implied basic unit. For the jazz musicians (filled circles), the implicit subdivision was quarter-note triplets, while in the laboratory experiment with classical musicians (empty circles), the implicit subdivision was quarter notes. The upper figure represents the data, while the lower figure adjusts the ratios of the jazz musicians by adding .10 of a ratio unit.

Collier and Collier (1994)

This study was triggered in part by our discovery, through an examination of alternate takes of a considerable number of jazz recordings, that there was a tendency for even celebrated jazz groups to change tempo, almost certainly unconsciously, at specific moments in a performance, as for example at the entrance of a particular soloist, consistently slowing down across a number of takes when soloist A entered, then speeding up with the entrance of soloist B.

We decided to examine performance tempos for a variety of effects, using as our "subjects" a large body of jazz records chosen to be representative of the development of jazz through several historical periods and associated styles. The artists selected were, in the main, major ones, and included several of the most celebrated of all.

As there is no practical way to subject this material to computer analysis, we resorted to a very primitive methodology, which involved timing segments of recordings, usually four, eight, or sixteen measures in length, with an ordinary runner's stopwatch. Depending on our aims, in some cases we timed all segments of a recording; in others, selected segments.

There are two main defects to this methodology. The first was that we could measure only relative large units of time, not the milliseconds electronic equipment can discriminate. The second was that it required the mechanical pressing of the off-on button of the stopwatch, which made a certain degree of error inevitable. However, many replications of a good many performances indicated that the method was sufficiently accurate for our purposes.

But even though the method had disadvantages, the compensating advantages were considerable, in that it allowed us to examine a large corpus of work in a practicable amount of time. We first examined a hundred performances we deemed to be representative of the development of jazz over its history. We followed this with a study of other performances in order to look at specific effects, for a total of 186 performances. With a corpus this large we could say with some confidence that the results we got were characteristic of jazz, rather than idiosyncratic, as may be the case with more limited samples.

Several findings emerged. Most notable was tempo stability: the majority of both groups and soloists did not vary more than five percent. However, even though the tempo shifts were minor, they were often deliberate, if unconscious, and systematic. For example, when we compared alternate takes of the same performances, in many instances there were statistically significant tempo changes coming at the same points in alternate takes. And this was true not only of alternate takes, but in some cases of performances of a tune by a group or a soloist made several years apart. For example, we discovered that some performers would systematically increase the tempo slightly when going into the bridge portion of a song to emphasize the structural change and increase excitement.

A second question we wanted to answer was whether jazz musicians preferred certain tempos to other ones. Broadly speaking, we discovered that the tempos were distributed along a smooth normal curve, suggesting no strong preferences for certain tempos, or what is more likely, that so many factors enter into tempo selection that they balance out. That is to say, extrinsic factors like the tempo of the previous tune, or how late in the evening the tune was played, may have as much to do with tempo selection as anything else.

Nonetheless, we found a mild tendency for certain tempos to appear more frequently than others, especially a slow tempo around MM 117, a medium tempo around 160, and a fast tempo in the 220–230 range. We found that tempos in the upper 100s range appeared less often than statistically expected, and that tempos below MM 80 and above MM 260 were rare.

One of our most puzzling findings had to do with tempos that emerged when groups went into "double-time." Our sample was necessarily limited, as the device has never been used extensively, and then mainly in the earlier periods of jazz history, but we were able to find enough examples to indicate something striking about the practice. For one thing, putative doubled tempos were always faster than strict doublings, sometimes substantially so, ranging from 2.11 to 3.73; in the case of one Ben Webster solo, the new tempo was three times as fast as the original. For another, in cases where the group returned to the supposed original tempo, it virtually always landed on a tempo that was neither the original tempo, nor half of the fast tempo, but somewhere in between, typically around ten percent faster than the original tempo. What was startling about this result was that it did not occur "sometimes" or "frequently," but in every case we studied.

We have theorized that in landing on tempos measurably faster than a true double, the musicians were attempting to avoid those tempos in the mid-range, around MM 170 to MM 190, which seems to be less popular than other tempos, and were at times required to go significantly beyond a true doubling in order to achieve this. However, we have not been able to explain why our subjects almost invariably returned to a tempo somewhat faster than the original one. We would not have been surprised to find that players had trouble returning to the original tempo, but we would have expected to see them fall randomly to one side or another of it. Nor would we have been surprised to find them falling back to a tempo that was approximately half the fast tempo. But they did neither. The explanation, when discovered, may have something significant to say about how the brain deals with time in general.

Cholakis (1995)

In the August 1995 issue of *Down Beat,* writer Will Parsons reported on some work in rhythm done by Ernest Cholakis "of WC Music Research, a company specializing in groove templates for sequencer software." Parsons writes, "The common assumption is that at a medium tempo, up to about 200 beats per minute, most drummers will play the offbeat as the third note of a triplet. At a slower tempo, it will move closer to the next beat, more like the last 16th. As the tempo increases, the offbeat will gradually approach a straight eighth."

To test this hypothesis, Cholakis isolated the drum portion of a number of recordings by major jazz musicians, featuring drummers like Max Roach, Philly Joe Jones, Elvin Jones, Art Blakey, and others similarly celebrated. The writers conclude, "Although there was an overall tendency toward the eighth note at faster tempi, it turned out to be much more an individual matter than we'd predicted."

However, on reanalyzing the data it appears that the tendency toward

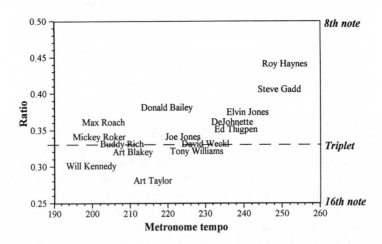

Figure 3. Plotting of data of Cholaskis's data from *Down Beat.* See text for details.

more even "eighths" at faster tempos is less idiosyncratic than the authors assert, and that it shows substantial consistency across all drummers examined. The strong tendency for the eighth to even out with increasing tempo can be seen by eye in Figure 3. This was confirmed statistically, with a quadratic regression accounting for more than 60 per cent of the variance.

These writers also noted that in the case of one drummer, Art Blakey, his undivided beats were consistently shorter than the divided ones. This tendency to play divided beats longer than undivided ones was noted by Rose (1989). Povel (1977) also noted the tendency of classical pianists to play some beats longer than others for expressive purposes.

One limitation of the Cholakis study is that all of the recordings examined were at speeds of MM 200 and above, a tempo range normally described as "fast" by jazz musicians. We have tested drummers in a laboratory setting on this phenomenon at tempos ranging from very slow to very fast and hope, when the data are analyzed, to shed additional light on this subject.

FUTURE DIRECTIONS

Our study of the papers discussed here suggests four specific technical issues we feel worth further investigation. They are:

The Phase Shift: Note Attack Relative to the Beat

The question of whether jazz musicians play ahead or "on top of the beat," behind the beat, or somewhere else in respect to it, has been the subject of a great deal of speculation almost from the beginning of jazz criticism. As early as 1925, Virgil Thomson suggested the jazz players start "a little ahead of the beat" (Thomson, 1925). It is apparent from the research in hand that jazz players do not attack precisely on the beat, and with electronic equipment it should be possible relatively quickly to discover if they attack around the beat in any systematic fashion. In technical terms, a stable change in note onset time relative to the beat—playing ahead of the beat, say—is called a shift in phase. A problem in studying this phenomenon is that the phase has to be shifted in comparison to something. For example, Rose (1989) noted that the bass, drum, and piano he studied sounded at slightly different points. How, then, do we decide which, if any of them, was playing the real beat and which were phase-shifted away from it? There is no reason, however, why more formal rules could not be established to define the beat, as for example by averaging the beat of the three instruments. Another solution is to provide a click track, as Ellis did (1991), although this establishes an artificial condition which needs to be taken into account.

A second problem, which is of particular interest to psychologists, is to determine how much of such a phase shift is due to musical strategies, conscious or unconscious, and how much arises out of mechanical "lags." There is always a time gap between the intent to produce a note and its actual sounding, as tuba players in particular are aware. Arms, hands, fingers, must move, lips form shapes, breath be expelled. We have called this sequence of actions, from intention to sounding of the note, its "trajectory."

Consider the delays observed by Ross (1989) in the light of the trajectory model. On average, the drum was heard first, followed by the piano and finally the bass. The order is roughly proportional to the rise times of these instruments, and we might hypothesize that all three musicians intended to sound the note at the same time but were thwarted by differing rise times. Or to put it in other terms, differing lags, not differing intentions, caused the instruments to be heard in sequence, not simultaneously. Laboratory examination of the trajectories of these instruments should allow us to determine how much of the delay is due to mechanical factors and how much is intentional.

Again, consider the delays found by Ellis (1991) in his studies of three saxophonists. We remember that they all consistently played behind the beat, but in general played further behind the beat as the tempo increased. Our examination of four models with different mixes of intentional and mechanical lag showed that the only model consistent with the data suggested that the increase in delay as tempos increased was largely mechanical, caused by the inability of the players to attack as closely behind the beat at fast tempos as they could at slow ones.

However, given the vast amount of lore in jazz on variations of the beat, it is hard to believe that a completely mechanistic explanation of the trajectory model we posit can fully explain these phase shifts. Nonetheless, it does provide a good base against which to pit intentional models. Indeed, Reinholdsson (1987) showed in his work that a bass player could play ahead or behind the beat on command. This suggests an interesting experiment. A click-track synthesized recording of the ride beat played by a cymbal could be coupled with a synthesized walking bass line. Different versions made by phase-shifting the bass line in vary-ing amounts ahead and behind the beat could be played for auditors of varying degrees of experience with jazz. Which versions would they pre-fer? Which ones, if any, would suggest the various styles of jazz?

The Swing Eighth Note Ratio

There is today no question that jazz players, in playing what is usually notated as pairs of eighth notes, or dotted eighth-sixteenth pairs, almost invariably make the first one longer. Indeed, this *doo ditta doo ditta doo* sound is so characteristic as to be almost a *sine qua non* of the music. Many theorists have concluded that these notes of unequal length are best described as quarter-eighth triplets.

However, researches such as those examined in this paper show that, in general, this ratio is neither even eighth notes (1 to 1), nor quarter-eighth triplets (2 to 1), but something in between. Reinholdsson found ratios between 1.48 to 1 and 1.82 to 1. Ellis observed a mean ratio of 1.7 to 1, with ranges between 1.47 to 1 and 1.87 to 1, strikingly close to the Reinholdsson ratios. There was one exception, the ratio of 2.38 to 1 found by Rose in the performance of "September Song"; it is hard to know how to explain this aberration without more study.

Further questions are raised by the fact that Collier and Wright (1995) obtained similar ratios when they tested a large number of classical musi-cians of various levels of training. These results raise the specter that this "swing" division of the beat exists in many types of music and may have more to do with the mechanics of playing music than with an intention to swing. It is possible, thus, that qualities other than elements of rhythm, like note duration and placement, are important to creating what is perceived as swing. It is obvious that here lies a rich open field for the investigator.

A final issue in the relationship of ratios at different rhythmic levels of analysis—that is, do jazz musicians balance beats, measures, and large units in the same way they do divisions of the beat? As figure 2 shows, the ratio used by jazz musicians *within* beats seems to fit the ra-tio pattern used by other musicians *between* beats, given a constant ad-justment factor. On the other hand, Collier and Collier (1994) discovered that when jazz musicians double the tempo, they almost invariably do so by a ratio of larger than two to one, implying that at least in some ways the swing eighth note ratio does not apply to larger units. We hope that our study of the ride beat, mentioned above, will address the question.

Fluidity Within Rigidity

The research available to date suggests that we can describe jazz rhythm generally as a system of "fluidity within rigidity." Rose (1989) found that AABA sections of jazz performance are quite exact in temporal length; Collier and Collier (1994) found that these sections vary only slightly from metronomic accuracy. At the same time, *within* measures there seems to be a pervasive tendency for "trade-offs" among beats. Rose, for example, found a slight elongation of the 2nd and 4th beats at the expense of 1st and 3rd beats. It is as if the rigid pulse of jazz swing is in fact an average: beats vary in length, but on the borrowing-from-Peter-to-pay-Paul principle, average out over a few bars, or even a single bar.

Individual Variation

Most of the work on the microrhythms of jazz discussed in this paper has concerned itself with universals—"grand consistencies"—that apply generally to jazz performances. Nonetheless, it is clear that there are individual differences in the rhythms used by jazz players. The Ellis paper, for example, showed that although his three saxophone players usually divided the beat according to the ratios cited above, each did it somewhat differently from the others. In the future, it is to be hoped, the study of microrhythms of jazz musicians will help us to understand those individual "styles" which have been so crucial to jazz criticism.

DISCUSSION

1. The study of jazz, using the tools of the cognitive psychologist, is still in its infancy. The research discussed above is, with the exception of the Ellis paper, exploratory rather than experimental; that is to say, it has looked at extant recordings, in the main, rather than basing itself on the testing of hypotheses in a laboratory setting.

2. Nonetheless, as limited as the research has been to date, it makes it clear that the study of jazz on this microscopic level has a great deal to offer to both the psychologist and the lover of the music. For the psychologist, the exquisitely subtle temporal substructure of jazz is rich with opportunities and challenges. For the jazz lover, it opens the way to an understanding of the music.

3. We are aware that many jazz people—musicians, critics, fans—resist this sort of theoretical approach—indeed resent it—for fear it will somehow "deaden the soul" of jazz. We believe this fear to be groundless. Anybody who studies classical music seriously learns a vast body of theory, especially as it concerns harmony, which takes years to acquire. Yet even when we can explain the exact function of every note in a Bach fugue or a Beethoven symphony, we can still be shaken by the music.

4. We believe that jazz ought to be given the same serious consideration that classical music has received for two centuries. Just as harmony is at the heart of classical music, so rhythm lies at the heart of jazz. A theoretical knowledge of the rhythmic properties of jazz is as essential to understanding it as harmonic theory is to understanding classical music. We believe it will enrich our pleasure in the music to know, for example, how the rhythms of, say, Charlie Parker and Bix Beiderbecke differ.

5. Jazz is essentially an improvised music, and as such cannot always be studied in the way that classical music has been. Generally, studies of classical music compare written scores with what has actually been played. This is not usually possible for jazz, although Reinholdsson (1987) managed to get around the problem by notating the Roy Haynes drum solo by hand and then comparing it to the recorded solo. Nonetheless, in the future, researchers into the micro details of jazz will probably approach it as students of classical music have done, by bringing into the laboratory musicians of various schools, persuasions, and levels of skill, and asking them to perform carefully chosen tasks on electronic equipment. The present authors have already begun to collect data in this fashion, by asking drummers to play the "ride beat" in various systematic ways.

6. One of the main purposes of such work is to isolate the various elements embedded in every note. It is clear enough, from studies of both classical music and jazz, that many, if not most, notes are inflected in a number of ways—shortened or lengthened, placed early or late in respect to the beat, played louder or softer, spiced with vibrato, changed during the course of their duration in respect to volume and pitch, and no doubt other practices we are as yet unaware of. We know—or at least we think we know—that out of a sequence of notes that make up a jazz performance there emerges a quality we call "swing." How much of this quality is due to relative dynamics, how much to microshadings of a beat, how much to other factors? As there is at present no way to break down a recorded performance into such qualities, it is only through carefully crafted laboratory experiments that we can find answers.

7. It should be clear that the papers examined above are few and limited in scope. They should be seen as only a start on the micro study of jazz. In truth, the best guess about the future is that it will contain surprises. That, really, is the fascination for the student of the music—that while we may see light at the end of the tunnel, we will not know what the view is from there until we reach it.

REFERENCES

Clarke, E.F. (1993). Imitating and evaluating real and transformed musical performances. *Music Perception.* 10, 3:317–341.

Collier, G.L. and Collier, J.L. (1994). An exploration of the use of tempo in jazz. *Music Perception.* 11, 3:219–242.

Collier and Wright, 1995. Temporal rescaling in simple rhythmic performance. *Journal of Experimental Psychology.* 21, 3:602–627.

Ellis, M.C. (1991). An analysis of "swing" subdivision and asynchronization in three jazz saxophonists. *Perceptual and motor skills.* 73: 707–713.

Palmer, C. (1989). Mapping Musical thought to musical performance. *Journal of Experimental Psychology: Human Perception and Performance.* 15, 12:331–346.

Parsons, W. with Cholakis, Ed. (1995). It don't mean a thang if it ain't dang, dang-a-dang! *Down Beat.* 62, 8 (August): 61.

Povel, D. (1977). Temporal structure of performed music: some preliminary observations. *Acta Psychologica.* 41:309–320.

Pressing, J. (1987). The micro- and macrostructural design of improvised music. *Music Perception.* 5, 2:133–172.

Reinholdsson (1987). Approaching jazz performances empirically: some reflections on methods and problems. In *Action and perception in rhythm and music.* A. Gabrielsson, ed. Stockholm: Royal Swedish Academy of music, No. 55:105–125.

Repp, B.H. (1990). Patterns of expressive timing performances of a Beethoven Minuet by nineteen famous pianists. *Journal of the Acoustical Society of America.* 88, 2:622–640.

Repp, B.H. (1992). Diversity and commonality in music performance: an analysis of timing microstructure in Schumann's "Traumerie". *Journal of Acoustical Society of America.* 95, 5:2546–2568.

Repp, B.H. (1992). Probing the cognitive representation of musical time: structural constraints on the perception of timing perturbations. *Cognition.* 44:241–281.

Repp, B.H. (1992). Detectability of rhythmic perturbations in musical contexts: bottom-up versus top-down factors. *Fourth Workshop on Rhythm Perception & Production.* Auxiette, Drake and Gerard (eds.):111–116.

Rose, R.L. (1989). An analysis of timing in jazz rhythm section performance. Unpublished doctoral dissertation. The University of Texas at Austin (University Microfilms No. 90-15520).

Shaffer, L.H. (1980). Analysing piano performance: a study of concert pianists. In *Tutorials in Motor Behavior.* Stelmach & Requin (eds.) Holland: North-Holland Publishing Company, 443–455.

Sloboda, J.A. (1983). The communication of musical metre in piano performance. *Quarterly Journal of Experimental Psychology,* 351:377–396.

Thomson, Virgil (1925). The future of american music. *Vanity Fair.* September: 62.

THE ART OF CHARLIE PARKER'S RHETORIC

Steve Larson

I enjoy listening to the *rhetoric* of Charlie Parker's famous 1946 performance of "Oh, Lady Be Good"—as if it were a stirring speech, compelling argument, rousing sermon, or engaging story.[1] (My transcription of the saxophone and bass parts is given in Example 1.[2])

Like the beginning of a good oration, the beginning of Parker's improvisation attracts my attention and promises to hold that attention. It first attracts my attention because it has an immediacy that is clearly Parker's—the timing, tone, and bluesy inflections define the style and identify the performer. Normally, this immediate information is all that it takes to get me interested. However, one reason it promises to hold my attention is that this opening statement also contains some other information. Like a good orator, Parker tells us what his solo will be about. He tells us that it will present his own distinctive conception of a familiar tune; he begins with a paraphrase of the original melody of "Oh, Lady Be Good." I will call this paraphrase Parker's "motto." Example 2c quotes the motto, and Example 2b quotes the beginning of the original melody of "Oh, Lady Be Good." Lines between these staves connect corresponding pitches to highlight the similarities.

But Parker's motto is more than simply a paraphrase. It alters the arpeggiated gesture of the original melody, turning it into a blues-inflected, forward-directed fifth-progression that supplies the thematic material for his improvisation and forecasts its fundamental structure. Example 2a shows that the motto prolongs the fundamental structural tone $\hat{5}$ with a fifth-progression of two thirds D-C-B and B♭-A-G. Note the appended embellishment of D with its upper neighbor, E. I will call this appended D-E the motto's "tail." This fifth-progression—together with its tail—is repeated in the fundamental structure that spans Parker's entire improvisation.

I can hear the motto as a summary of the whole improvisation because I know how it ends, because I know how Parker will tie up the threads of his

Example 1: Saxophone and Bass Parts of Oh, Lady Be Good

Example 1: Continued

Example 1: Continued

Example 1: Continued

Example 1: Continued

Example 1: Continued

Example 1: Continued

Example 1: Concluded

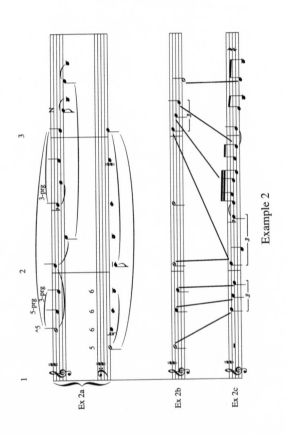

Example 2

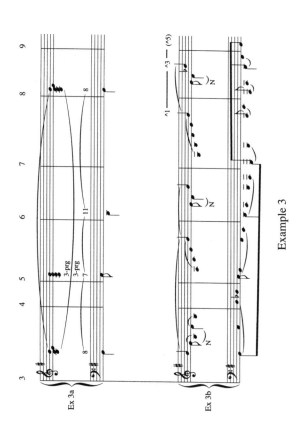

Example 3

story while avoiding every opportunity to cadence until the end, and because I know how this particular expression of the fifth-progression—together with its tail—describes the path of, and controls, the entire improvisation.

To hear Parker's improvisation in this fashion, without first hearing the ending, requires a certain faith that Parker will complete his opening thought in a way that will reward *Fernhören*—that long-range hearing that grasps spans of music as connected by the voice-leading of contrapuntal linear progressions. In fact, this faith must be present, or instilled, even if one is to hear in this way after repeated listening.

Fortunately, the music that immediately follows encourages this kind of listening. Example 3b shows measures 3–8. These measures demonstrate that the unity of linear progressions is not broken by the silence that intervenes. Every contrapuntal element of measure 3 initiates a contrapuntal strand that appears complete in the surface of the music. The E-D motive of the motto tail is notated with downward stems in Example 3b. Example 3a shows that the two third-progressions of measures 3–8 (the lower two voices on the upper staff) are the same two third-progressions that make up the fifth-progression of the motto. The underlying counterpoint, 7–11–8, rather than 7–10–8, is common in jazz.

The last note of measures 5–6 and the last note of measures 7–8 join in a middleground arpeggiation that is directed at regaining the fundamental structural tone 5 set out in measures 1–4. Example 4 shows that this arpeggiation is repeated and completed in the foreground in measures 9–10. The more foreground appearance of this arpeggio motive creates a nested hidden repetition. I call the foreground repetition of an idea simultaneously completed at a more remote structural level a "confirmation." (In the analyses, I symbolize such nested hidden repetitions with nested square brackets.) Here the confirmation focuses attention on the arrival in measure 10, making the inflection of D as D♭ more effective.

If I hear this middleground arpeggiation as striving to get back up to an initial point of departure, then I have oriented myself to a tonal space that has an up and down—one in which the idea seeks conclusion by giving in to "musical gravity" in order to return home to the tonic. Such an orientation to tonal space not only evokes and is evoked by my sense of *Fernhören*, but informs and is informed by my sense that ascending and descending gestures (respectively) have rhetorical implications of opening tonal space and closing it and thus have implications of beginningness and endingness.[3]

This sense enables me to enjoy the feeling that Parker is playing with beginningness and endingness in order to create a more cohesive statement. Example 5 shows that the ascending arpeggios of measures 5 and 7 (see the upward arrows below the staff) imitate the larger gesture of arpeggiation to

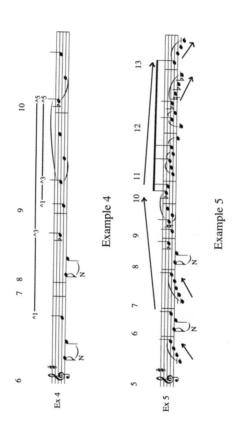

Example 4

Example 5

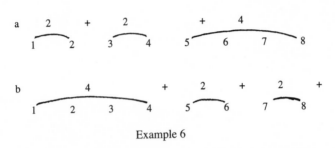

Example 6

measure 10 (see the upward arrow above the staff). Likewise, the larger descent of the fifth-progression of measures 10–13 (see the downward arrow above the staff), is rounded off by the descending arpeggios of measures 12 and 13 (see the downward arrows below the staff). Thus, Example 5 presents a rhetorical unit. An arpeggiation of ii7 begins and ends this unit.

This arpeggiation of ii7 becomes a marker. This marker sounds at the fifth bar of every A section (since Parker's "phrases" do not coincide with the 8-measure phrases of the original melody, I call these 8-measure units "sections" rather than "phrases"). By connecting the middle of the first line to the middle of the second line, this unit somewhat reduces the divisive effect of the potential cadence at measure 7.

This rhetorical unit not only connects the 4-measure group 5–8 to the 4-measure group 9–12 but also connects the 4-measure group 9–12 to the 4-measure group 13–16. The fifth-progression of measures 9–13 belongs to the tonic prolongation of measures 9–12, but the last note of this fifth-progression is delayed until measure 13 with a pattern that is common in Parker's improvisations.[4]

The rhythm of phrase-lengths in the first two lines helps me to hear measures 5–13 (shown in Example 5) as a unit. Example 6a shows that 2+2+4 phrase-length archetype that Schoenberg called a "sentence."[5] Rhythmically, the first eight measures of Parker's improvisation are incomplete in part because they are a kind of "reverse sentence." Instead of 2+2+4, Parker plays 4+2+2 (see Example 6b). In typical 2+2+4 sentences, the longer, final unit balances and completes the first two shorter units. Here, the two shorter units press forward.

I hear measures 14–16 as rhetorically parenthetical. Example 7 shows how they echo the fifth-progression of the motto (but with D-C-B Bb-A-G reversed to D-C-Bb, B-A-G). This example also suggests that postponing the final tone of this fifth-progression connects the second line to the bridge. But for me, the inner voices are what make this connection a cohesive one—and Parker's rhetoric seems to rely on this. Parker's line reduces the divisive ef-

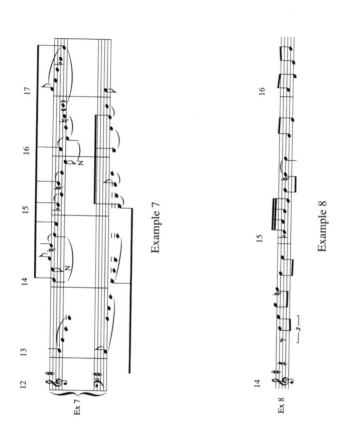

Example 7

Example 8

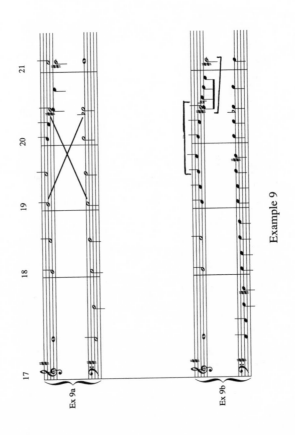

Example 9

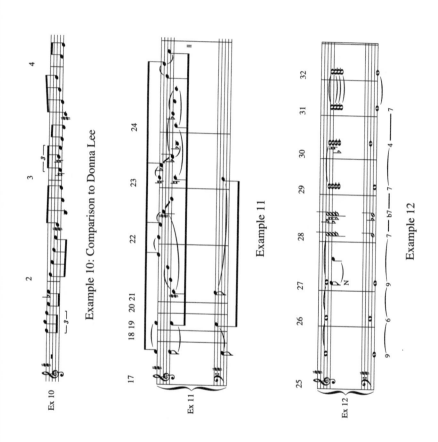

Example 10: Comparison to Donna Lee

Example 11

Example 12

fect of the potential cadence at measure 7 but suggests that it will close at the end of the second line. It could have; see Example 8. Instead, Parker ends this line with the F that signals the subdominant beginning of the bridge.

The bridge begins with an octave coupling that recalls the G5 of measure 14. This gesture prepares that register for measures 21–24. The bridge begins as if its first half will be a $1+1+2$ sentence. However, this sentence continues into the fifth bar of the bridge connecting the first half of this phrase to the second half. Here a sequential extension produces a gesture that may be recognized as a Parker formula. Example 9 shows the conceptual origin of this gesture as two descending third progressions. Example 10 shows the similarity of this lick to Parker's "Donna Lee." In this example, the beginning of "Donna Lee" is transposed to G major to make the similarities clearer.

What follows takes us repeatedly back to the register in which the bridge began. Part of the interest of this passage comes from its expansion of tessitura at this point. But there is more to it than just that. Each of these "rangy" gestures is connected by voice-leading strands to the gestures before and after it, and all the gestures together form a sensible unit—see Example 11.

Parker ends this bridge on A. Interrupting the line one step before its final note is a common technique at the half cadences that end bridges. After such an interruption, we may expect the reappearance of the fundamental structural tone. But instead of resuming with the structural $\hat{5}$ at the return to the A section, Parker continues the line down. In fact, in this way he not only connects his oration across the beginning of this line but also avoids cadencing at its end. Example 12 describes the counterpoint that arises as Parker's line descends by continually postponing resolutions until the resolutions are themselves dissonant, leading us directly into . . .

THE SECOND CHORUS

The first line of the second chorus is introduced by the figure (B-D-A) that introduced the last line of the first chorus. Example 13b shows this figure. The immediately following figure, Example 13c, seems a natural answer to 13b. If I think to myself "Parker has repeated this three-note figure and followed it with a very logical continuation," then I marvel at the continuity and logic of his playing. But I miss something. The beginning of the second chorus, Example 13c, also recalls the beginning of the second line of the first chorus, the nested hidden repetition shown in Example 13a. To make a return to an earlier idea seem like the natural result of the current one is a neat trick.

So, in telling his story, Parker brings us back to the simpler, more blues-inflected material that was important at the beginning of his improvisation. From this vantage point, I can now look back on the last A

Example 13

section of the first chorus as having "put the brakes on" after the energetic, more sophisticated gestures of the first-chorus bridge. (Parker's technique of resolving unstable notes only when their resolutions will now be heard as themselves unstable makes me feel the momentum behind those brakes carry all the way into this second chorus.) Hearing it this way, I experience some relief as Parker settles into more riff-like material (the other soloists also begin background riffs at this point). That simpler, more repetitive material seems now to celebrate the groove, to outline and reinforce the symmetry of the underlying meter. We hear the beginning of a clear 2+2+4 sentence. The short gesture of measures 32–33 is repeated with a change that emphasizes the motto tail as measures 34–35. I now expect a balancing 4-bar unit of similar material.

Instead, I hear an astonishing double-time lick. Notice how Parker's rhetorical skills have set me up. Because measures 32–35 lead me to expect something simpler, the surprise of the double-time material is more effective. And because measures 32–35 also focus my attention on the meter, my experience of its rhythmic excitement is also heightened.

But there is more to this lick than its rhythmic excitement. In fact, we can look at it in many different ways—and discover something of interest from each perspective. Traditional jazz harmonic analysis, chord-scale theory, and formulaic analysis all reveal interesting aspects of this lick. And looking at it Schenkerian terms allows us to tie those aspects together in a satisfying way.

I have already indicated how Parker marks the fifth measure of every A section with an arpeggio on ii7. Measure 36, the fifth measure of this A section, also begins with an arpeggio on ii7. Looking at this passage in terms of traditional jazz harmonic analysis, we can explain its harmonic richness by reference to extended and altered chords. Parker begins by extending his ii7 arpeggio into a complete eleventh chord. A D7 follows as expected, but we also get tensions of 9, ♭9, 13, and ♭13.

Chord-scale theory would allow us to catalog those same materials in a similar way. Such description and cataloging can be very interesting to "ornithologists" as well as budding improvisers.

And looking at this lick in terms of Parker "formulas" would allow us to relate it not only to ideas in this solo, but also to other Parker improvisations, giving some stylistic depth to our understanding of this passage.

Such descriptions might also be generalized as a possible account of Parker's apparent conception of the tonal space defined by the intersection of the affect of this performance, the way G major lies on his alto saxophone, and his aural/kinesthetic predisposition to resolve certain pitches in certain ways. Example 14 offers a visual representation of part of the generalized conception just described.

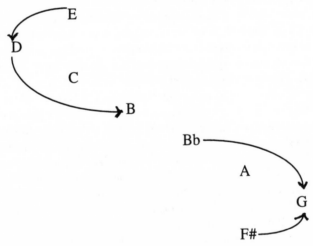

Example 14: A "Tonal Space" for Measures 37–39

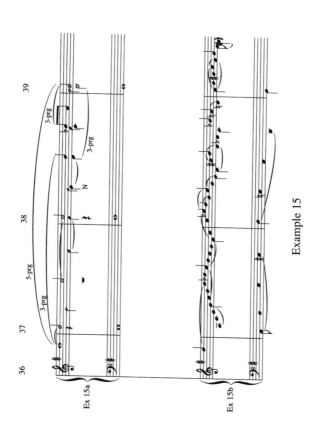

Example 15

But why are these materials used in just this way? What is so satisfying about this lick? Schenkerian analysis suggests that its coherence may result in part from the fact that it is based on an clear underlying structure—and that that structure is of *motivic* importance. Example 15b uses analytic notation to show all the notes in this lick. Example 15a uses durational notation to show how the basic pitches identified in Example 15b form a "compound melody" of three voice-leading strands. Notice that Example 15a strongly resembles Parker's motto: the fifth-progression D-C-B B♭-A-G complete with the appended embellishment of D by its upper neighbor E!

After the fireworks of measures 37–39, we might expect a pause, with activity to resume on the downbeat of measure 41—probably beginning with the fundamental structural tone D. Instead, Parker enters "too early" in measure 40. Not only is the lick early, but its first note is also early; the anticipation underscores the effect of getting the jump on the next section. In fact, there is another sense in which Parker gets the jump on the next section: The third progression D-C-B introduced by this early entrance corresponds to that of the original melody, so its D "belongs" on the downbeat of measure 41. Instead, the D appears before the downbeat and the gesture lands on C on the downbeat. The leap and rest after this downbeat interrupt the third progression D-C-B. In other words, the instability of this C over tonic harmony require the logic of Parker's line to continue.

When it does continue, it begins by retracing its steps with a confirmation that completes an immediate D-C-B at the same time that it completes the larger D-C-B motion (see the nested square brackets in Example 16c). As Example 16c shows, the underlying structure of these measures also strongly resembles that of both Parker's motto and the double-time lick of measures 37–39. One of the biggest differences is the absence of B♭; in its place, we get an E♭ that also echoes the E♭ of the previous bar (see the curly braces in Example 16c). Another difference, due to the "too early" quality of this statement, is that it reaches the tonic in measure 41 (over subdominant harmony) instead of in measure 42 (over tonic harmony).

This hearing of measures 40–43 as rhetorically underscoring the way it "gets the jump on" this section helps me to understand what follows in a more satisfying way. Listeners who have heard a lot of Parker's playing but don't understand its rhetoric might say "There's a string of Parker formulas I've heard before." But listeners attuned to that rhetoric will find there is more to it than just a string of formulas. And analysis can explain some of that. The G that "should" complete the motion to tonic over tonic harmony follows a rest and is stretched out into an arpeggio that not only completes the thought, but summarizes it as it does so—that is, the arpeggio of measures 43–44, shown in quarter notes in Example 16b, repeats

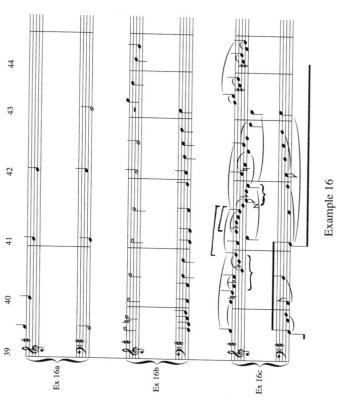

Example 16

the basic motion depicted in quarter notes in Example 16a. The repetition even preserves the metric shape (four times as fast) of that arpeggio.

The double-time lick of measures 37–39 is impressive. And the delayed and expanded arrival of G after the downbeat rest of measures 43–44 is also attractive. In this light, measures 45–48 are particularly interesting: they do both. In measures 45–46, Parker "gets the jump on" a repetition of the double-time lick of measures 37–39 so that it comes out a beat earlier. And he alters its ending by breaking off before we get the B♭-A-G that would complete it. Instead, just as in measures 43–44, we hear a rest followed by an expansion of G that fills the octave G5-G4. And that expansion recalls the material of the first bridge, as well as the measures that led to it. As Example 17 suggests, we might expect this expansion to end on G. Instead, it ends on F, like the analogous gesture that introduces the bridge in the first chorus, to prepare the subdominant that begins the following bridge.

The second bridge begins yet again with a figure that starts by arpeggiating ii7 in sixteenth notes. But this time, the same figure leads into another significant motive: the G-B♭-(G-B)-D two-level arpeggio. While the notation captures the fascinating play of motivic transformation, it cannot do justice to the incredibly expressive pitch bend in measure 50.

The second bridge has the same tight voice-leading structure that organizes the first bridge. But, in addition, it manages to recall the double-time lick of measures 37–39 as well as the way in which that same lick "gets the jump on" the section that begins in (or rather before) measure 41 with its smooth lead-in to the final 8-bar section of Parker's improvisation.

The last section is a remarkable ending to a remarkable solo (see Example 18). It not only ties up the story by bringing the unstable pitches finally (though teasingly) down to the tonic, but it also manages to refer to and integrate every motive that has played an important role within this solo. Measures 57–58 not only recall the motto of measures 1–2, but are also introduced in a way that recalls the "too early" entrance of the statement in measure 41 — but their descent to tonic is complete over subdominant harmony so must be repeated. Measures 59–60 not only recall the material of measures 9–10 but also integrate that material with a part of the motto — and while these measures end with tonic harmony, the melody (like that in the last A section of the first chorus) stops short of the tonic on $\hat{2}$. Measures 61–62 not only recall the double-time lick of measures 37–39, but also manage to refer to the ending material of all the previous A sections through its play with the motive tail (even its last structural motion, A-G-F#, may be taken as a summary of the final section of the first chorus) — yet it breaks off before the final tonic arrives.

Example 17

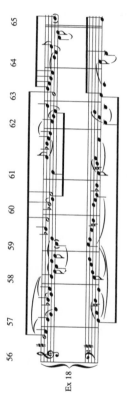

Example 18

Even measures 63–64, a kind of codetta, work in a final statement of skeleton of the motto with the tail transformed to resemble the A-D-G motive (transposed down a third)—while these measures finally supply $\hat{1}$ with an ending tonic harmony, they do so within a gesture that repeats the incomplete motions we've heard throughout Parker's improvisation.

While there is a great deal of beauty to this improvisation that cannot be captured in words or notation, I hope this discussion has conveyed not only my admiration for it, but also my feeling that some of its beauty lies in its rhetoric.

NOTES

1. Earlier versions of this paper were presented to the national meeting of the College Music Society in Washington, D. C. (October 1990) and to the annual meeting of the Texas Society for Music Theory in Nacogdoches (March 1987). The analytic method used here is described in my dissertation, "Schenkerian Analysis of Modern Jazz" (University of Michigan, 1987). Similar musical issues are discussed in my article "Dave McKenna's Performance of 'Have You Met Miss Jones?'," *American Music* 11, No. 3 (Fall 1993): 283–315.

2. Parker's solo on Gershwin's "Oh, Lady Be Good," recorded 28 January 1946 at a Jazz at the Philharmonic performance in Los Angeles, appears in the most recent edition of the *Smithsonian Collection of Classic Jazz,* which lists supporting personnel as Arnold Ross (piano), Billy Hadnott (bass), and Lee Young (drums). It also can be heard on *Bird: The Complete Charlie Parker on Verve,* CD 837 141-2. George Allan Russell, *The Lydian-Chromatic Concept of Tonal Organization for Improvisation, for All Instruments* (New York: Concept Publishing, 1959), presents an analysis of this performance. Readers may wish to compare my analysis with his to see how our analytic methods give different perspectives.

3. On the "musical forces" of "gravity, magnetism, and inertia" and their relation to *Fernhören,* see my article "The Problem of Prolongation in Tonal Music," *Journal of Music Theory,* forthcoming.

4. Thomas Owens, "Charlie Parker: Techniques of Improvisation" (Ph.D. diss., University of California, Los Angeles, 1974). I will refer here to several formulas that are common in Parker's playing. See Owens's list of motives.

5. William Rothstein, *Phrase Rhythm in Tonal Music* (New York: Schirmer, 1989).

JOHN COLTRANE'S *MEDITATIONS* SUITE: A STUDY IN SYMMETRY

David Liebman

BACKGROUND

There are several milestone recordings in the vast Coltrane repertoire. These works stand out because they represent a summation of a specific period of development for the great saxophonist who, in his two-decades-plus career, traversed several well-defined stages. Each period was marked by the compositions themselves, their harmonic implications especially, as well as certain saxophone and ensemble techniques.

The early years, roughly 1955 through 1959, included his tenure with Miles Davis and for a short period with Thelonious Monk. These years featured many dates as sideman, as well as leader dates under his own name. The repertoire consisted mainly of standards, blues, and originals, all within the well-defined bebop idiom. Coltrane's approach was unique even in this increasingly clichéd musical environment. It was complex, highly sophisticated concerning the chord changes, the speed as well as dexterity of his technique, and the saxophone sound itself. The "Giant Steps" recording on Atlantic (recently rereleased with alternate takes), along with nearly a dozen other tunes based on that complex harmonic progression, could be considered the culmination and apex of that first stage.

Beginning with "My Favorite Things" and the eventual formation of a steady and enduring group (Elvin Jones, McCoy Tyner, and Jimmy Garrison), Trane's modal period (1960–65) found its seminal recording in *A Love Supreme* (1964), which included four compositions loosely held together by a simple three-note motif, consistent pentatonic fourth-based voicings, chromaticism, and a spiritual underpinning. This famous and widely acclaimed album also marked the end of the quartet's basic premises, which were steady time and at least the semblance of a pedal point or ostinato harmony as the foundation for most of their repertoire. The frenetic pace of Coltrane's recordings in 1965 reflect the changes he

167

felt were necessary, first in the music and then in the personnel itself. Therefore, the recordings of that year bear witness to a change of concept—a freer approach to all the aspects of his music.

It is in this year that *Meditations* was recorded. Although *First Meditations* precedes the suite under analysis in this study, the original version can be viewed as a prelude to the full-blown suite finally recorded a few months later. Of significance is that the full suite recorded November 23, 1965, marks the last known record date for both Elvin and McCoy with Coltrane. (This does not include any possible bootleg recordings which may exist.) It also marks the first appearance of drummer Rashied Ali and nearly the first session with saxophonist Pharoah Sanders, both of whom would stay with Coltrane until his death in 1967. Although some of the newer stylistic innovations developed during this last period of Coltrane (1965–67) were present in subsequent recordings, nowhere are they as clearly presented and as complete as in this suite. Primarily this is due to the structure of the music, which gives it a unity and balance equal to the intensity that stands out in the Coltrane legacy.

OVERALL FORM

One should begin the discussion of what makes *Meditations* so unique with the nonmusical, spiritual underpinning which permeates the suite. Anyone familiar with Coltrane's sincere pronouncement of his self-awakening, so lucidly described in the liner notes to *A Love Supreme,* will notice how, during the last two years of his life, almost every composition bore some sort of spiritual significance in the titles themselves. The examples are many: "Dear Lord," "Peace on Earth," "Joy," "Ascension," "Dearly Beloved," "Amen," "Attaining," "Resolution," etc. Though it may seem presumptuous to speculate on such a private matter or attempt to deduce motives for this decidedly strong and obvious inclination, the five titles for the suite undeniably portray a strong religious quality: (1) "The Father and The Son and The Holy Ghost" (suggesting the Holy Trinity); (2)"Compassion"; (3) "Love" (the essential message of Christ); (4) "Consequences" (for those who don't follow the path?); (5) "Serenity" (the eventual resting place?). There are many interpretations which could be made for these titles, but when one hears the music and considers the possibilities, there can be no doubt as to the direction that Coltrane was at least implying.

But it is not only the nonmusical, perhaps programmatic, aspect which unites the suite. The compositions themselves have very definite musical intentions in both their outstanding sense of lyricism and how specific intervals were used to create the various moods. The question overriding this analysis is: Were these melodies written down to be played more or less literally, or were they improvised? As of this writing, I am not aware of what exactly occurred, but the strong harmonic undertones suggest the former scenario. (In a discussion with McCoy Tyner in early 1996, Tyner said that the basic chords were written out and they knew the general melodic structure, but most of the recording was freely improvised.) However, what shades this view is that nowhere during the performance does the piano play any direct harmony to the melodies, although, to my ear, they are so clearly suggestive of chords. This is what forms, for me, the essential crux of the suite. By and large the melodies are extremely diatonic, while the harmonies played by the bass and piano are nontonal, as are the improvisations. And herein lies the genius of *Meditations*—within the dense and dissonant overall color of the recording lies the most extreme and poetic lyricism. From the chaos of the firmament came perfect nature. In other words, the essential dichotomy of tension and release is not merely demonstrated as in any great art but is taken to an even higher level of contrast. Within the most complex lies the most simple.

MELODY AND HARMONY

Philosophy aside, a quick glance at the intervallic structures of the themes and their lyrical shapes is most instructive.

"The Father and The son and The Holy Ghost"

After beginning with some multiphonic colors peculiar to the tenor saxophone centered about A♭ (all references will be concert key), the first movement launches into a complete exposition of major triads beginning with the fifth as a pickup to the first, second, and third degree of the scales. For the most part, the key centers themselves descend by major thirds, except for a few cycles of fifths as the transposed motif evolves. The motif itself is unyielding and in its shape presents what must be the clearest example of tonality and melody in all musics—the 1,2,3,5 of the major key! To reiterate, what makes this simplistic melody not appear trite is the nonmatching bass and piano harmonic accompaniment as well as the flowing, nonmetrical rhythm underneath (see Example 1).

The Father, the Son & the Holy Ghost

Note: All chord symbols are the author's.

Example 1: Excerpt from "The Father and the Son and the Holy Ghost"

"Compassion"

This is another example of an interval tying the composition together. Except for occasional half-steps, fourths, and whole steps, the minor third permeates the piece. The eternal blues motif, full of yearning, unifies the transpositions which, although McCoy Tyner is freely comping harmon-

Compassion

Example 2: Excerpt from Compassion

ically, do occur over a D♭ centered bass line, set in a rolling 3/4 meter. The use of octaves in the recapitulation after the solo gives a dramatic finale to this wonderful, haunting, and mysterious melody (see Example 2).

"Love"

This piece represents the epitome of a diatonic, step, half-step melody which is completely song-like as a result. Though it seems to be centered around an A♭ tonality, the basic rising motif is transposed throughout (Example 3). What is remarkable about this section is first of all the length of the so-called melody, which brings me back to pondering the thought posed earlier about composed versus improvised. It seems here that much of the latter part of the melody may be spontaneous, especially in light of the earlier recorded version of "Love" on *First Meditations,* which is only a fragment of what appears full-blown here. Also, Trane lightens the tension dramatically in the middle by what seems a shift to the relative C minor before rebuilding to what for me is the midpoint of the entire suite, the altissimo melodies centered around his A (Example 4). Finally, the trills up and down A♭ major-seventh bring this dramatic section, the climax of the suite, to a close.

Love

Example 3: Excerpt from Love

Example 4: Excerpt from Love

"Consequences"

This movement is similar to other pieces from this late period in it not being so much a melody as a rhythmic motif which initiates a textural improvisation. One could say that "Consequences" represents the most elemental of structures functioning purely as a vehicle for the improvisation to follow. In other words, it is the truest free jazz piece of the suite,

Consequences

Themes

Example 5: Themes from Consequences

where the sole function of the "head" is to suggest a rhythm and texture. In actuality, though, even "The Father and The Son and The Holy Ghost" functions this way, although there is a motivic melody in that section at the outset. This is one of the parameters of Coltrane's last period, where melodies and ensuing improvisations are not necessarily directly related (Example 5).

"Serenity"

Finally, this tranquil and lyrical melody, based on what appears to be a phrygian motif, moves around several key centers in a V-I cycle when analyzed purely harmonically. As in "The Father," the accompaniment is not harmonically linked, so it appears on the surface that the melody was not intended to be tonally based. However, once again the point arises as to how clever was the juxtaposition of a diatonic-harmonic based melody opposite the nontonal, swirling background (Example 6).

RHYTHM AND COLOR

Quite possibly, it was the personal dynamics between the old and the new which gave the rhythm its essential character on *Meditations*. Legend suggests that there was an inherent tension between Elvin Jones and Rashied Ali. With the approval of the leader, the new kid on the block (Rashied) challenges the chief. After all, it was apparent from many of the 1965 recordings (which were not released contemporaneously) that Coltrane was heading towards an arhythmic, nonsteady pulse in his lines, as well as seemingly in the piano accompaniment. One hears on "Transition" and "Sun Ship" how Trane plays nonmetrically, yet Elvin still is

Example 6: Excerpt from Serenity

in time and in fact often marks off the 8- or 16-bar cycles, as was *de rigueur* in the quartet. As exciting as this kind of dialogue was, it had become clear that a change in the rhythm section was imminent. And in fact, as stated earlier, *Meditations* was McCoy's and Jones's last studio recording with Coltrane.

What Ali brought to the music was a flowing, bubbling feeling without dramatic cadence points which ordinarily emphasize tension and release. In other words, the rhythm became seamless—in a sense like prose without punctuation or paragraph markings. The familiar ups and downs of Coltrane's music receded. Instead, there was usually a quick ascent after the opening statement, rather than the peaks and valleys of the older format. Seemingly, the song form (and by extension modal forms) were pushed into the background from this period until the end of Coltrane's life.

But Jones was up to the challenge when necessary. With the two fairly well separated in the panning picture, it is apparent that much of the cymbal fluttering heard is Ali, while tom-toms are Jones. Ali also keeps a more-or-less steady cymbal/snare color throughout, which does in essence comprise the major component of his style. The bottom end of the drums were always important to Jones's approach, especially the characteristic, thunderous floor tom-tom rolls heard so much during these last recordings, often in rubato sections. Besides the 3/4 rhythm on "Compassion," which is typical of Jones's style, he does indeed play arhythmic and nonmetrical with no clear cadential mark-off points. Also, his particular way of playing of playing mallets is heard to great advantage in both "Father" and "Love" during cymbal and tom-tom rolls.

For Jimmy Garrison, the late period was really a perfect gift. After all, one of his earliest associations has been with free jazz pioneer Ornette Coleman. A large part of his style was well-suited for a nonpulse concept. Although his quarter-note-walking-feel fit like a glove with Jones's cymbal beat over the preceding years, one could sense that he liked to break up the time and play more freely whenever possible. In fact his normally long rhapsodic solos punctuated by flamenco-like strumming seemed to suggest a predilection for a more abstract rhythmic concept. Also evident in Garrison's playing were his simple, songlike melodies sometimes heard in the background but most clearly in _Meditations_ during the solo introduction to "Love."

The same could be said of McCoy Tyner, whose playing shines so brightly on this last recording. Through the years of accompanying and soloing, both his harmonic and rhythmic concepts had evolved to a point where Coltrane's late music seemed natural to him for the following reasons: (1) The chromaticism of his fourth and cluster voicings; (2) the complex and dense rhythms in the right-hand solo lines; (3) the grandiose left-hand and bass pedal-points which increasingly moved around many key centers; (4) the fluid and fast arpeggios in and around the basic pulse; (5) the contrary motion of left hand descending while right hand ascends, encompassing almost the entire range of the keyboard; (6) the sometimes droning right-hand tremolo opposed by left-hand bass notes or chordal movement; and (7) the independent, inner rhythmic conversations which would often be heard underneath the horns on top. All these contributed to a swirling, orchestral accompaniment perfectly matched to the late Coltrane dense style. Alice Coltrane's arpeggio approach, harplike and rubato orientation would replace Tyner's style through the final recordings. But there can be no doubt that Tyner found a way to enhance this new music as he has done so impeccably for the past years.

Finally the matter of color has to be addressed, for with the addition of another tenor sax and drums, as well as Ali's adding tamborine and bells, the entire sound of the group changed. Having Pharoah Sanders playing almost exclusively in the altissimo register as well as often employing a buzzing kind of growl to his normal sound and range, the sheer mass of the music grew both in density and extremes of tessitura. There were long portions of the late music (especially in live performance) where both tenors played simultaneously and quite intensely—Trane both high and low in rapid flashes; Sanders relentlessly high up; Tyner using the entire range of the piano; Ali almost always on cymbals and snare; Jones frequently playing tom-toms; Garrison playing counter melodies in the bottom. The color spectrum was in itself an assault upon the senses, especially to those who were used to the more traditional quartet sound.

PERFORMANCE

I would like to point out some highlights of the various solos taken. After a preliminary multiphonic coloring on the tenors, Trane plays the triadic melody to "Father" using a wide and lush vibrato, as was common in the late period. He makes extensive use of a repetitive triplet figure on one note, all over the fluttering nonpulse drums/bass accompaniment and Tyner's arpeggios. Trane's solo begins with fast, repeated runs eventually landing in the altissimo, ending with a technique common to the late-period improvisations, which is the impression of duets with himself—rapid high and low question/answer phrases. Finally Sanders enters with his buzzing tone and ultrahigh altissimo shrieks. With Trane up high also and the drummers burning, the first great peak of intensity has been reached, finally subsiding with a recapitulation of the melody and the same saxophone multiphonic from the beginning of the movement.

Into a quick segue, Elvin begins the rolling tom-tom oriented 3/4 rhythm with Garrison's bass line while Trane quickly plays the minor-third melody to "Compassion," again with a dramatic use of vibrato and a very dark tone. Tyner's solo is full of over-the-pulse lines, sequences and ostinatos in the right hand along with thunderous block chords towards the end played right in the pulse (see Example 7). Coltrane's recapitulation, as mentioned earlier, uses some dramatic octave leaps and lyrical altissmo playing before ending with a pause before the next movement.

Garrison takes one of his typical bass solos as an intro to "Love" using simple diatonic arpeggios and closely knit melodies in character with the coming theme. Tyner's background to the melody is rhapsodic and very scalar, albeit in various and changing key centers. With a lot of tom-toms from Jones, and Ali's cymbal, the balance behind Trane stays fairly

Analysis: Extended melodic shape; not exact transposition, but retaining the basic shape of downward motion, skip up, down again.

Example 7: Excerpt of McCoy Tyner's solo in "Compassion". This excerpt is taken from *A Chromatic Approach To Jazz Harmony and Melody* by David Liebman, published by Advance Music, 1991.

consistent throughout. Toward the middle of the theme a sensitive moment occurs as Trane quiets the whole band down and begins to build to the climax of the melody before resolving diatonically in A♭, concluding with rapid pianissimo trills. It should be noted that there are no solos in this movement or in the final "Serenity."

"Consequences" is the "burn" of the suite, featuring at first Sanders playing intensely, screaming and appearing to rip the horn apart. When Trane joins in, the two saxophonists raise the intensity to an unbelievable level along with Jones and Ali. The sheer physical energy here is awesome in itself, and its placement in the suite is crucial to the entire shape of the performance.

After a solo excursion by Tyner, which sounds like a mini-twentieth-century piano concerto in scope, intensity, and technique, the scene is set for the benediction—the beautiful, yearning, and finally peaceful goodbye melody, "Serenity." On the whole, as far as intensity is concerned, the form of the suite can be viewed as an A-A-B-A-B shape. The A sections are the intense "Father," "Compassion," and "Consequences," while B represents the more peaceful "Love" and "Serenity." There is also an interesting key relationship of fifths between "Love" (A♭), "Compassion" (D♭) and "Serenity" (G♭) when these movements are viewed harmonically.

PERSONAL VIEW

For me, every Coltrane release in the 1960s was an event. As I have written and said many times, seeing this group live was what inspired me directly to pursue jazz. I awaited each new release anxiously to see what to expect when I would go to the clubs in New York, as I did so often. It should be noted that the order of recording dates does not necessarily reflect the order of the actual releases at the time. In fact several of the 1965 recordings were released posthumously, possibly because of the enormous output or Trane's reluctance to make the music available. *Meditations* came out after an album called *The John Coltrane Quartet Plays*, which itself followed the acclaimed *A Love Supreme*. On *Quartet Plays*, the tune "Brazilia" gave an inkling as to the next stage of Trane's evolution. Besides the quartet being augmented by bassist Art Davis, the performance was very free in scope, and for me it was a big challenge to understand that tune. But it was *Meditations* with the addition of Ali and Sanders which gave conclusive evidence to the next period. Of course, record releases may have been stylistically dated, compared to what the group was doing in live performances. I had seen Sanders a few times with Coltrane, and his addition to the group mystified me. To hear Coltrane abandon eight-bar phrases and steady-time on *Meditations* was cataclysmic for me. All I can say is that hearing the group live was the strongest music I have heard since, or up to that time — bar none.

As the decades passed and my comprehension of the music itself increased beyond the heavy spiritual influence and direct inspirational effect it had upon me as a youth, I felt that Trane's late music has been by and large ignored by the audience and musicians alike. From the audience standpoint this was understandable, because their expectation of what Coltrane would play had been built up by so much repertoire from the quartet during the preceding five years. But I felt that musically, this period should be more studied and analyzed by musicians. In the mid-1980s with the help of my wife, Caris Visentin, who painstakingly transcribed all of the melodies of *Meditations,* I decided to perform the suite on each fifth anniversary of Coltrane's passing. As I write this article in 1995, I have just performed it several times in Europe and New York, befitting the thirtieth anniversary of the actual recording session.

The most interesting musical aspect of rediscovering this inspiring music was that the melodies often suggest, to my ears, very strong harmonic implications. So in these performances around the world over the years (and into the future I hope), I have added some chord changes to "Love" and "Serenity" in particular, as well as on occasion using keyboards and percussion to color the various sections. Also depending upon the performance, I have added guitar, synthesizer, percussion, and trumpet, as well as more horns. I treat the performance of *Meditations* as a spiritual event, a celebration of Coltrane's music and his massive effect upon me and so many musicians. This deep piece of music stands as a monument to John Coltrane's vision of revelation which imbues his late period and, in particular, the *Meditations* Suite.

NOTE

This article is part of an interactive Enhanced CD featuring a live performance by the Dave Liebman Group of the *Meditations* Suite, released by Arkadia Jazz.

OUTRAGEOUS CLUSTERS: DISSONANT SEMITONAL CELLS IN THE MUSIC OF THELONIOUS MONK

James Kurzdorfer

Although Thelonious Monk is considered by jazz musicians, critics, and musicologists to have been a seminal figure in the development of modern jazz in the 1940s (along with Charlie Parker, Bud Powell, and others), many of his compositions and improvisations are neither harmonically nor melodically congruent with the emergent bebop style of that period. Comparatively little of Monk's music, however, in contrast to that of his bebop contemporaries, has been systematically analyzed. Monk may be regarded as a transitional figure; his music, though firmly rooted in the traditional tonal jazz of the previous generation (James P. Johnson, Thomas "Fats" Waller, and others), in some ways foreshadows the often atonal "free" jazz of some of the musicians of the next generation (John Coltrane, Cecil Taylor, and others).

This article attempts to address one of the most idiosyncratic aspects of the compositions[1] of Thelonious Monk: the usage of dissonant semitonal cells as consonances. A few of the basic notations of pitch class (pc) set theory are used in the following discussion.[2] In pc set theory, the twelve pitch classes are numbered zero through eleven, with ten and eleven represented respectively in this article by the letters T and E. If C = 0, then $C_\sharp$ = 1, D = 2, . . . A = 9, $A_\sharp$ = T, B = E. Set classes are notated as pcs enclosed in parentheses without commas. For example, (01) is the set class name for the twelve possible (unordered) semitonal pc dyads—that is, (C,$C_\sharp$), ($C_\sharp$,D), . . . ($A_\sharp$,B), (B,C). Semitonal cells (hereafter, simply "cells") are defined here as transpositions of the (01) dyad, as well as transpositions of larger semitonal pc sets of cardinality three or greater—(012), (0123), etc.

Some special notation is necessary: in this article, pcs enclosed in angle brackets are used to notate root position chord types, with the root represented by zero and with chord members listed in ascending order within an octave. For example, the Dominant 7th chord (root, major 3rd, 5th, minor 7th) is notated <047T>.[3] This notation is a representation of ascending interval structure only, and does not refer to specific pcs. Scale orderings (modes) are notated in the same way as chord types. For example, the mixolydian mode notated <024579T>.[4]

In post-1940 tonal jazz, nine of the twelve possible transpositions of the dyadic cell, relative to a given chord root, are regarded as consonances in certain specific harmonic contexts—that is, two pcs related by interval class[5] 1 may both be considered to be consonant members of a single harmony. Particular transpositions of cells (relative to the roots of the harmonies of which they are subsets) are notated in this article as sets of two or more pcs enclosed in square brackets. For example, the Dominant 13th chord <0479T> includes the consonant [9T] cell—the 13th and the minor 7th—as a subset.

Before specific examples of Monk's usages of dissonant cells as consonances are presented and discussed, it would seem appropriate to review the harmonic contexts in which transpositions of the dyadic cell are usually regarded as consonant in post-1940 tonal jazz, including Monk's compositions. This will help isolating certain of Monk's usages as exceptional.

Four transpositions of the dyadic cell are commonly found as subsets of extended and/or altered Dominant 7th chords. The transpositions of this cell most likely to be found in this harmonic context are [01], [34], [67], and [9T]. Note that these four cells, taken together, form mode I of the octatonic[6] collection (known to jazz musicians as the "inverted diminished" or the "half-step whole-step diminished" scale), <0134679T>. From one to all four of these cells may be found as subsets of a single extended and/or altered Dominant 7th chord, if and only if the root of the chord is identical to the root of the mode. In other words, the minor 9th (pc 1), the augmented 9th (pc 3), the augmented 11th (pc 6), and the 13th (pc 9) may be added, singly or in any combination, to the complete Dominant 7th chord <047T>:

(1)	Dom7(13)	<0479T>	[9T]
(2)	″ (♯11)	<0467T>	[67]
(3)	″ (♯9)	<0347T>	[34]
(4)	″ (♭9)	<0147T>	[01]
(5)	″ (13,♯11)	<04679T>	[67] [9T]
(6)	″ (13,♯9)	<03479T>	[34] [9T]
(7)	″ (13,♭9)	<01479T>	[01] [9T]

(8)	" (♯11,♯9)	<03467T>	[34] [67]
(9)	" (♯11,♭9)	<01467T>	[01] [67]
(10)	" (♯9, ♭9)	<01347T>	[01] [34]
(11)	" (13,♯11,♯9)	<034679T>	[34] [67] [9T]
(12)	" (13,♯11,♭9)	<014679T>	[01] [67] [9T]
(13)	" (13,♯9,♭9)	<013479T>	[01] [34] [9T]
(14)	" (♯11,♯9,♭9)	<013467T>	[01] [34] [67]
(15)	" (13,♯11,♯9,♭9)	<0134679T>	[01] [34] [67] [9T]

All of the extended and/or altered Dominant 7th chords listed above, which are notated inclusive of their 5ths (pc 7), are subsets of octatonic mode I. Chord (15) is the verticalization of the complete octatonic mode I. Chord (5) is also a lydian dominant <024679T> (ascending melodic minor mode IV) subset, and chord (1) is also a mixolydian and a lydian dominant subset. If the 5th is omitted, as it often is in practice, then chords (3), (4), (8), (9), (10), and (14) are also super locrian <013468T> (ascending melodic minor mode VII) subsets, and chord (2)—the "Dominant-seventh-flat-five" chord—is also a super locrian, lydian dominant, and whole tone <02468T> subset. The majority of the extended and/or altered Dominant 7th chords found in post-1940 tonal jazz are subsets of one or more of these four scales: octatonic mode I, lydian dominant, super locrian, and whole tone.[7]

Four transpositions of the dyadic cell are also found as subsets of extended diminished 7th chords in post-1940 tonal jazz. The transpositions of this cell most likely to be found in this harmonic context are [23], [56], [89], and [E0]. Note that these four cells, taken together, form mode II of the octatonic collection (known to jazz musicians as the "diminished" or the "whole-step half-step diminished" scale), <0235689E>. From one to all four of these cells may be found as subsets of a single extended diminished 7th chord, if and only if the root of the chord is identical to the root of the mode.[8] In other words, the 9th (pc 2), the 11th (pc 5), the minor 13th (pc 8), and the major 7th (pc E) may be added, singly or in any combination, to the diminished 7th chord <0369>:

(1)	dim7(♭13)	<03689>	[89]
(2)	" (11)	<03569>	[56]
(3)	" (9)	<02369>	[23]
(4)	" (♯7)	<0369E>	[E0]
(5)	" (♭13,11)	<035689>	[56] [89]
(6)	" (♭13,9)	<023689>	[23] [89]

(7) " (♭13,♯7)	<03689E>	[89] [E0]
(8) " (11,9)	<023569>	[23] [56]
(9) " (11,♯7)	<03569E>	[56] [E0]
(10) " (9,♯7)	<02369E)	[23] [E0]
(11) " (♭13,11,9)	<0235689>	[23] [56] [89]
(12) " (♭13,11,♯7)	<035689E>	[56] [89] [E0]
(13) " (♭13,9,♯7)	<023689E>	[23] [89] [E0]
(14) " (11,9,♯7)	<023569E>	[23] [56] [E0]
(15) " (♭13,11,9,♯7)	<0235689E>	[23] [56] [89] [E0]

One of the set of four octatonic mode I cells—[67]—and three of the set of four octatonic mode II cells—[23], [56], and [E0]—are also found as subsets of non-Dominant/non-diminished extended and/or altered 7th chords. A few examples of these are given below:

(1) ma7(♯11,9)	<02467E>	[67] [E0]
(2) mi(6/9,♯7)	<02379E>	[23] [E0]
(3) mi7(9)	<0237T>	[23]
(4) mi7(11,9,♭5)	<02356T>	[23] [56]

These chords are subsets of modes of the diatonic and/or melodic minor collections. Chord (1) is a lydian <024679E> subset. Chord (2) is an ascending melodic minor <023579E> (mode I) subset. Chord (3) is both an aeolian <023578T> and a dorian <023579T> subset. Chord (4) is both a locrian <013568T> and an aeolian ♭5 <023568T> (ascending melodic minor mode VI) subset.

The foregoing account of the levels of transposition (relative to the roots of the harmonies in which they are found) and characteristic harmonic contexts of eight of the twelve possible transpositions of the dyadic cell leaves four transpositions of this cell unaccounted for. These are [12], [45], [78], and [TE]. The [78] cell is the only one of these four likely to be found as a simultaneity in post-1940 tonal jazz. This cell may typically be found as a subset of the Dominant 7th chord with added minor 13th and minor 9th, <01478T>. This chord, which often functions as dominant harmony in minor, is itself a subset of harmonic major[9] mode III, <013478T>. The remaining three dyadic cells—[12], [45], and [TE]—are rarely heard as simultaneities in tonal jazz for the following reasons:

The avoidance of the [45] cell is attributable to the ambivalence of harmonic function which results when both the 4th (suspension) and the major 3rd (resolution) occur simultaneously in the same harmony.[10] In a tonic harmonic context, the 4th (the 7th of V) implies the dominant function, while the major 3rd (the 3rd of I) implies the tonic function. Similarly, in a dominant harmonic context, the 4th (the 7th of ii or the 5th of IV) implies the pre-dominant function, while the major 3rd (the 3rd of V) implies the dominant function.

The usage of the [TE] and [12] dyadic cells, by definition, produces two trichordal cells—[TE0] and [012]—because in tonal jazz, these are always heard in conjunction with the roots of the chords (the "zero" of [TE0] and [012] of which they are subsets. This usage violates Pressing's dictum that " . . . vertical tonal jazz sets may use any level of secundal dissonance provided (012) [at any level of transposition] is not present . . . " Note that none of the supersets on Pressing's list (see note 7) includes the (012) trichord as a subset. Moreover, "Its [the (012) trichord] interval content effectively prohibits its use as a vertical sound object in tonal jazz."[11] The reason for this prohibition is not to be found in any inherent quality of "secundal dissonance" per se, however. Rather, the avoidance of the [TE0] and [012] cells is attributable to the ambivalence of harmonic function which results when both the minor 7th and the major 7th (pcs T and E), or when both the minor 9th and the major 9th (pcs 1 and 2) are present in the same harmony. Monk uses the trichordal cells [TE0] and [012] almost exclusively in the context of Dominant 7th chords. Although the Dominant 7th chord may function as either a dominant or a tonic chord in tonal jazz, the major 7th chord never functions as a dominant chord because it lacks the dominant tritone (major 3rd and minor 7th). Similarly, the Dominant 9th chord may function as either a tonic or a dominant chord in tonal jazz, but the "Dominant-seven-flat-nine" chord rarely functions as a tonic chord, probably because the unmistakable diminished-7th-chord sonority of its upper chord members—the "flat nine" in particular—so strongly demands resolution.

Monk's "consonant" usages of these three dissonant cells—[45], [TE0], and [012]—may have originated in his uniquely anachronistic approach to the blues. Many of the blues compositions of his bebop contemporaries feature convoluted melodic lines and complex harmonic progressions which rely extensively on transpositions of the "ii—V" (or "ii—V—I") progression and tritone substitute chords.[12] In stark contrast, the melodies of Monk's blues compositions are typically based on the repetition of simple riffs, and their accompanying harmonic progressions tend to be archaic, often using only the three chords of the basic blues progression—I7, IV7, and V7, all of which are Dominant 7th chords.

Although *Raise Four* (Example 1) was not recorded until the twilight

Example 1: Raise Four

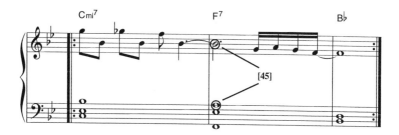

Example 2: Criss Cross B, mm. 1–6

of Monk's career (1968), it is one of his most primal blues compositions insofar as it is comprised entirely of the untransposed repetition of a single 6-note riff over a basic blues harmonic progression in B♭.[13] Note that Monk's sketchy left-hand accompaniment includes only the root and either the 3rd or the 7th of each chord. The "omitted" 7ths and 3rds are parenthesized in Example 1. The unordered pc content of the riff is a transposition of the (016) trichord,[14] (E,F,B♭). In the context of the B♭7 chord, these three pcs are respectively the "raised 4th" (augmented 11th), the 5th, and the root. This harmony thus includes the [67] cell—the augmented 11th and the 5th—one of the four dyadic cells commonly found as a subset of extended and/or altered Dominant 7th chords. In the context of the E♭7 chord, the pcs (E,F,B♭) are respectively the minor 9th (E = F♭), the major 9th, and the 5th. This harmony thus includes the [012] cell—the root, the minor 9th, and the major 9th. In the context of the F7 chord, the pcs (E,F,B♭) are respectively the major 7th, the root, and the 4th (11th). This harmony thus includes both the [TE0] cell—the "omitted" minor 7th, the major 7th, and the root—and the [45] cell—the major 3rd and the 4th (11th). Remarkably, this simple composition uses all three of the dissonant cells [45], [TE0], and [012] as consonances. Additional examples of Monk's consonant usages of these three cells, as well as a few larger cells which include them as subsets, are presented in the following section. A discography of the compositions from which the examples are drawn is provided at the end of this article.

Examples 2–8 are Dominant 7th harmonies which include the [45] cell—the major 3rd and the 4th (11th)—as a subset. This cell, deployed with the 4th (B♭), strongly emphasized in the melody, and with the major 3rd (A) just as strongly emphasized in the accompanying Dominant 7th chord (F7), is found in the B sections of two of Monk's compositions, "Criss Cross" (Example 2), and "Played Twice" (Example 3). The clashing

Example 3: Played Twice B, mm. 1–4

effect of these simultaneous suspensions and their resolutions is accen-
tuated by the repetition built into the structures of both of these compositions: the 3-measure phrase in "Criss Cross" is repeated twice, and the
8-note melodic figure in "Played Twice" is repeated three times.

The [45] cell, with the major 3rd and the 4th related by the pitch interval of a minor 2nd, is a subset of Dominant 7th chords in two other compositions. These are (F, G♭) in the D♭7 chord in A, m. 4 of "Thelonious"
(Example 4), and G♯,A) in the extended E7 chord in m. 7 of the final A section of "Ruby, My Dear" (Example 5). The E7 (13,11,9) chord in "Ruby,
My Dear" is the verticalization of the complete E mixolydian mode.

The second note of the ascending eighth-note-triplet figures which begin on the fourth beat of B, m. 1 in "Off Minor" (Example 6) and on the
fourth beat of A, m. 3 in "Boo Boo's Birthday" (Example 7) is the 4th
(11th), while the accompanying Dominant 7th chords both include major 3rds. These 4ths are disproportionately conspicuous, considering
their fleeting duration and unaccented metric position—each occupies

Example 4: Thelonious A, mm. 3–4

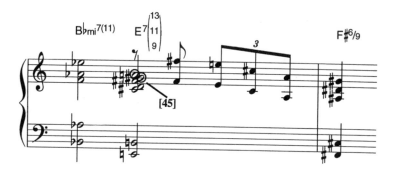

Example 5: Ruby, My Dear A, m. 7

the second eighth note of a triplet figure which itself occupies the fourth beat of the measure—possibly because they are not treated as traditional "nonharmonic" tones (passing tones, neighbor tones, suspensions, or appoggiaturas). Both 4ths are approached by ascending leap and neither resolves down by step.

The [4567] cell (B♭,C♭,C,D♭)—the major 3rd, perfect 4th, augmented 4th, and 5th of the dominant tritone substitute harmony G♭7—is found in B, m. 2 of "Boo Boo's Birthday" (Example 8). The chord progression of this passage is Gmi7(♭5)—G♭7—Fma7. Although these four pitches are played melodically, not simultaneously, and the C♭ on the downbeat of B, m. 2 is heard before the B♭, the effect of a 4-3 suspension is not produced. The dissonant sound of this melodic line is largely due to another voice-leading factor. The D♭ at the end of B, m. 1 is the chromatic "upper" neighbor (an octave lower) of the repeated C natural in B, m. 1. The

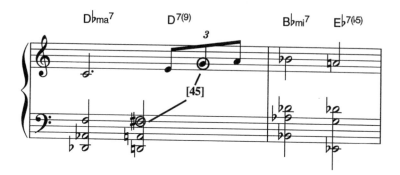

Example 6: Off Minor B, mm. 1–2

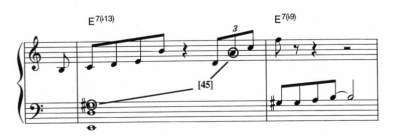

Example 7: Boo Boo's Birthday A, mm. 3–4

C♭ on the downbeat of B, m. 2, is an unorthodox resolution (by descending whole-step) of the immediately preceding D♭. If the "expected" C natural (scale degree $\hat{5}$ in F) is substituted for the C♭ on the downbeat of B, m. 2, this passage sounds harmonically and melodically orthodox,[15] but loses its characteristically dissonant Monkian flavor.

Examples 9–10 are Dominant 7th harmonies which include the [012] cell—the root, the minor 9th and the major 9th—as a subset. The closing B♭7 chords of "Blues Five Spot" (Example 9a), "Rhythm-a-ning" (Example 9b), and "Straight, No Chaser" (Example 9c) all include the [012] cell (B♭,C♭,C) as a subset. Although the voicings of the lower parts of these chords differ slightly, the two highest chord members are identically deployed in all three cases, with the minor 9th (C♭) and the major 9th (C natural) related by the pitch interval of an augmented octave. Since this chord clearly functions as the closing tonic in all three compositions, the minor 9th is a coloristic dissonance added to an otherwise consonant verticality.

If B♭ is heard as the root of the extended/altered Dominant harmony in B, m. 7 in "Off Minor" (Example 10)—B♭ is the lowest pitch in the bari-

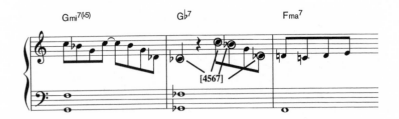

Example 8: Boo Boo's Birthday B, mm. 1–3

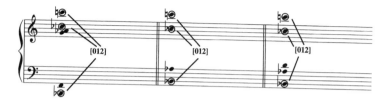

Example 9a: Blues Five Spot; 9b: Rhythm-a-ning; 9c: Straight, No Chaser

tone saxophone part, and the Dominant tritone (D,A♭) is embedded in the inner-voice counterline—then the pcs B♭, C♭, and C natural are respectively the root, minor 9th, and major 9th (the [012] cell). B♭7 functions as a tonic substitute chord in this composition, which is in G minor. In this interpretation, the E♭ on the downbeat in the inner voice functions as an appoggiatura. Although the string bass part is obscure during the first half of this measure, it clearly establishes D as the root of the harmony in the second half of the measure. The immediately following harmony in B, m. 8, the last measure of the B section D7(13,♯11♭9), <01469T>, an octatonic mode I subset. This is the extended/altered dominant 7th chord in G minor. If D is considered to be the root of the harmony in B, mm. 7-8 (parenthesized in Example 10), then the prominently heard low B♭ is a "nonharmonic" tone; all of the other pitches in these two measures are consonant chord members of D7(13,♯11♭9). In this interpretation, the pcs B♭, C♭, and C natural are respectively the minor 13th, major 13th and minor 7th (the [89T] cell). In both readings, the harmonic effect produced by this cell is one of extreme dissonance and functional ambivalence.

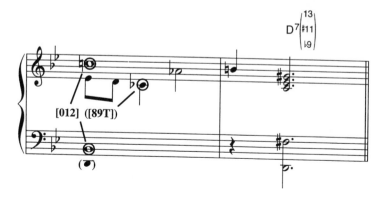

Example 10: Off Minor B, mm. 7–8

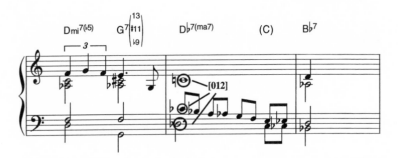

Example 11: Monk's Mood A, mm. 3–4

Examples 11–19 are harmonies which include the [TE0] cell—the minor 7th, the major 7th, and the root—as a subset. The [TE0] cell (C♭,C,D♭) is a subset of the D♭ harmony in A, m. 4 of "Monk's Mood" (Example 11). This harmony seems to function in two senses simultaneously. In one sense, as D♭ma7, it is a substitute for the expected tonic harmony. The tonic C is in the melody, and the chords preceding this harmony are Dmi7(11♭5)—G7(13,♯11,♭9).[16] In the other sense, as D♭7, it functions as the tritone substitute for the dominant of C major harmony (to which it briefly resolves on the fourth beat of A, m. 4). The dominant tritone (C♭,F =B,F) is unfolded in the inner-voice counterline.

The [TE0] cell (C♭,C,D♭) is a also subset of the D♭ harmony in A, m. 7-8 of "Boo Boo's Birthday" (Example 12a). This harmony is followed by tonic harmony (C major) at the beginning of the repeat of the A section. Although the C♭ and the C natural are sounded consecutively, the conflicting functions of these two pcs within the same harmony—C natural is the major 7th of D♭ma7, a tonic substitute chord, and C♭ is the minor 7th of D♭7, the dominant tritone substitute chord—produce an effect very

Example 12a: Boo Boo's Birthday A, mm. 7–8; 12b

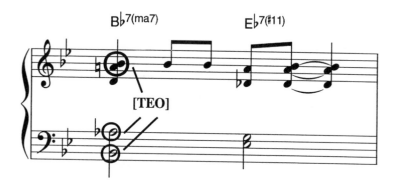

Example 13: Thelonious A, m. 7

similar to that heard in Example 13. This reading is confirmed when Monk plays the (C♭,C) dyad as a simultaneity in the D♭ harmony at the end of the first A section during the first saxophone solo chorus (Example 12b).

The B♭ chord on the downbeat of A, m. 7 of "Thelonious" (Example 13) includes both its minor 7th (A♭) and major 7th (A natural). In this context, this chord functions both as the tonic major 7th chord—the harmonic progression of "Thelonious" is a variant of "rhythm changes" in B♭—and as the Dominant 7th chord (V7 of IV) of the following E♭7(♯11) chord. The closing D♭ chord of "Introspection" (Example 14) also includes

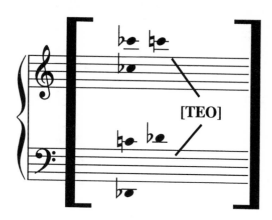

Example 14: Introspection

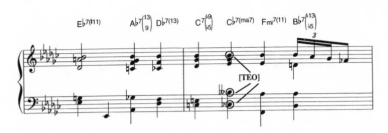

Example 15: 'Round Midnight Intro., mm. 7–8

both its minor 7th (C♭) and major 7th (C natural). In this context, however, the effect is coloristic; there is no confusion caused by conflicting
functions, since both the Dominant 7th chord and the major 7th chord
may function as tonics in jazz.

The [TE0] cell (B♭♭,B♭,C♭) is also found on the second beat of m. 8 of
the introduction in one of Monk's solo piano recordings "'Round Midnight" (Example 15). The chord progression of the last two measures of
the this 8-bar introduction is a slightly modified descending cycle-of-the-
5th sequence (I7—IV7—♭VII7—VI7—♭VI7—ii7—V7) leading to tonic
harmony (E♭ minor) at the beginning of the A section. The apparent major 7th (B♭) in the highest voice of the C♭7 chord (♭VI7) is the result of the
extension of scale degree $\hat{5}$ in the highest voice throughout this passage.

The C minor chord in B, m. 6 of "Ruby, My Dear" (Example 16) includes both its minor 7th (B♭) and major 7th (B natural). This is the only
instance of non-Dominant harmony I have found in Monk's compositions which includes the [TE0] cell as a subset. This harmony also im-

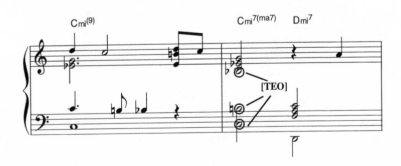

Example 16: Ruby, My Dear B, mm. 5–6

Example 17: Crepuscule with Nellie A, mm. 1–2

plies a certain degree of functional ambivalence in this context; although the minor 7th chord may function as a tonic in jazz, it usually functions as a pre-dominant. The minor-major 7th chord, however, typically functions as a tonic, and rarely as a pre-dominant.

Although the tonic of "Crepuscule With Nellie" (Example 17) ultimately proves to be A♭, the two opening harmonies are B♭7—E♭7, that is, I7—IV7 in the local "blues tonality" of B♭, with E♭7 harmony functioning as the subdominant prolongation of B♭7. The pungently dissonant three-note chord at the end of A, m. 2, is the result of the simultaneous sounding of the apparent major 7th (D natural)—scale degree $\hat{3}$ in the middleground-level arpeggiation of the B♭ major triad in the melody of this phrase—along with the minor 7th (D♭) and minor 9th (F♭) of an E♭7 chord. The E♭7 chord arpeggiated in the left hand at the beginning of m. 2 determines the harmonic context in which this trichordal cell is heard. This harmony thus includes the [TE01] cell (D♭,D,E♭,F♭) as a subset.

The [TE01] cell (D,E♭,E,F) is also found in the first half of A, m. 6, of "Monk's Mood" (Example 18). This cells is produced by the prolongation

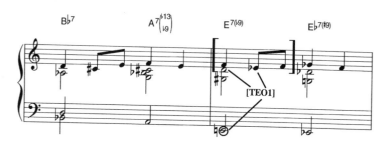

Example 18: Monk's Mood A, mm. 5–6

Example 19: Criss Cross A, mm. 5–8

of the F in the melody—the minor 9th of the E7(♭9) chord—by its whole-
step lower neighbor (E♭), heard in conjunction with the root (E) and minor 7th (D) of the chord. If, as in the similar situation discussed above in
"Boo Boo's Birthday" (Example 8), the expected lower neighbor (E natural) is substituted for the E♭ in A, m. 6, this passage loses its Monkian
astringency and sounds very bland.

The compound melodic figure in A, mm. 5-6 of "Criss Cross" (Example 19) is comprised of the descending chromatic line F—E—E♭—D
in the upper voice alternating with a repeated G natural in the lower
voice. This melodic figure, which begins on the downbeat of A, m. 5, is
heard in the harmonic context of Dmi7(11)—G7(♭5). In this context, the
E♭ in the descending chromatic line clearly functions as a passing tone.
In the following two measures, however (A, mm. 7-8), a metrically
shifted incomplete repetition of this melodic figure (F—E—E♭ in the upper voice alternating with G natural in the lower voice, and beginning on
the third beat of A, m. 7) is heard in the harmonic context of G♭7(♯5),
<048T>. In this context, the G natural in the lower voice of the com-
pound melody is also a consonant chord member (G = A♭♭, the minor
9th). The resultant chord, G♭7(♭9,♯5), <0148T>, is a super locrian subset.
Of the three pcs of the descending chromatic line of the upper voice, only
the E natural (= F♭, the minor 7th) is a chord member with respect to the
super locrian superset. The other two pcs, F and E♭, which are respectively the major 7th and the 13th, are emphasized by virtue of their metric positions on strong beats. This harmony thus includes the [89TE01]
cell (D, E♭, F♭, F, G♭, G) as a subset.

The examples discussed in this article demonstrate Monk's apparently
systematic exploitation of the [45], [012], and [TE0] cells as consonances. The sound of these "outrageous clusters"[17] is one of the factors
that gives many of Monk's compositions their unique flavor. Most of

Monk's compositions—including all of those discussed above except "Raise Four" (1968) and "Boo Boo's Birthday" (1967)—were composed and first recorded in the 1940s and the 1950s. Although Monk heard and used clusters in tonal contexts, his expansion of the jazz harmonic palette to include all of the possible dyadic semitonal cells, as well as a number of larger semitonal cells, prefigures the exploitation of chromatic clusters in the often atonal "free" jazz of the 1960s.[18]

NOTES

1. It is generally recognized that it is as a composer rather than as a performer that Monk has had the greater impact. In this article, Monk's compositions are understood to refer to the "heads" only—that is, the pre-composed melodies along with their underlying chord progressions—not to the solo improvisations. Many of Monk's compositions also include inner-voice counterlines and/or bass figures, as well as introductions and/or codas.
2. Pitch class (pc) set theory was originally devised for the analysis of the atonal concert music of the early twentieth century. Recently, however, a few theorists have begun to apply some of the analytical methods and terminology of pc set theory to both post-1940 tonal jazz and to atonal "free" jazz. See Jeff Pressing's "Pitch Class Set Structures in Contemporary Jazz," *Jazzforschung/Jazz Research* 14 (1982): 133–171; Steven Block's "Pitch-Class Transformation in Free Jazz," *Music Theory Spectrum* 12, no. 2 (Fall 1990): 181–202; and Block's "Organized Sound: Pitch-Class Relations in the Music of Ornette Coleman," *Annual Review of Jazz Studies* 6 (1993): 229–252.

   Readers unfamiliar with the terminology and notations of pitch class set theory are refered to Allen Forte's *The Structure of Atonal Music* (New Haven: Yale University Press, 1973); John Rahn's *Basic Atonal Theory* (New York: Schirmer Books, 1980); and Joseph Straus's *Introduction to Post-Tonal Theory* (Englewood Cliffs, NJ: Prentice-Hall, 1990).
3. In this article, Dominant (upper case D) refers only to the intervallic structure of this chord, whatever its harmonic function, while dominant (lower case d) refers to the dominant harmonic function of this chord, whatever the scale degree of its root. The Dominant 7th chord is broadly defined in this article to include any chord which is

comprised of or includes <04T> (root, major 3rd, and minor 7th) as a subset.

4. The angle bracket notations of chord types and scale orderings used in this article are adapted from Friedmann's notation of "modally ordered" supersets. See Michael Friedmann's *Ear Training for Twentieth-Century Music* (New Haven: Yale University Press, 1990), 115.

5. In terms of unordered pitch class, compound intervals are equivalent to simple intervals, and simple intervals wider than a tritone are equivalent to their "inversions" (octave complements). Thus there are only six interval classes (ics). For example, the category ic 1 includes the pitch intervals minor 2nd, major 7th (augmented prime, diminished octave), minor 9th, major 14th, etc. See Straus (cited above, 7-8).

6. The properties of the octatonic collection have also been widely exploited in the post-tonal European concert music of the early twentieth century, particularly in the music of Bartók and Stravinsky. See Straus (cited above, 97–101).

7. According to Jeff Pressing (cited above, 136), virtually all jazz chords are subsets of one or more of these seven "parent jazz sets/scales" (unordered pc collections):

(1) diminished (octatonic)	(0134679T)
(2) major (diatonic)	(013568T)
(3) ascending melodic minor	(013468T)
(4) harmonic minor	(0134689)
(5) Harmonic major*	(0135689)
(6) whole tone	(02468T)
(7) augmented	(014589)

*inversion of harmonic minor

Sets (2), (3), (4), and (5) each have seven possible modal orderings. Because they have higher degrees of transpositional symmetry (see Straus, cited above, 180–183), sets (1) and (7) each have only two possible modal orderings, and set (6) has only one possible modal ordering.

8. Diminished 7th chords (including extended diminished 7th chords) are subsets of octatonic mode II only when they function as common-tone chords in the prolongation of tonic or dominant harmony (e.g., I6—♭iii°7—ii7—♭II7—I, or V7—vi7—♯vi°7—V6/5). When diminished 7th chords function as leading-tone (dominant function)

chords, they are usually regarded by jazz musicians as "dominant-seventh-flat-nine" chords with their roots omitted, and are thus subsets of octatonic mode I.

9. The harmonic major scale, a designation coined by Nicolas Slonimsky in his *Thesaurus of Scales and Melodic Patterns* (New York: Scribner, 1947), may be constructed by disjunctly joining the lower tetrachord of the major scale to the upper tetrachord of the harmonic minor scale.

10. Chords in which both the 3rd and the 4th (11th) are present, but are related by ic 2 (whole tone), are common in post-1940 tonal jazz. Examples of these are the minor 7th chord with an added 11th, and the Dominant 7th or major 7th chord with an added augmented 11th. The so-called "sus 4" chord—a Dominant 7th chord in which the 4th is substituted for the major 3rd—and the Dominant 11th chord with its 3rd omitted, are also common.

11. See Jeff Pressing (cited above, 135, 137).

12. The tritone is the only pc interval which maps onto itself under the transpositional operation T6 (transposition by ic 6). A tritone substitute chord is considered to be functionally equivalent to the "original" Dominant 7th chord because the tritone-related pcs which comprise the major 3rd and minor 7th of one chord are respectively the minor 7th and major 3rd of the other chord.

Along with the basic operations of transposition and inversion, multiplicative operations have found application in some of the twelve-tone music of the mid-twentieth century. See Rahn (cited above, 40–58). For a brief description of the use of the multiplicative operation T6MI in tonal jazz harmony, which maps descending cycle-of-5ths progressions of Dominant 7th chords onto descending chromatic progressions of Dominant 7th chords, see Steven Block's "Organized Sound: Pitch-Class Relations in the Music of Ornette Coleman" (cited above, 234–236).

13. Monk's recorded blues compositions, all of which are in B♭, are "Ba-lue Bolivar, Ba-lues Are," "Blue Hawk," "Blue Monk," "Blues Five Spot," "Blue Sphere," "Functional," "Misterioso," "Monk's Point," "North of the Sunset," "Raise Four," and "Straight, No Chaser." See Philippe Baudoin's *"Compositions de Thelonious Monk,"* *Jazzophone* 13 (1982): 41–44, an annotated list of Monk's compositions, with incipits.

14. The (016) trichord, one of Monk's signature pc collections, is also exploited motivically in "Well, You Needn't," "Brilliant Corners," and "Ba-lue Bolivar, Ba-Lues Are."

15. The extension of scale degree $\hat{5}$ is one of the upper voices of the
    ii7($\flat$5)—$\flat$II7—I progression produces the common variant ii7(11$\flat$5)—
    $\flat$II7($\sharp$11)—I.

16. The ii7—V7—$\flat$IIma7 progression, a deceptive cadential formula in
    post-1940 tonal jazz, is typically used when scale degree $\hat{1}$ is in the
    melody in the expected tonic harmony.

17. This colorful phrase is excerpted from the introduction to Stuart
    Isacoff's *Jazz Masters: Thelonious Monk* (New York: Amsco,
    1987), a collection of transcriptions of eight of Monk's composi-
    tions and piano solos.

18. For example, chromatic clusters are a prominent feature of many of
    the compositions of pianist Cecil Taylor. See Ekkehard Jost's *Free
    Jazz* (Vienna: Universal, 1974). For set-theoretical analyses of se-
    lected compositions of Taylor, Coltrane, Ornette Coleman, and An-
    thony Braxton, see Steven Block's "Pitch-Class Transformation in
    Free Jazz" (cited above, 181–202).

DISCOGRAPHY

All examples transcribed by the author from the following sources:

Blues Five Spot (1962)	*Monk's Dream*, Columbia CS 8765.
Boo Boo's Birthday (1967)	*Underground,* Columbia CS 9632.
Crepuscule with Nellie (1963)	*Criss Cross,* Columbia CS 8838.
Criss Cross (1951)	*The Best of Thelonious Monk: the Blue Note Years,* Blue Note CDP 7-95636-2. (Originally issued on *The Complete Genius,* Blue Note BN-LA 579-2LP.)
Introspection (1947)	*Thelonious Monk: Genius of Modern Music,* Blue Note CDP 7-81510-2. (Originally issued on *The Complete Genius,* Blue Note BN-LA 579-2LP.)
Monk's Mood (1947)	*The Best of Thelonious Monk: the Blue Note Years,* Blue Note CDP 7-95636-2. (Originally issued on *The Complete Genius,* Blue Note BN-LA 579-2LP.)
Off Minor (1959)	*The Thelonious Monk Orchestra at Town Hall,* Riverside RLP 12-300.

Played Twice (1959)

Raise Four (1968)

Rhythm-a-ning (1962)

'Round Midnight (1968)

Ruby, My Dear (1965)

Straight, No Chaser (1963)

Thelonious (1959)

Monk by Five by Monk, Riverside RLP 12-305.

Underground, Columbia CS 9632.

Criss Cross, Columbia CS 8838.

Greatest Hits, Columbia CS 9775.

Solo Monk, Columbia CS 9149.

Tokyo Concerts, Columbia, C2 38510.

The Thelonious Monk Orchestra at Town Hall, Riverside RLP 12-300.

HOW WEIRD CAN THINGS GET?
(MAPS FOR PANTONAL IMPROVISATION)

Tim Dean-Lewis

INTRODUCTION

Improvising "outside the changes" whilst other performers continue "within the changes" is a common occurrence in modern jazz—bitonality and polytonality are part of the sound of the style. Musicians such as John Coltrane often circumnavigate the "home" key using relatively short devices played in other keys, returning to this home key (and their colleagues) relatively swiftly.[1] In a development of this approach, practitioners such as Ornette Coleman incorporate bitonality and polytonality freely, whilst adding pantonality to their palette of improvisation techniques. Here the use of other keys is sufficiently complex and long-term among the whole group to disrupt any sense of the home key. A good understanding of this pantonal approach is not possible using conventional chord-based analysis techniques. The mathematical complexities of 12-note music have been examined in depth with regard to classical music, but these principles are rarely extended to the performance or analysis of jazz music. Most jazz musicians and composers develop a relationship with dissonant sounds through trial and error, incorporating these sounds as they seem appropriate. While the author considers this trial-and-error approach to be essential to the development of any musician, this paper is designed to reveal some truths about exactly how "weird" things can actually get in such bitonal, polytonal, and pantonal environments; with the aim of focusing, and giving perspective to, such personal musical experiments. The author includes several "maps" for making and understanding planned, limited journeys through such music.

TONALITY, BITONALITY, POLYTONALITY, PANTONALITY, AND HARMOLODICS

Some definitions

Tonality: This means to be in one key, e.g. C major—although it is important to remember that music really moves around within a key, and that it takes a gradual revelation of notes in time for a tonality to be defined to an audience.

Bitonality: This means to be in two keys at once. It is

> . . . a way of expanding the tonal system without completely breaking the rules governing tonality, which, on the contrary, are essential to it. Originally developed as a humorous effect in polyphony based on the clash of two different keys (e.g., Mozart's *Ein musikalischer Spass,* K. 522, and Hans Neusidler's *Juden Tantz* (1544), it has since developed a more serious musical status and emotional credence as a sound of its own through the works of composers such as Prokofiev, Shostakovich, Hindemith, Ives, and Les Six (Milhaud in particular).[2]

Polytonality: This means to be in two or more keys at once.

Pantonality: This is a word first used by Rudolph Reti in his book *Tonality, Atonality and Pantonality* (London, 1958), to explain the continued extension of the tonal language of classical music found in the work of Wagner, Debussy, etc. The approach which these composers took is often clearly more than polytonal, but certainly less than atonal. Pantonality is well defined as:

> . . . being characterized by the notion of "movable tonics"; that is, it recognizes and uses tonal relationships in intervals, melodic figures and chord progressions without defining, or even implying, a key centre in any large-scale sense.[3]

Reti applied this description to much of the music of Bartok and Berg, as well as to early Stravinsky and Hindemith (up to about 1920). A vast twentieth-century repertory of "pantonal" music has followed from the developments of these composers.

Shortly after the publication of Reti's book, in 1960, George Russell cowrote an article for *Jazz Review,* which was later added as an appendix to his own book *The Lydian Chromatic Concept of Tonal Organization,* in which he applied the term "pantonal" to the improvisational style of Ornette Coleman and other jazz musicians, making the point that this music is often neither polytonal nor atonal in structure.[4]

Harmolodics: Coleman himself has since titled his improvisational method as "harmolodics," i.e., a synthesis of "harmony, movement, and melody."[5]

It is hard to find better quotations on this nebulous subject than those used by John Litweiler in his book, *Ornette Coleman: A Harmolodic Life*. Don Cherry (Coleman's trumpet-playing colleague) once described this harmolodic theory as:

> . . . a profound system based on developing your ear along with technical proficiency on your instrument. . . . We have to know the chord structure perfectly, all the possible intervals, and then play around with it. . . . If I play a C and have it in my mind as the tonic, that's what it will become. If I want it to be a minor third or a major seventh that has a tendency to resolve upward, then the quality of the note will change.[6]

Cherry has also said, in a lecture, that:

> In the harmolodic concept, you're reaching to the point to make every note sound like the tonic. . . . [7]

And Charlie Haden, the bassist, described playing with these musicians like this:

> Technically speaking, it was a constant modulation in the improvising that was taken from the composition, and from the direction inside the musician, and from listening to each other. . . . [8]

Clearly, then, we need to include pantonality in any assessment of "Harmolodics," or of Coleman's music per se (and Russell is correct to make the connection). However, although it is true to say that Coleman and his colleagues are melodically driven, often producing heterophonic textures, it should be recognized that these melodic patterns are carefully structured in tonal, bitonal, polytonal, and pantonal ways at various (specifically composed) points within a piece. This variety of textural approach can be heard from Coleman's earliest recordings up to, and including, his recent work with Prime Time—e.g., "Tone Dialing" (Harmolodic, 1995). For example, while the melody of a particular piece may be tonal in parts, bitonal in others, the improvisations that follow may be polytonal and/or pantonal. The author believes that in a study of Coleman's music the issue of detuned notes is no more an issue than in any other music; all music is "out of tune" at various points and to varying degrees. The note you "nearly heard" is just that—it's the note you nearly heard.

LESSONS IN JAZZ

Courses of study in learning to play a musical instrument "in a jazz style" progress in various manners, whether from a book, a teacher or by trial and error. Over time, however, the student is likely to be introduced to the sound of, as well as the techniques for performing, various complex systems characteristic of the style:

(a) a "Blues" scale (i.e., C E♭ F F# G B♭) improvisation over a diatonic (often major scale) chord progression with the same tonic (e.g., a simple 12-bar "Blues" using C, F and G major triads, or C / Am / F / G, etc.). This "panacea" scale sounds good in most situations and avoids the "naive" sound of the major scale from which the chords are built. Of course, this is not music constructed from two keys played simultaneously (a traditional definition of bitonality); these are two different scales that share a tonic, and other, note(s)!

(b) the same "Blues" scale, but played over increasingly complex chord progressions—at first the chords may be only slightly chromatic, later increasingly chromatic (e.g., at first C / A7 / D7 / G7; later Cmaj7 / A7+− / D7♭9 / G7♭9b13; or a 12-bar "Blues" with many "substitutions," etc.). These chord alterations and substitutions are sometimes designed to "fit better" with the Blues scale, but there are often still points of conflict between the chords and the scale (which, ironically, may be deliberately ignored to provide stylistic "color").

(c) modes and new scales, generally seen as useful as "better fits" for modal and chromatic chords (e.g., C Dorian—C D E♭ F G A B♭—for Cm7; C Altered Scale—C D♭ E♭ E G♭ A♭ B♭—for C7♭9♭13, etc.), learned and mastered conventionally, then used more freely to create new effects; for example: using C Lydian over a Cmaj7 chord, C Phrygian or C Dorian ♭2 over a Cm7 chord, etc.

(d) synthesizing new scales, either as a compositional extension of the Blues/diatonic system of (a) above, or, perhaps, in order to deal with potential/actual chromaticisms in other parts of the music (e.g., a complex walking bass line), or to solve metrical problems, such as those of using 7-note scales in duple/quadruple meter.

(e) "playing outside the changes," i.e., deliberately playing material not in the "key" of the piece (or a part of the piece). Student musicians are often encouraged to improvise in a key "a semitone up" or "a semitone down."

By undergoing such a course, a musician is not only learning how to make "a jazz sound" but is also becoming aurally familiar with music of varying dissonance. From the musician's perspective, they are enlarging (and becoming more fluent with) their "vocabulary of the familiar."

Conventional analysis provides us with an understanding of consonance and dissonance with regard to a tonal gravity, or a tonal center. This is useful for bitonal and polytonal music. In order to assess accurately what happens when musicians in a group deliberately leave a "home" key, each transposing to a key of their choice, and then constantly modulating (see Haden, above)—i.e., creating "pantonal" music (as Russell defines it), we need to ask an additional question: "How Weird Can Things Get?"

THE 2048 SCALES

There are 2048 different possible scales using 12 semitones, starting from a given note (for example, C):

1 × 1-note scale	(= C)
11 × 2-note scales	(from C D♭ to C B)
5 × 3-note scales	(from C D♭ D to C B♭ B)
165 × 4-note scales	(from C D♭ D E♭ to C A B♭ B)
330 × 5-note scales	(from C D♭ D E♭ E to C A♭ A B♭ B)
462 × 6-note scales	(from C D♭ D E♭ E F to C G A♭ A B♭ B)
462 × 7-note scales	(from C D♭ D E♭ E F F# to C F# G A♭ A B♭ B)
330 × 8-note scales	(from C D♭ D E♭ E F F# G to C F F# G A♭ A B♭ B)
165 × 9-note scales	(from C D♭ D E♭ E F F# G A♭ to C E F F# G A♭ A B♭ B)
55 × 10-note scales	(from C D♭ D E♭ E F F# G A♭ A to C E♭ E F F# G A♭ A B♭ B)
11 × 11-note scales	(from C D♭ D E♭ E F F# G Ab A B♭ to C D E♭ E F F# G A♭ A B♭ B)
1 × 12-note scale	(= C D♭ D E♭ E F F# G A♭ A B♭ B)

$$1+11+55+165+330+462+462+330+165+55+11+1 = 2048$$
(note the symmetry of this sum)[9]

These scales represent the 2048 different interval patterns that are possible with 12 semitones. These 2048 interval patterns can, of course, be started on any of the 12 notes available on chromatic instruments (C, D♭,

D, E♭, E, F, F#, G, A♭, A, B♭ or B); making a grand total of 24,576 possible scales! If we number these scales in natural order from 1 to 2048, with scale number 1 being the 1-note scale, and scale number 2048 being the 12-note chromatic scale, we find that commonly used scales occur at the following positions:

No.	Scale
1361	Major (Ionian mode)
1325	Dorian mode
1197	Phrygian mode
1371	Lydian mode
1360	Mixolydian mode
1323	Aeolian mode
1191	Locrian mode
1326	Melodic minor ascending (or "Jazz Melodic")
1199	Dorian ♭2 (2nd mode of Melodic minor ascending)
1374	Lydian Augmented (3rd mode of Melodic minor ascending)
1370	Lydian ♭7 (4th mode of Melodic minor ascending)
1358	Mixolydian ♭6 (5th mode of Melodic minor ascending)
1317	Locrian #2 (6th mode of Melodic minor ascending)
1171	Super Locrian (7th mode of Melodic minor ascending) — also known as "Altered Scale"
1324	Harmonic minor
1193	2nd mode of Harmonic minor
1364	3rd mode of Harmonic minor
1335	4th mode of Harmonic minor
1232	5th mode of Harmonic minor
1427	6th mode of Harmonic minor
1170	7th mode of Harmonic minor
936	Blues Scale (= C E♭ F F# G B♭)
785	Major Blues Scale (= C D E♭ E G A)
393	Pentatonic
465	Minor Pentatonic
1739	Diminished
1636	Auxiliary Diminished

If we sort the above list into numerical order, it is easy to see that many of these commonly used scales are "neighbors," or, at least, "relatively near neighbors":

No.	Scale
393	Pentatonic
465	Minor Pentatonic
785	Major Blues Scale (= C D E♭ E G A)
936	Blues Scale (= C E♭ F F# G B♭)
1170	7th mode of Harmonic minor
1171	Super Locrian (7th mode of Melodic minor ascending)—also known as "Altered Scale"
1191	Locrian mode
1193	2nd mode of Harmonic minor
1197	Phrygian mode
1199	Dorian ♭2 (2nd mode of Melodic minor ascending)
1232	5th mode of Harmonic minor
1317	Locrian #2 (6th mode of Melodic minor ascending)
1323	Aeolian mode
1324	Harmonic minor
1325	Dorian mode
1326	Melodic minor ascending (or "Jazz Melodic")
1335	4th mode of Harmonic minor
1358	Mixolydian ♭6 (5th mode of Melodic minor ascending)
1360	Mixolydian mode
1361	Major (Ionian mode)
1364	3rd mode of Harmonic minor
1370	Lydian ♭7 (4th mode of Melodic minor ascending)
1371	Lydian mode
1374	Lydian Augmented (3rd mode of Melodic minor ascending)
1427	6th mode of Harmonic minor
1636	Auxiliary Diminished
1739	Diminished

It seems surprising, at first glance, that so often these commonly used scales should be simple chromatic versions of each other. However, an analysis of the internal interval structure of these scales reveals some common threads.

HOW WEIRD THINGS CAN GET—
"MOST DIFFERENT" KEYS

If two musicians improvise in different keys using a major scale each, there will always be at least two common notes between these keys. If the two musicians change to another scale type, the number of common notes may change.

It is important to recognize that in any piece of music where two scales/keys are being used at once then each scale/key will exert its own "pull" on the ear of the listener to a lesser or greater degree. The most familiar scale/key will exert the strongest pull (a melody played in one key with the same melody played in parallel in another key will result in a single, stronger pull!). A scale can be familiar for different reasons: it may have been just heard in the piece, or it may be a commonly recognized convention, e.g., a major scale, a blues scale, a famous melody, etc. The familiar is incredibly strong. It is perhaps not surprising that many of the pantonal excursions of Ornette Coleman and his colleagues are based around these conventions.

It is possible to calculate for any given scale type the "key-defining cell(s)"; i.e., the shortest lists of notes that contain intervals which only occur in, and thus define, one particular key. It is often surprising how many of these key-defining cells there are for a given scale type, and, indeed, how small they can be. For example, there are five possible key-defining cells for the major scale (and its modes), each made up of three notes, thus (the following example is for C major): {C,F,B}, {D,F,B}, {E,F,B}, {F,G,B} and {F,A,B} (notice that, in this case, each of these cells consists of the tritone, F and B, and one of the other five notes of the scale). While these key-defining cells are of academic interest, they often do not provide sufficient aural information to define the relevant key in the mind of a listener (for example, most of these cells do not contain the tonic). Most musicians express themselves through the various levels of solidity/ambiguity allowed by the use of more complete/complete scales, whether in a tonal, bitonal, polytonal, or pantonal environment. And, after all, a small part of one scale could easily be mistaken for a similar part of a different, more familiar, scale. This approach results in an "ambiguity" of tonal purpose.

When playing "outside the changes" musicians are often keen to express real difference with the tonic key—perhaps to repeat a familiar device (i.e., something already performed or already known) "out of position," in order to heighten our understanding of the device's individuality, its importance, its defiance. This will be most effective in keys that are "most different," i.e., where ambiguity can be reduced to a minimum. For example, the scale of D major is obviously more chromatic to C major than G major is. But how can we calculate the minimum number of common notes between two different keys of any given scale? What are the "most different" keys of any given scale? The answer to these questions lies in the interval frequency structure of these 2048 different scales. For example, if we search a scale like a major scale for the number of minor 2nds, the number of major 2nds, and so on, we get the following results:

from \ to	C	D	E	F	G	A	B
C	×	Ma2	Ma3	Perf4	Perf5	Ma6	Ma7
D	mi7	×	Ma2	mi3	Perf4	Perf5	Ma6
E	mi6	mi7	×	mi2	mi3	Perf4	Perf5
F	Perf5	Ma6	Ma7	×	Ma2	Ma3	Aug4
G	Perf4	Perf5	Ma6	mi7	×	Ma2	Ma3
A	mi3	Perf4	Perf5	mi6	mi7	×	Ma2
B	mi2	mi3	Perf4	Aug4	mi6	mi7	×

(Note that all similar sounding intervals have are given the same "standard" name for this exercise—for example, all diminished 5ths are called "Augmented 4ths.")

Frequency of Intervals (compiled from diagram above):

mi2	Ma2	mi3	Ma3	Perf4	Aug4	Perf5	mi6	Ma6	mi7	Ma7
2	5	4	3	6	2	6	3	4	5	2

Notice the symmetry of this result about the central axis of Aug4— there is a lot of symmetry to be found in this type of analysis![10]

We can see that in a major scale each of the 11 interval types is represented at least once; this is true of many of the other 7-note scales (although not all of them), but is never true of scales that contain less than 4 notes. This Frequency of Intervals table is useful in that it allows us to calculate (a) the name of the keys that are most different to any given tonic scale, and (b) the minimum number of common notes between any two keys of a given scale; all achieved by simply noting which intervals have the smallest results in the table above, thus:

mi2					Aug4					Ma7
2	5	4	3	6	**2**	6	3	4	5	**2**

This result means that the keys a minor 2nd, an Augmented 4th, and a major 7th above a major scale are the most different to that major scale (i.e., ♭II, #IV and VII are most different to I), and that these keys each contain two notes in common with that major scale. So, if C major is our given scale, then D♭, F#, and B are the "most different" keys (and each only share two notes with the scale of C major); all defined by the table above. This confirms the good sense of a common described/prescribed "map" for "playing outside the changes" where a musician will play up or down a semitone from the "home" key in order to create a really strong sense of "difference" with the underlying tonality; musicians often repeat a melodic pattern "out of key" by performing it, or a close variation of it, up or down a semitone. In this way, musicians are being as weird as they can get (with transpositions of a major scale) without sacrificing the identity of the scale or device being played! Indeed, if we examine all of the (previously mentioned) commonly used scales in the same way, we find that playing up or down a semitone will indeed create this sense of "difference" most clearly in each case:

No.	Scale	"Most Different" Keys (tonic = C)
1361	Major (Ionian mode)	D♭ F# B
1325	Dorian mode	D♭ F# B
1197	Phrygian mode	D♭ F# B
1371	Lydian mode	D♭ F# B
1360	Mixolydian mode	D♭ F# B
1323	Aeolian mode	D♭ F# B
1191	Locrian mode	D♭ F# B

(2 common notes between each of D♭ F# B and the tonic major scale)

No.	Scale	Keys
1326	Melodic minor ascending (or "Jazz Melodic")	D♭ B
1199	Dorian ♭2 (2nd mode of Melodic minor ascending)	D♭ B
1374	Lydian Augmented (3rd mode of Melodic minor ascending)	D♭ B
1370	Lydian ♭7 (4th mode of Melodic minor ascending)	D♭ B
1358	Mixolydian ♭6 (5th mode of Melodic minor ascending)	D♭ B
1317	Locrian #2 (6th mode of Melodic minor ascending)	D♭ B
1171	Super Locrian (7th mode of Melodic minor ascending)	D♭ B

(2 common notes between each of D♭ B and the tonic Melodic minor scale)

No.	Scale	Keys
1324	Harmonic minor	D♭ D B♭ B
1193	2nd mode of Harmonic minor	D♭ D B♭ B
1364	3rd mode of Harmonic minor	D♭ D B♭ B
1335	4th mode of Harmonic minor	D♭ D B♭ B
1232	5th mode of Harmonic minor	D♭ D B♭ B
1427	6th mode of Harmonic minor	D♭ D B♭ B
1170	7th mode of Harmonic minor	D♭ D B♭ B

(3 common notes between each of D♭, D B♭, B and the tonic Harmonic minor scale)

| 936 | Blues Scale (+ C E♭ F F♯ G B♭) | D♭ E F♯ A♭ B |
| 785 | Major Blues Scale (= C D E♭ E G A) | D♭ E F♯ A♭ B |

(2 common notes between each of D♭, E F♯ A♭, B and the tonic Blues/Major Blues scale)

| 393 | Pentatonic | D♭ F♯ B |
| 465 | Minor Pentatonic | D♭ F♯ B |

(0 common notes between each of D♭, F♯ B and the tonic Pentatonic scale)

| 1739 | Diminished | C D♭, D E F G A♭, B♭, B |
| 1636 | Auxiliary Diminished | C D♭, D E F G A♭, B♭, B |

(4 common notes between each of C D♭, D E F G A♭, B♭, B and the tonic Diminished scale)

It can also be seen from the data above that all of the modes of any scale share the same results—the reason being that all of the modes of any scale have an identical interval pattern as the scale itself. Note, however, that not all scales reveal their "most different" keys to be ♭II and VII; there are many scales for which playing up or down a semitone will not be as weird as it would first seem to be. For example, an analysis of the frequency of intervals in the "Augmented" scale (C D♯ E G A♭ B) reveals

mi2	Ma2	mi3	Ma3	Perf4	Aug4	Perf5	mi6	Ma6	mi7	Ma7
3	0	3	6	3	0	3	6	3	0	3

and thus the fact that II, #IV, and ♭VII are, in fact, the most different transpositions. It is possible to assess the "most different" keys for any of the 2048 scales in this way—by simply adding up the number of times that each of the 11 intervals occurs. It's good to draw a "from . . . to . . . " table like the one above to avoid forgetting to go beyond the octave—otherwise the result will not be symmetrical around the central Aug4 position—a good check of your counting! Another good check is to make sure that the following is true:

Sum of Frequency of Intervals =
(No. of notes in scale × No. of notes in scale)–No. of notes in scale

An example (major scale):

$$(2+5+4+3+6+2+6+3+4+5+2) = 42 = (7 \times 7) - 7 \ldots . .\text{true!}$$

Another example (Augmented scale):

$$(3+0+3+6+3+0+3+6+3+0+3) = 30 = (6 \times 6) - 6 \dots \text{.true!}$$

Commonly used scales, then, often display the characteristic that their "most different" keys include those a semitone away (is their common usage symbolic of a kind of cultural chromatic "obsession"?). But why are the other scales (all 2021 of them) so little used, even if they display this characteristic (e.g., scale number 1052, C D♭, D E♭, F G A— "most different" (to C) at D♭, E♭, A and B)? Of course, there are many musicians who have tried to exploit this resource; the European school (both classical and jazz) is famous for such experiments. However, before musicians choose a scale and rushes off to calculate weird keys and practice them, they should understand the following in order to choose well.

If we sort the 2048 scales into groups (i.e. scales with one note, scales with two notes, scales with three notes, etc.), and then order these groups by their frequency of interval data (starting with those that contain the lowest number of minor 2nds, then major 2nds, then minor 3rds, and so on) several interesting features are revealed. Firstly, all of the scales that are modes of each other are collected together as "neighbors." Secondly, commonly used scales appear at or very near to the top of their respective groups—because they often contain a relatively small number of "small" and (by default) "large" intervals (e.g., mi2 [thus also Ma7], Ma2 [thus also mi7], etc.), compared to the number of "medium-sized" intervals (e.g., Aug4, Perf4 and Perf5, etc.). For example, the top of the list of 7-note scales looks like this (note that this list is spelled with the notes of the C chromatic scale for convenience, i.e., C D♭, D E♭, E F F# G A♭, A B♭, B):

No.	Scale	Frequency of Interval	Common Name =/ ~
1191	C D♭, E♭, F F# A♭, B♭	2 5 4 3 6 2 6 3 4 5 2	= Locrian mode
1197	C D♭, E♭, F G A♭, B♭	2 5 4 3 6 2 6 3 4 5 2	= Phrygian mode
1323	C D E♭, F G A♭, B♭	2 5 4 3 6 2 6 3 4 5 2	= Aeolian mode
1325	C D E♭, F G A B♭	2 5 4 3 6 2 6 3 4 5 2	= Dorian mode
1360	C D E F G A B♭	2 5 4 3 6 2 6 3 4 5 2	= Mixolydian mode
1361	C D E F G A B	2 5 4 3 6 2 6 3 4 5 2	= Major scale (Ionian mode)
1371	C D E F#G A B	2 5 4 3 6 2 6 3 4 5 2	= Lydian mode
1171	C D♭, E♭, E F# A♭, B♭	2 5 4 4 4 4 4 4 4 5 2	= Super Locrian
1199	C D♭, E♭, F G A B♭	2 5 4 4 4 4 4 4 4 5 2	= Dorian ♭2
1317	C D E♭, F F# A♭, B♭	2 5 4 4 4 4 4 4 4 5 2	= Locrian #2

1326	C D E♭ F G A B	2 5 4 4 4 4 4 4 5 2	= Jazz Melodic
1358	C D E F G A♭ B♭	2 5 4 4 4 4 4 4 5 2	= Mixolydian ♭6
1370	C D E F# G A B♭	2 5 4 4 4 4 4 4 5 2	= Lydian ♭7
1374	C D E F# A♭ A B	2 5 4 4 4 4 4 4 5 2	= Lydian Augmented
1101	C D♭ D E F# A♭ B♭	2 6 2 6 2 6 2 6 2 6 2	~ Whole Tone +♭II
1200	C D♭ E♭ F G A B	2 6 2 6 2 6 2 6 2 6 2	~ ♭II Whole Tone +VII
1297	C D E♭ E F# A♭ B♭	2 6 2 6 2 6 2 6 2 6 2	~ Whole Tone +♭III
1352	C D E F F# A♭ B♭	2 6 2 6 2 6 2 6 2 6 2	~ Whole Tone +IV
1368	C D E F# G A♭ B♭	2 6 2 6 2 6 2 6 2 6 2	~ Whole Tone +V
1373	C D E F# A♭ A B♭	2 6 2 6 2 6 2 6 2 6 2	~ Whole Tone +VI
1375	C D E F# A♭ B♭ B	2 6 2 6 2 6 2 6 2 6 2	~ Whole Tone +VII
1170	C D♭ E♭ E F# A♭ A	3 3 5 4 4 4 4 4 5 3 3	= 7th mode of Harmonic minor
1177	C D♭ E♭ E G A♭ B♭	3 3 5 4 4 4 4 4 5 3 3	= 3rd mode of Harmonic major
1190	C D♭ E♭ F F# A♭ A	3 3 5 4 4 4 4 4 5 3 3	= 7th mode of Harmonic major
1193	C D♭ E♭ F F# A B♭	3 3 5 4 4 4 4 4 5 3 3	= 2nd mode of Harmonic minor
1232	C D♭ E F G A♭ B♭	3 3 5 4 4 4 4 4 5 3 3	= 5th mode of Harmonic minor
1234	C D♭ E F G A B♭	3 3 5 4 4 4 4 4 5 3 3	= 5th mode of Harmonic major
1319	C D E♭ F F# A B♭	3 3 5 4 4 4 4 4 5 3 3	= 2nd mode of Harmonic major
1324	C D E♭ F G A♭ B	3 3 5 4 4 4 4 4 5 3 3	= Harmonic minor
1335	C D E♭ F# G A B♭	3 3 5 4 4 4 4 4 5 3 3	= 4th mode of Harmonic minor
1336	C D E♭ F# G A B	3 3 5 4 4 4 4 4 5 3 3	= 4th mode of Harmonic major
1359	C D E F G A♭ B	3 3 5 4 4 4 4 4 5 3 3	= Harmonic major
1364	C D E F A♭ A B	3 3 5 4 4 4 4 4 5 3 3	= 3rd mode of Harmonic minor
1427	C E♭ E F# G A B	3 3 5 4 4 4 4 4 5 3 3	= 6th mode of Harmonic minor
1430	C E♭ E F# A♭ A B	3 3 5 4 4 4 4 4 5 3 3	= 6th mode of Harmonic major
1167	C D♭ E♭ E F# G A	3 3 6 3 3 6 3 3 6 3 3	~ most of Auxiliary Diminished

etc . . .

(the other 426 × 7-note scales)

By examining all of the 2048 scales in this way we find that a great many of commonly used patterns and scales contain relatively few small/large intervals:[11]

Scales with 3 notes that contain relatively few small/large intervals:
The four triads (Major, minor, Augmented and diminished) with their inversions, then Suspended 4th chords, etc.

Scales with 4 notes that contain relatively few small/large intervals:
All common 6th and 7th chords: diminished 7th, minor 6th, Dominant 7th, major 6th with their inversions (includes minor 7th), etc.

Scales with 5 notes that contain relatively few small/large intervals:
Major Pentatonic scale, and its modes (including the minor), Dominant 9th chords, etc.

Scales with 6 notes that contain relatively few small/large intervals:
Whole tone scale, etc.

Scales with 7 notes that contain relatively few small/large intervals:
Major scale and its modes, Jazz Melodic and its modes, etc.

Scales with 8 notes that contain relatively few small/large intervals:
Auxiliary diminished and diminished scales, followed by the modes of major and minor scales, each with an additional chromatic note.

(Note that all of the commonly used patterns and scales listed here are also at their "most different" at a semitone's distance away from a given tonic. Also, note the absence of the Blues and Major Blues scales from this list — see below.)

While this evidence alone is insufficient to suggest that scales that exhibit this characteristic of containing relatively few small/large intervals are "easy to hear," it is, however, striking that so much of the material from which music has been constructed for so much time, and by so many cultures, demonstrates this characteristic low frequency of small/large intervals. What seems to stop many musicians from going further is a combination of the aural unfamiliarity of these other scales, combined with the relatively closer (i.e., less exaggerated) relationship between "familiarly dissonant" keys and a given tonic — all of this being determined by the relatively different interval structure of these numerous other scales. This is not to suggest that a personal program of study could not well provide a musician with a new vocabulary, based upon one or more of these other scales, but it is clear that the aural skills necessary for the effective musical use of these other scales would need to be developed. (Consider for a moment the 8- and 9-note scales that are used to explain the work of bebop musicians; these are often 7-note modes with an additional note or two to provide metric solutions to music founded on swung quavers, triplet quavers, and semiquavers played over 4 beats to a bar. They are not principally "new sounds"; these metric strengths overcome the tonal problems mentioned above through rhythmic implementation.) A musician needs to be very determined to learn what these other scales sound like, and what they imply, in various situations in order to use any of them effectively. This determination will have to be shared by the musician's colleagues (perhaps these "colleagues" could be a computer!).

However, an interesting anomaly found in this analysis is that the (very commonly used) Blues and Major Blues scales do not contain relatively few small/large intervals compared to other 6-note scales. Indeed, these scales occur deep into the list of 6-note scales: at position numbers 106 and 117 out of the $462 \times$ 6-note scales (they are relatively near neighbors!). When a Blues scale is used in an improvisation over an essentially diatonic chord progression, the shared tonic seems to act like a magnet on the listener/performer, drawing them back to this "home" note with especial force. Familiarity is clearly what allows us to accept this complex sound. Or, accepting that jazz started as a confluence of African and European influences in New Orleans, and has developed in a linear fashion since, perhaps this comparatively massive difference in interval structure is a part of the African contribution? Interestingly, a comparison of the relevant data for the Blues scale and the major scale actually reveals a great deal of similarity in the contour of the frequency of intervals:

	mi2	Ma2	mi3	Ma3	Perf4	Aug4	Perf5	mi6	Ma6	mi7	Ma7
Major scale	2	5	4	3	6	2	6	3	4	5	2
Blues scale	2	3	3	2	4	2	4	2	3	3	2

This similarity is even more striking when we remember that the sum of the frequency of interval data for the (7-note) major scale is 42, compared to the (6-note) Blues scale, which is 30. From this perspective, then, the Blues scale is not quite so "weird"!

THREE OTHER WAYS OF GETTING WEIRD

Map 1. Pivoting On (or Avoiding) Notes Shared by Different Keys

The keys that are "most different" to C major are D♭, F# and B major, as we have seen above. It is worth pointing out, however, that of these three "most different" keys, D♭ actually contains the tonic note C (this is not true in keys of F# and B). Would it not be better to avoid the tonic note for most difference? Perhaps a measurement of the "weirdness" of bitonal (etc.) music would be how much the tonic note of one performer is avoided by another performer/other performers. Another approach would be for a musician to choose from the list of keys that contain a particular note, pivoting on this note as they improvise through these various keys.

Calculating keys that contain (i.e., can pivot on) or do not contain (i.e., can avoid) a particular note in a given scale type is really quite simple:

(i) Examine the interval pattern of the scale being used, including the last step up to the octave: e.g., major scale: Maj2, Maj2, min2, Maj2, Maj2, Maj2, min2;

(ii) Reverse this list: min2, Maj2, Maj2, Maj2, min2, Maj2, Maj2;

(iii) Calculate the notes of this new scale, starting on the given note: min2, Maj2, Maj2, Maj2, min2, Maj2, Maj2 = (e.g.) C D♭ E♭ F G A♭ B♭— this is, in fact, C Phrygian!

(This scale provides us with a list of all of the keys of the major scale that include the note C).

(iv) Calculate the complement set of this scale (i.e., find out the names of the keys not represented by stage (iii) above. The author finds that this is most easily done by sorting 12 small squares of paper, each with a different note of the chromatic scale written upon it): = D E F# A B—this is, in fact, D Pentatonic!

(This scale provides us with a list of all of the keys of the major scale that do not include the note C).

So, we can say that the list of major scales that contain the note C are those that start on the notes of C Phrygian, and that the list of major scales that do not contain the note C are those that start on the notes of D Pentatonic. Any musician wanting to use this system while improvising will clearly have to prepare and learn/notate one or two pivoting/avoiding systems in advance (or do a very quick mental calculation during the drum solo!)—just as the scale(s) that these system(s) will be based on has had to be prepared and learned/notated in advance. This kind of preparation is also necessary for the other maps, below.

Map 2. Using Scales with Palindromic Interval Construction

Recognizing that the Phrygian mode is constructed from the same intervals as the major scale, but in reverse order, it seems sensible to examine all of the seven modes for their "retrograde partner":

Dorian	<	>	Dorian
Ionian	<	>	Phrygian
Locrian	<	>	Lydian
Aeolian	<	>	Mixolydian

Indeed, we find something significant in that Dorian mode maps onto itself. This is because its interval pattern is palindromic (i.e., it reads the same forwards and backwards; the word "palindromic" is used to avoid confusion with other so-called "symmetrical" scales, such as the Diminished scale, that do not display this palindromic quality):

Dorian = Maj2, min2, Maj2, Maj2, Maj2, min2, Maj2
= T S T T T S T

We find a similar result if we examine the modes of the Jazz Melodic minor scale:

Mixolydian ♭6	<	>	Mixolydian ♭6
Lydian ♭7	<	>	Locrian #2
Lydian Augmented	<	>	Super Locrian
Dorian ♭2	<	>	Jazz Melodic

Here (as with Dorian mode above) Mixolydian ♭6 maps onto itself because it contains a palindromic interval pattern:

Mixolydian ♭6 = Maj2, Maj2, min2, Maj2, min2, Maj2, Maj2
= T T S T S T T

What this all means is that for any scale type constructed with a palindromic interval pattern, then the keys that contain a given note are those keys named by the very notes of the same scale type, starting from the given note. An example: improvising in the scale of C Dorian (a palindromic scale), we might stop on any note of the scale, for example, D. The list of all of the keys of the Dorian mode that contain this note D is, in fact, the same as the notes of D Dorian: D E F G A B C. The improvisation may then progress by pivoting on this common note (D) between any keys that share it (i.e., D, E, F, G, A, or B Dorian), the rougher sounds of these more dissonant keys contrasting with the familiarity and "good fit" of D Dorian. This is one option. The movement between keys will always seem smoothest, however, if the improvisation is continued in a linear way, shifting between keys on a new "pivot" note each time. This "smoothness" will, of course, be more or less offset by the relative differences between these various keys and the scale(s) used for any accompanying parts.

In fact, there are 64 of these scales constructed with a palindromic interval pattern:

1 × 1-note scale	(= C)
1 × 2-note scale	(= C F#)
5 × 3-note scales	(C D♭ B, etc.)
5 × 4-note scales	(C D♭ F# B, etc.)
10 × 5-note scales	(C D♭ F G B, etc.)
10 × 6-note scales	(C D♭ D F# B♭ B, etc.)
10 × 7-note scales	(C D♭ D F G B♭ B, etc.)
10 × 8-note scales	(C D♭ D E♭ F# A B♭ B, etc.)
5 × 9-note scales	(C D♭ D E♭ F G A B♭ B, etc.)
5 × 10-note scales	(C D♭ D E♭ E F# A♭ A B♭ B, etc.)
1 × 11-note scale	(= C D♭ D E♭ E F G A♭ A B♭ B)
1 × 12-note scale	(= C D♭ D E♭ E F F# G A♭ A B♭ B)

$$1+1+5+5+10+10+10+10+5+5+1+1 = 64$$
(note the symmetry of this sum)[12]

Once any of these 64 palindromic scales is chosen, it is a simple matter to work out which keys do not contain a given note by noting down the members of the complement set of the chosen scale, as for Map 1 above.

Map 3. Conjugate Pairs—A Balancing Act

Another way of mapping a route through the world of playing "outside the changes" is for a performer to answer an initial "out of key" phrase with an equally "out of key" reply, this reply being at the same distance from the tonic of the home key as the initial phrase but on the opposite "side" of the tonic, creating a kind of tonal "symmetry." For example, if the home key is C major, then after improvising in the key of D♭ major for a while, the musician will "balance" this (5-flat) "excursion" with the (5-sharp) key of B major (note that the type of scale used is irrelevant to the success of this operation—any of the 2048 scales can be used). The pair of keys chosen will always be at a conjugate distance to the central, home key (this home key will not necessarily be heard—it may just exist in the mind of the performer, and may, or may not, be based on an underlying tonality or chord/scale concept). Steve Coleman is one practitioner who has described the use of just this kind of symmetrical system.[13]

There are 6 types of "conjugate pairs." Here they are, expressed against a home key of C:

Type 1	D♭	< C >	B	(up and down a min 2)
Type 2	D	< C >	B♭	(up and down a Maj 2)
Type 3	E♭	< C >	A	(up and down a min 3)
Type 4	E	< C >	A♭	(up and down a Maj 3)
Type 5	F	< C >	G	(up and down a Perf 4)
Type 6	F#	< C >	F#	(up and down an Aug 4)

Note that in conjugate pair Type 6, F# maps onto itself (the tritone).[14]

The author finds these conjugate pairs most easy to visualize when they are laid out in a pattern not unlike the shape of a Common Ash leaf (the stem represents the home key, the 11 leaflets represent the 11 possible destination keys; the conjugate pairs are arranged so as to be directly opposite each other, the tritone mapping onto itself). As above, this example (Figure 1) uses C as the home key.

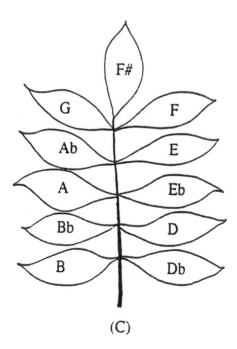

Figure 1: Conjugate Pairs with a Home Key of C

Which of these conjugate pairs will sound the "weirdest" for any given scale type will depend upon the interval construction of that scale type. For example, for improvising in a major scale, or one its modes, then the weirdest of these conjugate pairs is Type 4, represented in the diagram above by an improvisation set against the tonic key of C, first moving to the key of E, then to the key of A♭; or vice versa. It is noteworthy that, for any given conjugate pair, one key will contain the tonic note of the "home" key (i.e., the mediant of A♭ major), while the other will not (i.e., E major). This may affect the order in which a musician chooses to explore the members of a conjugate pair, dependent upon any desired tonic/antitonic effect of the improvisation. Interestingly, conjugate pair Type 4 is also the easiest to learn for all tonic keys, as the three notes concerned form an Augmented triad (e.g., C E A♭ [A♭ = G#]),[15] and there are only four of these in a chromatic scale. Also, experience has shown that once you leap away from the tonic key up or down a given interval (a major 3rd), it is easier then to remember to continue to move up or down by the same interval (another major 3rd), with a final, equal shift of key (a major 3rd again!) bringing you back to the tonic (which you may, or may not, sound). Examining the "difference factors" of the other conjugate pairs, we find that, for a major scale, Types 1, 3, and 6 are also fairly weird, but Types 2 and 5 (being less different to the tonic scale, and each other) are much less weird (see below for how to do this calculation for any scale).

So, the most weird conjugate pair for any given scale type will be that conjugate pair that has the highest "difference factor" between the three keys concerned: i.e., between the tonic key and the first key of the conjugate pair, between the tonic key and the second key of the conjugate pair, and (less obviously, but crucially) between the first and second keys of the conjugate pair. To calculate these "difference factors" for the six conjugate pairs of any given scale type (and thus be in a position to choose the most weird conjugate pair) we can simply multiply together the number of differences between the three keys concerned.[16] Follow this procedure:

(i) Calculate the frequency of interval data for the given scale, e.g., major scale:

mi2	Ma2	mi3	Ma3	Perf4	Aug4	Perf5	mi6	Ma6	mi7	Ma7
2	5	4	3	6	2	6	3	4	5	2

This result, as explained above, tells us how many notes are shared by keys at each of the 11 intervals of transposition.

(ii) Subtract each of these entries from the number of notes in the given scale (in this case, 7):

7	7	7	7	7	7	7	7	7	7	7
− 2	5	4	3	6	2	6	3	4	5	2
= 5	2	3	4	1	5	1	4	3	2	5

This result provides us with a modified frequency of interval table which tells us how many notes are *not* shared by keys at each of the 11 intervals of transposition, thus:

mi2	Ma2	mi3	Ma3	Perf4	Aug4	Perf5	mi6	Ma6	mi7	Ma7
5	2	3	4	1	5	1	4	3	2	5

(iii) Insert this data in the form below into a new table (note that we only actually need the data from the mi2 to the Aug4 intervals, whatever the scale type; this is due to the symmetry of the data):

Conjugate Pair Type	1	2	3	4	5	6
(from tonic to first of conjugate pair =)	mi2	Ma2	mi3	Ma3	Perf4	Aug4
(from tonic to second of conjugate pair =)	mi2	Ma2	mi3	Ma3	Perf4	Aug4
(from first to second of conjugate pair =)	Ma2	Ma3	Aug4	Ma3	Ma2	unison*

To continue our example, completing this new table with the relevant data for the major scale, we get this:

Conjugate Pair Type	1	2	3	4	5	6
(from tonic to first of conjugate pair =)	5	2	3	4	1	5
(from tonic to second of conjugate pair =)	5	2	3	4	1	5
(from first to second of conjugate pair =)	2	4	5	4	2	1*

The asterisk (*) denotes that for conjugate pair type 6, where the tritone maps onto itself, the data is considered a "unison," which always translates as a multiplier of 1.

(iv) Finally, multiply the three interval values together for each conjugate pair, and examine the results:

(iv) Finally, multiply the three interval values together for each conjugate pair, and examine the results:

Conjugate Pair Type		1	2	3	4	5	6
		5	2	3	4	1	5
		5	2	3	4	1	5
	×	2	4	5	4	2	1
Difference Factors	=	50	16	45	64	2	25

So, from this result we can see that conjugate pair Type 4 (i.e., up and down a major 3rd) is, as noted above, the most weird for a major scale, and that conjugate pair Type 5 (up and down a Perfect 4th) is the least weird.

Note that while these "difference factors" are only really "rules of thumb" created by multiplying three relevant interval values together, they do offer a fairly accurate gauge of the relative weirdness of each of the six conjugate pairs as they relate to a given scale, and thus they allow musical decisions to be made.

NOTES

1. For example, the four-note device (F A♭, F B♭) used in *A Love Supreme* (Impulse, 1964).
2. Eric Blom, "Bitonality," in Stanley Sadie, ed., *The New Grove Dictionary of Music and Musicians* (London: Macmillan, 1980), vol.2, p. 747.
3. William Drabkin, "Pantonality," in ibid., vol.14, p. 163.
4. George Russell, *The Lydian Chromatic Concept of Tonal Organization* (New York: Concept, 1959), appendix.
5. A description of harmolodics by Ronald Shannon Jackson (drummer and composer), in Gary Giddins, "Harmolodic Hoedown," in *Rhythm-a-ning: Jazz Tradition and Innovation in the '80s* (New York: Oxford University Press, 1985) (a collection of previously published articles), pp. 235–49.
6. Conrad Silvert, "Old and New Dreams," *Down Beat* 47, 6 (June 1980):16–19; quoted by John Litweiler, *Ornette Coleman: a Harmolodic Life* (New York: Morrow, 1992), p. 148.
7. Don Cherry, in a lecture at Ann Arbor, Michigan, March 28, 1980, quoted in David Wild and Michael Cuscuna, *Ornette Coleman 1958–1979: a Discography* (Ann Arbor: Wildmusic, 1980), p. 76.

8. Robert Palmer, "Charlie Haden's Creed," *Down Beat,* 39, 13 (July 1972): 16–18; quoted by Litweiler, op. cit., p. 148.

9. Note that this list of numbers (1,11,55,165,330,462,462,330,165, 55,11,1) occurs as the 12th "line" of Pascal's Triangle, and, as such, is not a surprising pattern (see note 12 below).

10. Students of atonal music will recognize this Frequency of Intervals table as being similar, but not identical, to the "interval vector" array (introduced to atonal music theory by Donald Martino in 1961 in "The Source-Set and Its Aggregate Formations," *Journal of Music Theory* 5, no. 2.). The structure and implications of this array are well explained by Allen Forte in his book, *The Structure of Atonal Music* (New Haven: Yale University Press, 1973). By altering this established convention, it is the author's intention to provide a tool directly relevant to the analysis and construction of maps for pantonal (rather than atonal) music. The key difference lies in the counting of the tritone (Aug 4) interval(s). The "atonal" method sees a pair of tritone intervals within an octave as a single equivalent interval, whilst this "pantonal" method sees them not only as discrete sounds in/against another tonality, but also as essential data in the comparison of keys (discussed later in the main text). It is, however, a simple matter to "translate" between the two systems (in either direction) should a musician wish to use, for example, a table of prime forms and interval vectors (e.g., Forte, op. cit., Appendix 1) by: (i) ignoring/recreating the symmetry of the Frequency of Intervals data, and (ii) dividing/multiplying the tritone (Aug 4) result in the relevant table by 2 (this subtle but essential change is shown below in bold type for clarity); so, for the major scale:
Pantonal—Frequency of Intervals = 25436**2**63452
Atonal—7–35 interval vector = [254361]
     (Martino, Forte, etc.)

11. Note that this analysis reveals results found in any "equal divisions of the octave" table. However, importantly, these results also include many of the so-called "symmetrical" and "synthesized" scales.

12. Note that (similar to note 9 above) this list of numbers (1,1,5,5, 10,10,10,10,5,5,1,1) (sum = 64) is closely related to the 6th "line" of Pascal's Triangle, which in fact reads (1,5,10,10,5,1) (sum = 32). Note also that 2048/32 = 64.

13. Steve Coleman interviewed by Michael Hrebeniak: "Black Scientist," *Jazz FM Magazine* (an Observer Newspaper Publication, London), Issue 7, 1991, p. 20.
14. These six types of "conjugate pairs" correspond at a basic level to the six "interval classes" described by Forte (op. cit., p. 14); however, their applications are quite different.
15. In the interview cited in note 13, Steve Coleman points out that the symmetry found in this particular triad is relevant to his work.
16. The results of merely *adding* these numbers together would not sufficiently reflect the true difference between each of the conjugate pairs.

HEARING CHORDS

Armen Donelian

INTRODUCTION

The purpose of any ear training method is to provide a practical aural foundation which helps the student to process music easily and confidently.

By practicing certain techniques of embodiment—singing, rhythmic tapping, recognition, identification, transcription—the student cultivates an internal connection between a musical sound and the concept it represents.

Aural approaches vary according to the particular musical language they are designed to inculcate. For example, Indian and Arabic music each give rise to different procedures for absorbing these respective styles. The same is true for jazz. While jazz shares common elements with the Western European tradition, jazz improvisers require special aural training. Of foremost concern for the jazz apprentice is rhythm, particularly Afro- and Latin-American styles; also, blues- and bebop-based melodic lines; and, chord/scale relationships, chord voicings and harmonic progressions. Once acquainted with diatonic and chromatic intervals, root position triads, major and minor scales, basic blues chord progressions and other aural rudiments, the student embarks on a study of intermediate level jazz harmony.

The purpose of this article is to provide instructors and self-motivated students with some suggestions for an aural approach to this subject.

RECURRING ISSUES

Time and again, students ask for exercises they can use to improve the way they hear chords. The following includes a number of recurring issues raised by students, with some suggestions.

INVERSIONS OF TRIADS

Q: The student can hear root position triads well, but when it comes to inversions, he/she can't tell one from the other. What to do?

A: First, be sure the student can really hear root position triads. To do this, the student works with a partner. The partner plays, the student listens.

1. The partner plays any root position triad on the piano and names only its root. The student listens to it.

Advise the student to really focus on it for a good ten seconds. Many hearing problems occur because of unfocused listening. (Important: Partner should play the chord in the resonant middle register of the piano, near middle C, which is also a good vocal range.)

2. The student sings and names its top, bottom, and middle note; names the interval between each note and the adjacent pitch; names the chord.

Advise the student to fully sing each note with a straight, unwavering tone for at least three seconds. Anything that can't be sung within a reasonable vocal range indicates an area ripe for aural growth. Singing is not only an indicator of aural ability, but the best method of improving it. The student identifies notes by pitch name (for example, "E♭") and by chord function ("♭5").

3. Partner changes the chord quality.

4. Student sings and names the note(s) that changed; names the new intervals; names the new chord.

5. Student and partner cover all root position triads (major, minor, diminished, augmented) in several keys in a similar manner.

6. Variation: In 1 above, partner names only the 3rd, or 5th, of the triad. Student proceeds as in 2 above.

When the student is warmed up, move on to inversions.

1. Partner plays any inverted major triad on the piano and names only its root. The student listens to it. Advise the student to listen for what's on top, what's on the bottom and what's in the middle.

2. Student sings and names top, bottom and middle notes; names the interval between each note and the next; names the chord and its inversion.

Ask the student to start by singing only what he/she actually hears most prominently. In this way, student proceeds first from his/her own aural experience, as the realistic foundation for improving his/her awareness of the given sound. The partner, without naming the inversion, tells student only whether the note he/she sang is in the chord or not.

Here is where most errors in inversion recognition are made. The student often displaces a note by an octave, placing it above or below its actual place in the chord. Partner can say, "That note is in the chord but you sang it in the wrong octave. Listen to it again and sing it again."

Partner re-strikes chord, and student re-listens to it and re-sings what he/she hears. They repeat this process as necessary. Repeat until student can hear and sing the chord tones exactly as they appear in the chord and name everything he/she has sung. Only if this proves impossible for the student, partner may then arpeggiate the chord, and proceed as in 2 above.

This may take some practice, but after all, this is why the student can't hear inversions in the first place. He/she needs more practice.

3. Tip: A 4th indicates the inverted position of the chord's root and 5th. The presence of a 4th is a vital piece of aural data. It says, "This chord isn't in root position, it's inverted." The placement of the chord's 3rd above or below this 4th indicates which inversion the chord is in.

4. Student and partner cover all inverted major and minor triads in several keys in a similar manner.

5. Variation: In 1 above, partner names only the 3rd, or 5th, of the triad. Student proceeds as in 2 above.

6. Inverted diminished triads require special attention. The diminished triad's first and second inversions are often mistaken for each other. Another common error is to add a note to an inverted diminished triad, as if to complete a dominant or diminished 7th chord. Inverted diminished triads can be practiced as follows:

Alternation. While student listens, partner plays and holds for about ten seconds a first inversion diminished triad (say, E°—from the bottom G, B♭, E). Then, a second inversion diminished triad whose root is a minor third lower (in this case, C♯°—G, C♯, E). The outer two notes (G and E) are common to both chords, while the middle note moves (from B♭ to C♯).

While partner slowly alternates from one chord to the other and back again, student listens to and appreciates the subtle differences between them (size and order of intervals, tensions they create). In particular, advise the student to notice the location of the augmented 4th in each chord, which represents the inverted root and 5th.

Student and partner proceed as in 1 and 2 above in several keys until these chords are clear to student.

7. Inverted augmented triads sound identical to those in root position. The following exercise clarifies this aural enigma.

Student sings an augmented triad (say, C, E, G$\sharp$), arpeggiating up and down the chord. Then, student lowers the *top* note by a half-step and re-arpeggiates. Instructor: "Sounds like CΔ in root position, right? Obviously, the first chord sounds in retrospect like it was C$^+$ in root position."

Next, student re-sings the first (augmented) chord. Then, he/she lowers only the *middle* note by a half-step and sings this chord. Instructor: "Sounds like A$\flat\Delta$ in first inversion (hear that 4th on top?). So the previous augmented chord can be interpreted in retrospect as A$\flat^+$ in first inversion (root on top, $^+$5th in the middle)."

Finally, student re-sings the first chord. Then, he/she lowers only the *bottom* note by a half-step and sings this chord. Instructor: "Sounds like EΔ in second inversion (fourth is now on the bottom). So, the augmented chord must have been E$^+$ in second inversion (root in the middle, $^+$5th on bottom)."

Repeat as necessary until the harmonic function of each note in each inverted augmented chord is aurally clear to the student.

INVERSIONS OF 7TH CHORDS

Q: The student can recognize the harmonic quality of an inverted seventh chord, but can't identify its inversion. What to do?

A: Again, start by reviewing root position 7th chords.

There are 9 of them: major, augmented-major, minor, minor-major, dominant, dominant-$\flat$5, augmented-dominant, diminished and half-diminished 7th.

1. As before, partner plays a root position major 7th chord on the piano and names only its root. Student listens to it.

2. Student sings and names its top, bottom and middle notes; names the interval between each note and the next; names the chord.

3. Partner changes the chord quality.

4. Student sings and names the note(s) that changed; names the new intervals; names the new chord.

5. Student and partner cover all 9 root position 7th chords in 2 or 3 keys in this manner.

6. Variation: In 1 above, partner names only the 3rd, 5th, or 7th, of the chord. Student proceeds as in 2 above.

Now, on to inverted 7ths:

1. Partner plays any inverted major 7th chord on the piano and names only its root. Student listens to it.

2. Student sings and names its top, bottom and middle notes; names the interval between each note and the next; names the chord and its inversion.

Again, ask the student to start by singing only what he/she actually hears most prominently. Partner should look out for the student's tendency to displace a note by an octave, or to add a note to complete another kind of chord.

Sometimes, a second inversion major 7th chord is identified as a rootless minor 9th chord. Rather than a problem, look on this as an opportunity to clarify the student's perception of the harmonic function of this chord by practicing hearing/singing/naming it both ways.

Partner re-strikes chord, and student re-listens to it and re-sings what he/she hears. They repeat this process as necessary until student can identify the chord and its inversion. Only if this proves impossible for the student, partner may then arpeggiate the chord, and proceed as in 2 above.

3. Tip: A minor 2nd indicates the inverted position of the chord's root and major 7th. The presence of a minor 2nd is, again, a vital piece of aural data. It says, "This chord isn't in root position, it's inverted." The placement of the remaining chord tones above or below this 2nd indicates which inversion the chord is in.

4. Student and partner cover all inverted major, minor, dominant 7th and half-diminished chords in several keys in a similar manner. Remind student to "seek the second" (root & 7) when listening.

Inverted minor 7ths, and inverted half-diminished 7ths, are often identified, respectively, as major 6th or rootless major 9th chords, and as minor 6th or rootless dominant 9th chords. As before, encourage student to practice hearing these chords each of these ways.

5. Variation: In 1 and 4 above, partner names only the 3rd, or 5th, or 7th of the chord. Student proceeds as in 2 above.

6. Inverted diminished 7ths sound identical to those in root position. As with inverted augmented chords, try this exercise to clarify this aural enigma.

First: ask the student to consider the root of the diminished 7th chord as equivalent to the 3rd of a rootless dominant seven-flat 9th chord (for example, C°7 = A♭7, ♭9).

Now, student sings this diminished 7th chord (C, E♭, G♭, A), arpeggiating up and down the chord. Then, he/she lowers the *top* note by a half-step and re-arpeggiates. Partner: "That's A♭7 in first inversion, right? (Hear that 3rd, C, on the bottom?) Therefore, the first chord you sang can be interpreted in retrospect as C°7 in root position (3rd of A♭7 = root of C°7)."

Next, student re-sings the first (diminished 7th) chord. Then, he/she lowers only the *second note from the top* (G♭) by a half-step and sings this chord. Partner: "That's F7 in second inversion (hear that 5th, C, on bottom?). So the previous diminished 7th chord was an A°7 in second inversion (5th of F7 = 3rd of A°7)."

Third, student re-sings the first (diminished 7th) chord. Then, he/she lowers only the *second note from the bottom* (E♭) by a half-step and sings this chord. Partner: "That's D7 in third inversion (hear that 7th, C, on bottom?). So the previous diminished 7th chord was an F♯°7 in second inversion (7th of D7 = 5th of F♯°7)."

Finally, student re-sings the first (diminished 7th) chord. Then, he/she lowers only the *bottom* note (C) by a half-step and sings this chord. Partner: "That's B7 in root position (hear that root, B, on bottom?). So the previous diminished 7th chord was D♯°7 in third inversion (9th of B7 = 7th of D♯°7)."

Repeat as necessary until the harmonic function of each note in each inverted diminished seventh chord is aurally clear to the student.

7. Root position and inverted minor-major, augmented-major, dominant-♭5 and augmented-dominant 7ths require special attention. They can be practiced using the alternation technique described earlier.

Minor-major 7ths

After student practices the root position of E-Δ7, partner plays and holds for about ten seconds its first inversion (G, B, D♯, E) while student listens. Then, partner *lowers the major 7th* (D♯) to a D and plays this chord. Then, back to the first chord again. Then, partner *raises the minor 3rd* (G) to a G♯ and plays this chord. Finally, the first chord again.

While partner slowly alternates between these three chords, student listens to and appreciates the subtle differences between them (size and order of intervals, tensions they create). Again, advise student to "seek the second" in each chord, which represents the inverted root and seventh. With partner, student proceeds in this manner in several keys with all inversions of the minor-major 7th chord, including root position if necessary, until they are all clear.

Augmented-major 7ths

After student practices the root position of E♭+Δ7, partner plays and holds for about ten seconds its first inversion (G, B, D, E♭) while student listens. Then, partner *lowers the augmented 5th* (B) to a B♭ and plays this chord. Then, back to the first chord again.

While partner slowly alternates between these two chords, student listens to and appreciates the subtle differences between both of them (size and order of intervals, tensions they create). Again, advise student to "seek the second." With partner, student proceeds in several keys with all inversions of the augmented-major 7th chord, including root position if necessary.

Dominant 7th-♭5's

After student practices the root position of E♭7, ♭5, partner plays and holds for about ten seconds its first inversion (G, A, D♭, E♭) while student listens. Then, partner *raises the diminished 5th* (A) to a B♭ and plays this chord again. Then, the first chord again. Then, partner *raises the root* (E♭) to an E and plays this chord. Finally, the first chord again.

While partner slowly alternates between these three chords, student listens to and appreciates the subtle differences between them (size and order of intervals, tensions they create). Student is advised to "seek the second" and to notice the aural whole step between the diminished 5th and the 3rd, as well as that between the 7th and the root; student repeats as necessary until the harmonic function of each chord tone is aurally clear. With partner, student proceeds in several keys with all inversions of the dominant 7th-♭5 chord, including root position if necessary.

Augmented-dominant 7ths

After student practices the root position of this chord, partner plays and holds for about ten seconds a first inversion augmented-dominant 7th (say, G, B, D♭, E♭) while student listens. Then, partner *lowers the augmented 5th* (B) to a B♭ and plays this chord. Then, the first chord again.

While partner slowly alternates between these chords, student listens to and appreciates the subtle differences between both of them (size and order of intervals, tensions they create). Student is advised to "seek the second," to notice the aural whole step between the augmented 5th and the minor 7th, as well as that between the 7th and the root, and repeat as necessary until the harmonic function of each chord tone is aurally clear. With partner, student proceeds in several keys with all inversions of the augmented-dominant seventh chord, including root position if necessary.

DOMINANT CADENCES (II-V-I)

Q; I'd like to be able to hear jazz chord changes better. How do I practice?

A: Given that the bulk of jazz chord movement is based on the cycle of 5ths (what is called "functional" harmony), the place for the student to begin working is with the II-V-I cadence, and its many variations. A strong aural grounding in this area will enable the student to deal with other types of chord changes more effectively.

Limiting our harmonic scope just to the use of unextended 7th chords, tritone substitution (see * below), secondary dominants, chords of the minor key, and certain rudimentary chord substitutes (I-Δ7 for I-7, I$^+\Delta$7 for IΔ7, and V7, ♭5 or V$^+$7 for V7), a vast number of combinations can be devised for a thorough aural workout on the II-V-I cadences used in jazz.

In Chart 1, any II (or ♭VI*) can resolve to any V (or ♭II*), and in turn to any I, with the exception of ♭VI-7 which resolves only to ♭II7. Thus, 84 dominant cadences are possible.

Dominant Cadences		
II ($\flat$VI*)	V ($\flat$II*)	I
In the key of FΔ/F$-$		
G-7	C7	FΔ7
G7	C$^+$7	F$^+\Delta$7
Gϕ7	C7,$\flat$5	F$-$7
D$\flat\Delta$7*	G$\flat\Delta$7*	F$-\Delta$7
D$\flat$7*	G$\flat$7*	
D$\flat-$7* (to G$\flat$7)		

Chart 1: Dominant Cadences

How to use Chart 1: Start by composing your own cadence.
1. Choose any II (or $\flat$VI).* Student writes it in root position.
2. Choose any V (or $\flat$II).* Using the chord inversion which achieves the smoothest possible resolution from the first chord, student writes it.

Basically, if the root movement is by cycle of 5ths (i.e., tritone substitution is not used), this chord should be in second inversion, which retains the most common tones and resolves with the least intervallic movement from the first (root position) chord.

However, if *either* chord you choose is a tritone substitute*—causing chromatic root movement, such as II-$\flat$II or $\flat$VI-V—then the smoothest possible resolution from the first (root position) chord is achieved by using the root position of the second. If *both* chords are tritone subs—causing $\flat$VI-$\flat$II root movement by cycle of 5ths—the smoothest resolution from the first (root position) chord is achieved by using the second inversion of the second chord.

3. Choose any I. Using the smoothest resolution, student writes it. Again, the type of root movement from the previous chord—cyclic or chromatic—will determine which inversion to use.

4. Chord inversion can then be applied to these 84 Dominant Cadences. Inverting the starting chord, proceed as in 2 and 3 above. Thus, a total of 336 inverted, voice-led cadences are possible (84 $\times$ 4)!

5. The student may practice these in any number of ways. Here are some suggestions for practice alone. (Note: Use the number of the chord function of each note—1, 3, 5 or 7—as a syllable to sing on.)

1. Sing by arpeggiating up each chord.

2. Sing by arpeggiating down each chord.

3. Sing by arpeggiating up and then down each chord.

4. Sing by arpeggiating down and then up each chord.

5. Sing by arpeggiating up the first chord, down the second chord, etc.

6. Sing by arpeggiating down the first chord, up the second chord, etc.

7. Sing through the entire cadence on each of the four chord voices, one at a time.

8. Sing through the entire cadence on two selected chord voices simultaneously, by alternating between one chord voice and the other (6 SATB possibilities: BT, BA, BS, TA, TS, AS).

9. Reverse the intervallic direction of #8 (TB, AB, SB, AT, ST, SA).

10. Sing one chord voice, play root progression on piano (4 possibilities).

11. Sing root progression, play one chord voice on piano (4 possibilities).

12. Sing one chord voice, play another voice on piano (6 possibilities).

13. Switch the voice and piano part of #12 (6 possibilities).

14. Make your own listening tapes as needed.

15. Play on the piano. Listen.

Here are some suggestions for practice with a partner.

1. Sing #1–9 above in unison.

2. Sing #8 above by assigning a different chord voice to each partner.

3. Sing #8 again, switching parts with your partner.

4. Sing #10–13 above, with partner on piano or other instrument.

5. Sing #10–13 above, switching parts with your partner.

6. Give each other harmonic dictations.

7. Play for each other. Listen.

Here are some suggestions for practice in a group (4 or more).

1. Sing #1–9 above in unison.

2. Sing #8 above by assigning a different chord voice to each of 2 sub-groups.

3. Sing #8, switching parts between sub-groups.

4. Sing the entire cadence in SATB fashion (4 sub-groups).

5. Switch parts (24 possibilities).

6. Group dictations.

7. Group listening.

With **29 techniques and 336 cadences, over 9,700 different exercises can be created by the instructor or motivated student!** You're encouraged to find original ways to apply this material to your specific needs.

CHORD EXTENSIONS (9, 11, 13)

Q: I need help hearing and naming chord extensions. Also, I have trouble hearing the right scale to play with a chord having harmonic extensions.

A: First, be sure the student can sing the root of the chord containing the extension.

Preparatory Exercise #1. Student sings from the same pitch several random descending intervals larger than the octave. Instructor or partner then strikes each interval on piano (unarpeggiated) to verify student's intonation.

Preparatory Exercise #2. Instructor or partner plays on piano a simply-voiced chord (no clusters or extremely wide intervals) containing one (or more) harmonic extensions. Student listens to it and sings the extension(s), and then the root, and identifies the size of the resulting interval(s) between the extension(s) and the root.

Then, the student can try the following.

Chord Extension Exercise. Observe Chart 2.

1. Using the number for the chord function of each note, student sings each chord ascending from 1, and then descending from 13. Also, ask student to sing the mode or scale which corresponds to the chord.

2. Tip: Ascending, pause on the 7th of the chord (⌒↑), and then reiterate it and continue upward. Descending, pause on 7 (⌒↓), and then reiterate it and continue downward. Pausing separates the chord into two constituent chords (the base chord and its upper-structure triad), making it easier to assess and adjust intonation. Once he/she can do this easily, ask student to eliminate the pause and sing straight up and down the entire chord.

3. Variation: For a more challenging exercise, sing descending from 13 immediately (!).

4. Variation: Student or partner creates a series of chord number, and student sings them on each chord type. Apply retrograde and inversion techniques, and sing again.

	Basic Chord Type			
	Δ7	7	−7	⌀7
	Sing Extensions Up/Down			
	13	*13*	*13*	*♭13*
	+11	*+11*	*11*	*11*
	Δ9	*Δ9*	*Δ9*	*Δ9*
⌢↓	Δ7	−7	−7	−7
⌢↑	Δ7	−7	−7	−7
	5	*5*	*5*	*♭5*
	3	*3*	*−3*	*−3*
	1	*1*	*1*	*1*
	Sing Scale/Mode			
	Lydian	Lyd Dom	Dorian	Locr+2

Chart 2: Chord Extensions

Example: Sing 1-↑5-↓3-↑7-↓5-↑9-↓7-↑11-↓9-↑13-↓11.
Reverse the order: 11-↑13-↓9-↑11-↓7-↑9-↓5-↑7-↓3-↑5-↓1.
Invert the intervallic direction: 1-↓5-↑3-↓7-↑5-↓9-↑7-↓11-↑9-↓13-↑11.
Reverse the order: 11-↓13-↑9-↓11-↑7-↓9-↑5-↓7-↑3-↓5-↑1.

Truly, there is no limit to the way in which this material can be manipulated to create fresh exercises. For example, the intervallic leaps can be increased in size, i.e.: 1-↑7-↓3-↑9-↓5-↑11-↓7-↑13-↓9, etc.

The series can be patterned (as above) or unpatterned, i.e.: 1-↑5-↑7-↓3-↑9-↑13-↓11, etc.

5. The student can utilize these techniques to create his/her own exercises for singing an extended chord corresponding to virtually any scale:
• Major modes or their alterations
• Diminished scale
• Whole tone scale
• Minor melodic/harmonic modes or their alterations
• Altered dominant scale
• Any other scales commonly used in jazz

CHORD PROGRESSIONS

Q: I would like to be able to listen to a record of someone playing a standard tune, and really know what's going on harmonically. Besides practicing II-V-I's, how can I improve at hearing jazz chord changes?

A: Before the student attempts a harmonic transcription of a tune which uses functional root progressions, he/she should thoroughly absorb the 84 Dominant Cadences in Chart 1. The student should transpose, notate, and sing them in several keys using the suggested techniques for practice, as well as compose and improvise melodic lines over them, and arrange and play them in two-hand shell-voicings on the piano.

The next step is to apply these cadences in a similar manner in modulations to different key areas. I have found Arnold Schoenberg's *Chart of the Regions*[1] useful in organizing this study (see Chart 3 below). By practicing modulatory phrases in isolation, the student is more apt to identify them correctly when encountering them in the context of a chord progression. Hearing the harmonic movement from, say, the A section to the bridge in a standard tune—for example, *The Song Is You* (Jerome Kern/Oscar Hammerstein), in which A modulates from I to III at B—becomes less daunting for the student once he/she has an aural handle on these seminal harmonic modules. Eventually, even more complex and frequent modulations become easier to hear, recognize and identify.

1. Begin by having the student modulate from a given chord (I) to the keys most closely related to it in the cycle of 5ths—I, V and IV—by means of the 84 Dominant Cadences. These closely related keys belong to Level 1 of the Modulation Chart. For example, see Chart 4.

Modulation Chart			
Level 1 *Closely related keys*	IV	I	V
Level 2 *Relative Minors*	II	VI	III
Level 3 *Relative Majors*	♭VI	♭III	♭VII
Level 4 *Tritone Subs*	VII	♭V	♭II

Chart 3: Modulation Chart

Given Key	84 Dominant Cadences of Level 1 Keys		Level 1 Key Goal
I (i)	II (♭VI*) of I (i)	V (♭II*) of I (i)	I (i)
I (i)	II (♭VI*) of V (v)	V (♭II*) of V (v)	V (v)
I (i)	II (♭VI*) of IV (iv)	V (♭II*) of IV (iv)	IV (iv)
I.E., from ...	through ...		to ...
FΔ/F−	84 Cadences of FΔ/F−		FΔ/F−
FΔ/F−	84 Cadences of CΔ/C−		CΔ/C−
FΔ/F−	84 Cadences of B♭Δ/B♭−		B♭Δ/B♭−

Chart 4: Modulations to Level 1 Keys

Modulations to or from parallel major and minor keys are accomplished by a simple chord color change in either the initial chord, cadence chords, or the goal chord (or all, as the case may be), which has no effect on the function of the cadential root progression.

2. Similarly, modulate to the relative minors of the Level 1 keys. These are called Level 2 keys of the Modulation Chart. For example, see Chart 5.

Given Key	84 Dominant Cadences of Level 2 Keys		Level 2 Key Goal
I (i)	II (♭VI*) of VI (vi)	V (♭II*) of VI (vi)	VI (i)
I (i)	II (♭VI*) of III (iii)	V (♭II*) of III (iii)	III (iii)
I (i)	II (♭VI*) of II (ii)	V (♭II*) of II (ii)	II (ii)
I.E., from ...	through ...		to ...
FΔ/F−	84 Cadences of DΔ/D−		DΔ/D−
FΔ/F−	84 Cadences of AΔ/A−		AΔ/A−
FΔ/F−	84 Cadences of G♭Δ/G♭−		GΔ/G−

Chart 5: Modulations to Level 2 Keys

Given Key	84 Dominant Cadences of Level 3 Keys		Level 3 Key Goal
I (i)	II (♭VI*) of ♭III (♭iii)	V (♭II*) of ♭III (♭iii)	♭III (♭iii)
I (i)	II (♭VI*) of ♭VII (♭vii)	V (♭II*) of ♭VII (♭vii)	♭VII (♭vii)
I (i)	II (♭VI*) of ♭VI (♭vi)	V (♭II*) of ♭VI (♭vi)	♭VI (♭vi)
I.E., from . . .	**through . . .**		**to . . .**
FΔ/F−	84 Cadences of A♭Δ/A♭−		A♭Δ/A♭−
FΔ/F−	84 Cadences of E♭Δ/E♭−		E♭Δ/E♭−
FΔ/F−	84 Cadences of D♭Δ/D♭−		D♭Δ/D♭−

Chart 6: Modulations to Level 3 Keys

3. Next, modulate to the relative majors of the Level 1 keys. These are called Level 3 keys of the Modulation Chart. For example, see Chart 6.

4. Finally, modulate to the tritone substitutes of the Level 1 keys. These are called Level 4 keys of the Modulation Chart. For example, see Chart 7.

Given Key	84 Dominant Cadences of Level 4 Keys		Level 4 Key Goal
I (i)	II (♭VI*) of ♭V (♭v)	V (♭II*) of ♭V (♭v)	♭V (♭v)
I (i)	II (♭VI*) of ♭II (♭ii)	V (♭II*) of ♭II (♭ii)	♭II (♭ii)
I (i)	II (♭VI*) of ♭VII (♭vii)	V (♭II*) of ♭VII (♭vii)	VII (vii)
I.E., from . . .	**through . . .**		**to . . .**
FΔ/F−	84 Cadences of BΔ/B−		BΔ/B−
FΔ/F−	84 Cadences of G♭Δ/G♭−		G♭Δ/G♭−
FΔ/F−	84 Cadences of EΔ/E−		EΔ/E−

Chart 7: Modulations to Level 4 Keys

Thus, the student is preparing the ear for most modulatory eventualities he/she is likely to encounter in reading, listening to, and playing standard tunes.

5. Related Activity. Student can compile a list of examples from the jazz repertoire which demonstrate the use of these modulations, singing and playing them in several keys.

SUMMING UP

Embodiment techniques play a critical role in embracing any musical language. Singing, listening, naming, tapping, transcribing, and playing are useful in the judication as well as the development of aural foundation.

A few examples of the application of these techniques to intermediate level jazz harmony are presented in this article. While the harmonic subject matter I have chosen is somewhat limited in scope, it is evident that a creative approach can generate many effective exercises targeted towards the specific aural needs of young jazz improvisers.

NOTE

1. Arnold Schoenberg, *Structural Functions of Harmony* (New York: Norton, 1969), p. 20.

TRANSCRIBING A SOLO USING A TAPE CONSTRUCTED FROM A COMPACT DISC PLAYER WITH A/B REPEAT FUNCTION

Patrick C. Dorian

In the mid-1990s students, educators, and professionals have access to hundreds of published, written transcriptions of improvised solos of the jazz masters. A dilemma may exist in that some students (possibly a majority) are not transcribing solos because of the availability of written transcriptions of landmark improvisations. Many of the great improvisers transcribed solos from several artists to gain a greater understanding of the melodic material and expressiveness of each artist. They were transcribing decades before published transcriptions became available.

Transcription is one of the most challenging yet beneficial exercises that aspiring and accomplished jazz artists undertake. Meticulous transcription becomes a lesson in total ear training. Improvisation is an aural discipline combined with theoretical knowledge and technical ability. Students of improvisation need to enhance their abilities through the cultivation of aural skills. Some students and teachers may be so visually oriented ("page-locked") that reading transcribed solos becomes their primary orientation of studying improvisation. They may read melodic patterns instead of hearing them. Students whose main frames of reference are published solos are in a similar situation as students who have been given the answers to an exam. They will not benefit from reading the text, taking notes, and studying the material that is required.

Listening to the entire solo many times is usually not sufficient for learning the solo. There is too much detailed information to absorb in terms of pitches, rhythms, phrases, nuances, etc. It is much more efficient to learn the solo aurally through the repetition of short melodic fragments. Students whose primary learning style is not aural would especially benefit from such an approach. A useful tool for learning a solo is a cassette tape comprising repeated loops of each melodic fragment of the solo.

Improvisers who are committed to learning a specific solo in an accurate, efficient manner will save time in the long run if they construct such a looping and repetitive melodic-fragment tape. During the construction of the tape, transcribers will also have done enough initial listening so that they have begun the first phase of truly learning the solo. Depending on the length of a solo, some tapes can be made in less than one hour.

I.   Start with a compact disc of the solo, a blank cassette tape, a cassette recorder, and a compact disc player that contains an *A/B repeat function.*
  A.   A/B repeat function allows user to set up a loop from less than one second in length to the entire length of the disc: from any point A to any point B.
  B.   Many CD players do not contain the specific A/B repeat feature.
    1.   Many repeat features are not A/B: may only repeat entire disc or a song, not fragments of a selection.
    2.   Be careful if purchasing; ask for a demonstration.
  C.   Start recording mode on a blank cassette tape; control the length of the CD melodic fragment by pushing the A/B button at desired beginning of melodic fragment; push button again to end fragment; CD player emits this desired time span repeatedly until CD "play" button (or other appropriate button) is pushed to deactivate A/B repeat function.
  D.   Record five immediate repetitions of each melodic fragment of the solo.
    1.   Even though a melodic fragment seems to end when performer rests for a few pulses or takes a breath (ending a phrase), include the next few notes when the soloist resumes, overlapping into the next melodic fragment. Will assist the transcriber to learn the entire solo with flow and continuity, learning exact pulse placements where the soloist reenters for each new fragment.
    2.   Each repetition will be followed immediately by the next repetition.
  E.   Press "pause" on CD player and cassette player.
  F.   Record five seconds of silence after taping the five repetitions of each melodic fragment.
    1.   Allows the ears to absorb this information.
    2.   Allows a moment to prepare for the next set of repetitions of the next melodic fragment.

G. Resume taping the next melodic fragment by including the final few notes of the previous fragment to assist learning melodic continuity, thus overlapping the melodic fragments.

H. Loop and record remaining fragments until entire solo is completed.

II. At the beginning of an additional cassette tape, record the solo in its entirety (or refer back to the CD). Also can loop entire solo several times, filling up entire side or both sides of a tape to avoid rewinding.

A. Use to review complete solo immediately before and after each immersion listening session.

B. Both tapes may be utilized almost anywhere.

1. Automobile cassette stereo.

2. Walkman while walking or riding bus, jet, etc.

III. Attempt to aurally learn each melodic fragment until each can be sung along with tape at pitch with all stylistic inflections and nuances.

A. Primary goal is to hear the solo, not see it on paper (writing it out comes later).

B. Some fragments are "easier" to learn than others because of simpler rhythms and/or intervals.

1. Use the repeated listenings of these easier melodic fragments to immerse oneself in the tone quality and expressiveness of the master improvisor.

2. Don't skip them to save time.

IV. Construct additional practice tape with periods of silence that are the exact length of the melodic fragment in between the five repetitions of the fragment being learned. Five times: listen to fragment, emulate (sing) fragment during silence; fragment sounds again immediately, sing.

V. Be able to sing entire solo from beginning to end along with CD at pitch with all stylistic inflections and nuances.

VI. If student is an instrumentalist, learn the solo on one's instrument in the same manner.

VII. Write solo in standard music notation as exactly as possible in the same manner. Once the transcriber has an understanding of melodic intervals and rhythmic notation, the solo can be written, quite possibly with confidence and momentum, writing entire melodic fragments at a time, instead of one or two notes at a time.

BOOK REVIEW

Barry Kernfeld, *What to Listen For in Jazz* (New Haven: Yale University Press, 1995, 247 + xvii pp., $40.00)

Reviewed by William Bauer

What must a listener bring to the experience of jazz in order to get the most out of it? Authors of most jazz texts tackle this question by arming the reader with an arsenal of facts about the music's history, thus enabling the reader to understand the circumstances in which the music developed. Two general assumptions motivate this approach: first, that music's meaning comes from its sociocultural context; second, that we can understand music better if we know about the forces that have shaped it. For the readers of such texts, information about the lives of the people who made the music, and the world in which they made it, forms a backdrop for their experience of the sounds of jazz and can allow them to identify with listeners who first encountered these sounds as they were being made. While authors usually provide descriptions of how jazz has changed over the course of its history, discussions of the music itself have tended to avoid technical matters, and have stayed fairly general.

As jazz increasingly makes its presence felt in the classroom, teachers are coming to realize that reading about the music's history is not enough to help the student understand jazz. In order for inexperienced listeners to make sense of the sounds of jazz, they also need to develop essential listening skills. A few jazz texts have sought to address this problem by including sections designed to give the reader guidelines for approaching the sound of the music itself (Martin Williams's notes to *The Smithsonian Collection of Classic Jazz,* Mark Gridley's *Jazz Styles* and more recently, Lewis Porter and Michael Ullman's *Jazz: From Its Origins to the Present,* to name a few). In so doing, the latter authors acknowledge that listeners do not automatically know how to deal with sounds and the intricate ways musicians often put them together. The wonderful aural tapestry that gives jazz the richness and complexity so compelling to experienced listeners can easily leave novices wondering where they should direct their attention. Clearly the need exists for a way to help the listener make sense of the music by sharpening his musical perceptions.

Barry Kernfeld's latest book, *What to Listen For in Jazz,* seeks to remedy this situation. The dust jacket portrays the book as "a thorough, accessible introduction to jazz . . . [that] provides the background necessary to fully enjoy this musical art." For Kernfeld, this means giving the reader "a practical, commonsense explanation of how [various] concepts work in jazz with clear examples drawn from a set of great recordings" (74). The design of the book was inspired by his frustration with what he terms "the stylistic approach," leading him to suggest a method of listening independent of style (184). Kernfeld hopes that, with the background the book provides, the listener may approach the subject in a "concretely musical way before tying up musical elements into stylistic packages" (185). He makes use of over one hundred notated musical examples to illustrate jazz rhythm, form, arrangement, composition, improvisation, style and sound. Kernfeld ends the book with short biographies of the musicians that figure prominently in the recordings.

Kernfeld has built the text around twenty-one recorded selections assembled onto an accompanying compact disc which adds to the book's usefulness. In addition, he has made good use of the digital timer to key musical examples and discussions to precise moments in the listening selections. He exploits this tool to provide a verbal "score" for especially difficult music, such as John Coltrane's "Ascension," which allows him to indicate at what point the most obvious changes in texture or the crucial structural moments occur. When listening to the selections in continuous succession, however, the listener must beware jarring changes in volume level between tracks, such as the beginning of "Trumpet No End" (track 7).

Curious about how Kernfeld would go about training the reader's musical perceptions, I read *What to Listen For in Jazz* from two perspectives. Knowing that jazz educators might wish to use the book as a textbook, I read it from the vantage point of the uninitiated student. Knowing that such books add to the ongoing dialogue about the meaning of the music, I also read it with the weather eye of the historiographer. From both angles I found the book at turns provocative, insightful, uncertain of its pedagogical and aesthetic focus, and biased in its approach to jazz history.

Throughout the book, Kernfeld does not sustain a consistent stance toward the reader. At times he assumes the reader has a considerable degree of musical sophistication and thus misses opportunities to teach basic skills. At other times he gives the reader little credit for prior musical knowledge and spells out what would seem obvious. He explains that "the focus is on fundamental examples, some requiring no special knowledge, others requiring the ability to read music and a rudimentary acquaintance with music theory" (2), and certain of his recorded selections do illustrate fundamental aspects of the music. Basie's "Jumpin' at the Woodside" and The New Orleans Rhythm Kings' "Tin Roof Blues," for example, provide the raw material for discussions about swing rhythm and blues harmony, to which even a nonmusician might relate. In general, however, Kernfeld does not present the music in a way that moves the student through listening skills of increasing difficulty. While knowledgeable readers will get restless at times, neophytes will be deterred by the book's pedagogical unevenness.

As early as the second chapter, Kernfeld thrusts the reader into fairly involved discussions that require a solid grasp of such concepts as syncopation (we get the following obscure explanation for this term several pages after Kernfeld has already used it: "technically, to syncopate is to attack a note in a rhythmic position weaker than one through which it carries" [29]), structural design, theme statement, 5/4 time, polyrhythmic, polymetric, three against four, four against six, metric modulation, structural downbeat, and aperiodic rhythm.

To a trained musician these elements are obvious, yet a beginner can find even so fundamental a concept as beat elusive. Kernfeld acknowledges the complexities that beat sometimes presents for the inexperienced listener: "Recognizing double-time requires one to pin down the tempo; [however,] identifying the beat can sometimes be difficult . . . because musicians present two tempos" (8). He nevertheless assumes the reader already has in place the ability to distinguish the rhythmic surface from the various levels of pulse that constitute the metric infrastructure.

He also assumes that the reader already knows how to separate foreground from background, as reflected in the different levels of rhythmic activity between instruments. In "Black Bottom Stomp," for instance, the reader must be able to aurally identify the rhythmic interaction between banjo and bass in the accompaniment.

Had Kernfeld broken these skills down or provided exercises for developing them, the book would be much more useful to beginners. His instruction to hum the melody of "St. Thomas" during Max Roach's drum solo, for example, elicits the reader's active engagement with the music (135). Such engagement is a strong pedagogical tool that would help to develop the reader's aural skills. Even here, however, refinements are in order, for to do this activity a reader would need to know when to begin humming the tune and how to align it with the solo. One can only assume this skill in a reader with a degree of musical background.

Also problematic for beginners but obvious to musicians, the reader must have the capacity to hear large scale formal designs. Early on, Kernfeld appeals to this skill when he refers to the bar numbers of individual theme statements in "Black Bottom Stomp." Kernfeld also assumes that the reader has the ability to interpret musical scores and formal schemata in considerable detail. His later inquiry into form assumes as well that the reader has a thorough mastery of harmony. In other chapters he continues to make assumptions about the reader's prior listening experience and understanding.

Without seeming to notice any incongruity, Kernfeld stops occasionally to explain terms that a listener with a rudimentary knowledge of music theory would already know, perhaps in an effort to give a nonmusician access to the book's contents. In the most extreme instance of this he explains how a stride pianist would play the interval of a tenth (188).

Some of Kernfeld's explanations of familiar terms offer special applications of these terms, but most of them do not. At first, for example, Kernfeld describes form broadly as "any aspect of music that contributes to the organization of a specific piece" (40), and adds that interrelationships among pieces can generate "abstract and intricate structural models" that also qualify as form, possibly meaning his "Ur-blues form." Later, Kernfeld narrows his definition of form to focus upon the harmonic scheme upon which "any respected musician" would be expected to be able to improvise variations.

Some of the issues that come up in *What to Listen For in Jazz* are inherent in writing about music in general, and Kernfeld points out that certain musical relationships are simpler to understand in sound than in words (135). At times, he uses language effectively to bridge the gap between nonmusician and musician. In his imaginative use of onomatopoeic language, for example, Kernfeld has found a simple, yet effective way to convey some of the subtleties of jazz rhythm and timbre through the sonic qualities of words. Indeed, one can hear the echoes of scat at times (173–4).

At one point Kernfeld uses the "oom-pah"s of marches and rags to illustrate two-beat meter (7). Later he builds an entire sonic shorthand around Lester Young's expression "tinkety-boom" to explore the abundant methods that a rhythm section player can use to express swing feel in keeping time (14–5; 31). Kernfeld's use of vocal sounds to point to articulation and accentuation works well because, as he himself points out several times, jazz has many speechlike characteristics. In these places Kernfeld builds upon what a nonmusician knows intuitively about sound in order to enrich his understanding of the music. His phonetic analysis of Louis Armstrong's scat solo in "Hotter Than That" hints at an important aspect of jazz aesthetics by illustrating "the African-American conception of sound upon which jazz timbre is founded" (167).

On a deeper level, when Kernfeld probes the music's moods with vividness and eloquence he underscores the incredible impact music can have on the listener. At such times he does not intend to give the reader a programmatic basis for listening, for he earlier clarifies that "those who seek a direct connection between sound and story would do better to invent a personal interpretation than to look for stories in a book such as this" (3). But with his colorful descriptions he succeeds in revealing the music's power to go beyond itself.

In his discussion of one of the Miles Davis Quintet's 1956 versions of "'Round Midnight," for example, Kernfeld effectively captures the emotional character of the group when it plays the interlude that sets up Coltrane's entrance. He describes it as the "tightening [of] a giant spring, which then uncoils in a sudden burst as Coltrane begins his solo" (83). The quintet's wordless ecstatic shouts here are not meant to have literal verbal content. But Kernfeld's powerful imagery validates this moment's profound emotion for the listener, especially one who cannot yet translate the emotional gestures of jazz into a meaningful expressive vocabulary.

Such descriptions serve a crucial function in writing about music, for they reinforce the miraculous fact that musicians who succeed in making the music *speak* go beyond impressive technical virtuosity to win our hearts with their artistry. As with any endeavor, the empty application of technique in music is not enough to make the activity meaningful, and a discussion of technique alone will not suffice to reveal the music's depth and beauty. Furthermore, such discussions actually limit the reader's experience of the music, for to discuss the sounds of jazz as though they were self-referential is to imply that they have no connection at all to life. Kernfeld does begrudgingly concede that music "in some sense" expresses life, but all too often he leaves the listener seeking between the lines for evidence of it.

The problem this issue poses for a writer is how to go beyond technical descriptions without sounding trite. In such passages as the one about

" 'Round Midnight," cited above, Kernfeld demonstrates a remarkable sensitivity to the music's expressive impact and an ability to communicate it effectively with words. Had he so illuminated the other musical passages he wrote about, his readers would have profited immensely.

Kernfeld has a musician's fascination with the methods of music-making, and fellow musicians will benefit from the great care with which he has analyzed them. In fact, the book is a potent antidote to the anti-intellectualism of some jazz critics and musicians, whose reticence about technique perpetuates the myth that the improviser's artistry springs from some mysterious process that words cannot elucidate. However, because Kernfeld focuses the discussion of musical elements on their technical aspects, the reader does not get the strong sense that musicians do much more than cleverly manipulate them. The reader needs to know more about how musicians use technical devices to generate the expressiveness of jazz.

Kernfeld's chapter on rhythm serves as a case in point. In it, Kernfeld tells us that the back-beat is sometimes used to add intensity and that syncopation in jazz does not always have the surprise impact that one might expect. But he is generally more concerned with rhythmic procedures than he is with what expressive function they serve. This same issue crops up again and again throughout the book with regard to other musical elements. Occasionally Kernfeld sprinkles asides about emotion, but this aspect of the music does not seem to intrigue him as much as the procedures he has so carefully elucidated. Certainly an introduction to jazz needs to highlight the musicians' power to move the listener, and how their technique contributes to this power, especially since moving the listener is one of their basic goals.

In addition to the book's pedagogical difficulties, certain aesthetic issues undermine its usefulness as a jazz primer. Kernfeld favors looking at the music synoptically (i.e., as an architectural structure), over listening to it diachronically (i.e., as events emerging over time). As a result, jazz appears to lack the formal sophistication one finds in classical music. In his closing remarks on form, for example, he observes that "no one would mistake Mingus' [formal] achievement [in "The Fables of Faubus"] for the heady architecture of Mozart and Beethoven," and asserts that the musician's "attempts to move toward the elaborate formal constructions of classical music" are often motivated "by a desire to equalize the . . . sociocultural status of jazz and classical music" (73). This seems unfair to Mingus, who deserves to be judged on his own terms.

Kernfeld's caution that "jazz is an inherently imperfect art" (161) further clouds the aesthetic issue. His explanation that "some imperfections should merely be disregarded . . . [because] a desire for perfection clashes with the aesthetics peculiar to jazz" comes off as an apology for the ways that jazz does not meet the aesthetic standards of classical music (161).

While the classical audience judges music according to standards of excellence specific to that world, the jazz audience gauges success according to its own rigorous criteria. Part of the difficulty stems from the nature of jazz as a hybrid art form with roots in European-American and African-American cultural values. Thus, at various times in its history jazz has either embraced or repudiated classical aesthetics in varying degrees. Because of this, the issue of jazz aesthetics requires a complex approach that lies beyond the scope of Kernfeld's book. Nevertheless, the reader needs to know what constitutes perfection in terms of the aesthetics of jazz.

The reader may find Kernfeld's position on jazz aesthetics in an endnote (232n). In it he states that, while "jazz literature can usefully borrow a terminology that has been refined over centuries and that is more precise than jazz jargon, . . . the literature need not borrow the evaluative standards that come along with that terminology." If Kernfeld had expressed this sentiment at the outset and kept it in focus throughout rather than burying it in an endnote he would have given the reader a more appropriate frame of reference for experiencing the music. As it stands now, regardless of how much the endnote qualifies his remarks about jazz's "imperfections," it does not displace his emphasis on synoptic form, which obliquely invites the reader to look for complex design in the music's large dimension when this is often not a primary goal of the music. Furthermore, because Kernfeld does little to elaborate upon the aesthetic stance required of a jazz listener, as distinct from that of a classical listener, the book lacks a philosophical compass.

Several features of the music require the listener to adopt a mode of experiencing the music unique to jazz. The extraordinary nature of the challenge that jazz poses for the performer is one such feature. Kernfeld's division of formal procedures into arrangement, composition, and improvisation emphasizes distinctions that many players find less significant or discrete than he does. An improvising musician must inevitably explore the entire spectrum between planning on the one hand (which encompasses arranging, composing, and certain kinds of improvising) and spontaneity on the other (which entails spur-of-the-moment decisions made in the course of improvising). The function of making fine distinctions within this continuum is unclear, if not sometimes misleading. Jazz musicians take an exceptional approach to the issue of control. Typically they will combine a remarkable command of their instrument with an equally remarkable openness to the exploration of a wide range of possibilities. This is why a diachronic approach to form can help us account for the music's sophistication so much more effectively than a synoptic one does.

Some of the ways that jazz relates to other styles of African-American music and to West African music can help us to distinguish the jazz aesthetic from the classical aesthetic. Kernfeld does not mention important organizing principles which relate these musics to jazz, such as call-and-response and the use of time-cycles. The omission of call-and-response seems especially glaring because of its obvious use in the recorded selections, such as during Earl Hines's opening statement of "Sweet Sue."

Similarly, Kernfeld neglects to associate the unique way jazz uses syncopation to the West African use of interlocking rhythmic patterns whose rhythmic gaps leave spaces for others to fill. Making this connection can give us insights into the phrasing of Miles Davis, who uses silence to make the presence of the rhythm section felt as well as to leave us waiting in suspense until he reenters. In Kernfeld's discussion of microscopic note placement (24–5) one does not get the sense that Davis's line grows from his striking way of relating to the supporting players.

Kernfeld's self-imposed methodology precludes tracing the historical roots of every musical aspect, and he is under no obligation to do so. But to look at jazz with no consideration of its roots may distort how the jazz community responds to the music in the present. In creating textures built upon dialogue, both call-and-response and jazz syncopation reveal how jazz evokes the conversational tone of much West African and African-American musics. These cultures emphasize the interaction among musicians and between the musicians and the audience as an essential part of a musical experience. While Kernfeld hints at the conversational qualities of jazz when he observes its speechlike aspects, the reader needs the historical connection to be mentioned explicitly, for the aesthetic reasons stated earlier.

Integration of the participants into the entire fabric of a music event also plays a crucial role in West African and African-American culture. Any approach which considers the music of these cultures separately from the context of its performance has edited out more than a peripheral detail. While this may hold less true for certain kinds of jazz, the interdependence among its participants is as important in experiencing jazz as the topics considered in *What to Listen For in Jazz.*

The application of classical analytic methods to jazz poses aesthetic problems that Kernfeld ignores. Standard methods of musical analysis encourage us to experience a musical work as an art object that stands removed from ordinary life. The analyst seeks to objectify the music, and examine it for its intrinsic worth. While one may analyze a jazz recording in a cultural vacuum, a jazz musician's greatness stems from his or her subcultural status as well as it does from the intrinsic worth of his or her output. This may explain why so many writers have underrated Lester Young's impact on jazz. Parker's "Koko" provides a good case in point. Whatever its inherent value as a work of art, its critical assessment must also come from its function as a bebop manifesto, and from the ways it reveals Parker's ability to embody the subcultural ideal. Only then will the music, and the enormous impact it had on jazz history, make sense to neophytes in the face of its apparent incoherence.

Furthermore, the question of how a work transcends the bounds of its time to become a masterwork comes from a tradition in which the creator seeks the work's attainment of this status. Especially outside of the recording studio, improvising musicians have a different, more immediate, perspective on their transitory medium; one in which no particular performance represents a final statement of its content. Unlike classical composers, who create new thematic material in each work, thus setting it apart from their other works, such musicians continue repeatedly to rework the same materials. Every musical element serves as a vehicle through which the musicians collectively and individually reflect their taste, skill and, above all, their power to move the audience.

Kernfeld's emphasis upon formalistic analytic procedures suggests an eagerness to demonstrate how his selections have transcended their era to become masterworks; and perhaps they have. His perspective inevitably proceeds from his focus on "historic" studio recordings, rather than on live jazz, and it results in his readiness to accept that jazz has now entered a repertory phase. These recordings undoubtedly document an important part of jazz history. But as they constitute only a portion of the music's performance tradition, we cannot base our conclusions about what to listen for on them alone.

Certain aspects of the recording industry have influenced how the music developed and how it has been preserved. As Kernfeld himself points out, the amount of music a 10-inch 78 rpm disc could hold dictated the short length of most recorded jazz until the early 1950s, whereas players at a jam session might improvise on one tune for several hours (42). Record producers also had an impact on jazz history by deciding whom to record, and musicians tell of great players who never set foot in a studio. The aesthetic criteria that musicians and producers applied to recordings differ in many ways from the ones that musicians and audiences applied to live jazz, and this determined what recordings ultimately got released. In the case of bebop especially, the music was created as much for the pleasure of the musicians as it was for the audience, which accounts for its complexity. Recorded jazz is therefore not entirely representative of the performance tradition. Related to this issue is Kernfeld's own selection of recordings, which emphasizes music in which the musicians' ongoing decision-making process depends less on responsive interaction than it does on advance planning of some kind. In some ways, a jazz record is the sonic residue of a rich process that involves much more than sound alone, a process that sound recording can only hint at. Anyone who has felt the emotional sparks that someone like Betty Carter can ignite in a crowd would not willingly relegate jazz to the archives.

Because Kernfeld chooses to examine "historic recordings of jazz masterpieces" purely as sound objects, *What to Listen For in Jazz* would better serve readers who want to learn how to enjoy the music's past triumphs than those who want to know how to experience a live jazz performance as it takes shape before their very ears. As great as the recordings are, for many listeners nothing can rival the thrill of being present during a jazz performance and feeling a part of its unfolding process.

Because of Kernfeld's self-imposed limitations, he cannot adequately address the question of meaning in jazz. The title of *What to Listen For in Jazz* implies a breadth of scope, yet its contents suggest a narrow approach in which we mostly listen for formalistic constructs. In a rare exception to this approach, Kernfeld briefly hints at the significance that pitch can have in modal jazz besides its organizational uses, by considering the borrowing of scales from regional musics in light of its meaning rather than its sound (67). To Kernfeld, the impulse to evoke an exotic flavor via ethnic borrowings helped inspire Ellington's pseudo-African "jungle style." This acknowledgment that jazz can refer to something beyond itself opens up a realm of possibilities that Kernfeld leaves relatively unexplored.

Other constructive elements that Kernfeld discusses seem hollow when removed from their cultural context. His preference for terminology borrowed from classical music over jazz jargon, mentioned above, embodies this dislocation. Introducing the use of licks in improvisation, Kernfeld lists several terms as though they were interchangeable, and then opts for the term "formula," ostensibly for the sake of clarity (137). But since he implies that the terms all serve equally well, why not adopt the musicians' perspective? Even if an analyst does seek to make certain distinctions clear by using nonjazz terminology, it is worth knowing whether the players make such distinctions themselves. This may help keep the discussion focused upon issues significant to the makers of the music, and guide us to hear the music as they do.

Even in terms of formalistic analysis Kernfeld sometimes falters. He points out that the musician builds improvised lines from fragments, adding that "seldom could the fragments be described as melodic in the tuneful sense" (136–7). While he qualifies this, saying that the importance of a lick emerges from hearing it in its context, and in the ways that licks are combined and manipulated, his discussion sheds little light on the purposes of linear fragmentation. Kernfeld implies that the absence of tunefulness seems a flaw instead of a strength, when in fact licks often serve a percussive function that fuels the rhythmic impulse of the music. The fragmentation of the line also spurs the interaction between solo line and accompaniment. Those listening for a tune will miss these crucial features of the music. Furthermore, in the emergence of bebop, the untunefulness of the solo line also has an extramusical resonance associated with the style. Kernfeld's inability to address this exemplifies the hazards of looking only at the notes.

Kernfeld downplays the significance of the bebop revolution, choosing instead to emphasize the musical continuity between swing and bop styles. According to him, the "stylistic perspective from a later time . . . corrected the first impression" formed in the heat of battle (192). For Kernfeld this correction in perspective comes from the "truly revolutionary style" of free jazz (195). This radical revision of jazz historiography ends up distorting the meaning of the music by leaving out the social significance of these changes in musical style.

I interpret the creation of bebop as an act of empowerment by African American musicians who, by reacting against the mainstream status that big bands had given to jazz, created a tightly knit musical subculture with its own language and its own conventions. While Kernfeld concedes that his book is not the place to consider the extramusical elements that added to the sense of revolution created by the leaders of the bebop movement, he does not seem to recognize that this self-imposed limitation undermines his ability to help the listener make sense of the music on its own terms. In fairness, Kernfeld does not wish to provide a social context for the sounds of jazz, even when he takes a "whistle-stop tour" through general styles in the book's Epilogue. On the contrary, he seems to view such context as inimical to approaching the subject "in a concretely musical way" (185) as well as being beyond the scope of the book.

In order to form an accurate impression of jazz, however, we need to hear it in light of the extramusical elements that Kernfeld dismisses as irrelevant. We can certainly hear the jaggedness of bebop lines, which lessened the music's tunefulness, as the result of some abstract musical exercise. But by seeming incoherent to outsiders the musicians also sought to reclaim jazz for blacks. The serrated edge of the music carved out a closed circle that warded off squares. Kernfeld himself admits that, even now, newcomers to bebop find Parker's "Koko" incomprehensible. A formalistic approach to the music can not fully account for the music's meaning because it does not address the dramatic social function that bebop filled. This also explains why Kernfeld's made-up term "swing-bop" is not an accepted term in the field: the two styles satisfied different cultural ends.

The usual forum for sociocultural considerations has been jazz history texts. Kernfeld claims that the readers of these books do not necessarily come to understand what unifies jazz amidst all of its stylistic diversity (184). Regardless of this, a formalistic analysis should not *obscure* the cultural factors responsible for this diversity. The issues raised by Kernfeld's book suggest that the truth lies between the historical and the theoretical approaches. Any author who seeks to present a complete and truthful perspective will have to reconcile the two.

In the past, jazz scholars have had to justify to the academy the formal study of a musical style that originated as entertainment in red-light districts, tent shows, night clubs and theaters. The music has not been taken seriously in the university until recently, and in some fronts the battle to assert its legitimacy wages on. That jazz is now routinely presented in such elegant settings as Carnegie Hall and Lincoln Center poses a different challenge to all students of the music, one which is elusive but no less urgent: How do we connect our experience of the sounds of jazz to the music's meaning when it is presented out of its original context? In some ways, *What to Listen For in Jazz* embodies this question.

Kernfeld's approach to jazz gives us important insights into specific aspects of the music and useful tools for discussing these aspects concretely. But we should beware using it to introduce students to jazz or to form critical interpretations of live jazz. For, while *What to Listen For in Jazz* rewards the reader with the astute observations about the techniques of jazz, it lacks an awareness of the function music plays in peoples' lives. In his zeal to prove that jazz deserves scholarly attention by assigning to certain works the label "masterpiece," and analyzing these works for their intrinsic value, Kernfeld has presented the music as though it had no cultural frame of reference. Let us teach future generations of listeners to experience jazz in relation to the music's own aesthetic, with its own social function and emotional significance. Only then will listeners bring to the music what it calls upon from them.

CD REVIEW

Big Band Renaissance: The Evolution of the Jazz Orchestra, the 1940s and Beyond (Smithsonian RC/RD 108, 1995) 5 CDs boxed, $64.96; cassettes, $54.96)

Reviewed by Max Harrison

Jay McShann: Swingmatism; **Boyd Raeburn:** Dalvatore Sally; **Ray McKinley:** Idiot's Delight; **Duke Ellington:** On a Turquoise Cloud, Such Sweet Thunder, Perdido, Tourist Point of View, Blood Count; **Benny Goodman;** Undercurrent Blues; **Charlie Barnet:** Eugipelliv; **Artie Shaw:** Lucky Number, Similau; **Count Basie;** Bambo, L'il Darlin', Blues in Hoss' Flat, Basie; **Woody Herman:** Stompin' at the Savoy, Sister Sadie, Summer of '42; **Stan Kenton:** Intermission Riff, Cuban Carnival, Young Blood, A Trumpet, Egdon Heath; **Sauter-Finegan Orchestra:** The Loop; **Ted Heath:** The Man I Love; **Harry James:** The Jazz Connoisseur, That's Thad; **Maynard Ferguson:** On Green Dolphin Street; **Buddy Rich:** Goodbye Yesterday; **U.S. Air Force Airmen of Note:** Noël; **Herb Pomeroy:** Theme for Terry; **Johnny Richards:** Nipigon; **Dizzy Gillespie:** I Remember Clifford, Chorale; **Terry Gibbs:** Cottontail; **Gerry Mulligan:** Weep; **Quincy Jones:** Meet B.B.; **Gerald Wilson:** Viva Tirado; **Kenny Clarke-Francy Boland:** Now Hear My Meanin'; **Thad Jones-Mel Lewis:** Cherry Juice, Willow Weep for Me; **Duke Pearson:** New Girl; **Clare Fischer:** Miles Behind; **John Dankworth:** Sailor; **Don Ellis:** Chain Reaction; **Rhythm Combination and Brass:** Green Witch; **Toshiko Akiyoshi:** Sumie; **Boss Brass:** Portrait of Jennie; **Sam Jones:** Antigua; **Bob Belden:** Treasure Island; **Miles Davis:** Israel; **Hal McKusick:** Blues for Pablo; **Miles Davis-Gil Evans:** Blues for Pablo; **Gil Evans:** Barbara Song; **Bill Potts:** I Got Plenty o' Nuttin'; **Frank Rosolino-Les Brown:** Pizza Boy; **Charles Mingus:** Revelations; **Les and Larry Elgart:** Soon; **George Russell:** Manhattan; **Benny Carter:** Blue Star; **Curtis Fuller-Manny Albam:** Savannah; **Billy May:** Dat Dere; **Thelonious Monk:** Four in One; **J. J. Johnson:** El Camino Real; **John Lewis:** Animal Dance; **Henry Mancini:** 'Round about Midnight; **Oliver Nelson:** Heidi; **Doc Severinsen:** Sax Alley; **Sun Ra:** Street Named Hell; **Charlie Haden:** Interludes; **Willem Breuker:** Congratulation Cigar; **Tom Pierson:** Planet of Tears; **Muhal Richard Abrams:** Hearinga.

This is Bill Kirchner's follow-up to Martin Williams and Gunther Schuller's *Big Band Jazz: The Beginnings to the 50s* (Smithsonian RC/RD30) of 1983. That meant to trace the growth and development of the jazz orchestral idiom from its beginnings to an arbitrary yet unavoidable cut-off point around mid-century. Having considerable reservations, to put it mildly, about how this was done, and in particular about much of what was said in the accompanying booklet, it was with no little caution that I approached the successor to that Grammy-winning issue. But sets like this have to be taken seriously. A press release sent with the above intimates that the Smithsonian's *Classic Jazz,* for example, "went platinum in 1979 and is still selling well. It has also been widely used as a jazz text in college music courses." So, if one cares about what people think and believe about jazz, the matter of what goes into such compilations and what is left out are questions for real concern.

Most pressing among the immediate problems is that no two competent people would agree completely about the contents of such a package; they might not even concur as to the principles on which the items ought to be selected. One should not read too much into a subtitle like "The Evolution of the Jazz Orchestra," yet what does "evolution" mean in musical contexts? Elsewhere the term refers to the development of an organism, design, concept, or argument and most particularly, in biology, to the origination of a new species by gradual development through modification of earlier forms. This seems promising because the most satisfactory—or at any rate the least unsatisfactory—way of regarding the processes of jazz history is as the growth of a musical language. To what extent can the big band be said to have evolved, both as a medium and as a form, since its emergence within jazz during the 1920s?

In fact does Bill Kirchner's selection of recordings for the Smithsonian Institution demonstrate a continuing evolution? Following on from Williams and Schuller, does it show a further variety of ways of writing for large jazz ensembles and improvising inside them? Does it especially demonstrate that composing and scoring for big bands got better in terms of craft—which presumably would mean a fuller diversity of textures, colors, etc.—and that an advance had occurred with regard to art—which presumably would mean a greater variety and depth of expression? To put this more simply, when the touring bands came off the road there was still an enormous amount to be done musically with the large jazz ensemble and we need to ask if Kirchner's choice shows just how much. One can fit a lot of music on five CDs, but would a different selection have told us more?

He opens the quite substantial 88-page 5¼-inch by 11¼-inch explanatory booklet with a piece of approximately 1,300 words on the "Big Band Renaissance." This makes the familiar yet highly relevant point that during the earlier years of the period he covers, if not sooner, big band music, led by such people as Ellington and Goodman, was changing from dance music into art music, or trying to; and that others, like Shaw and Kenton, "chafed under the limitations imposed upon them by the entertainment industry." Next is explained the division of this box's contents into four sections, these being Road Bands, the survivors of the so-called Swing Era; Part-Time Bands, such as Jones-Lewis, which are sometimes misleadingly called rehearsal bands; Studio Bands, assembled for recording dates and concerts; and a small Avant-Garde section. The dead hand of categorization can all too easily thwart creative diversity, yet this is a helpful division.

There follows a longer piece, of about 2,000 words, called "The Rise, Fall and Rebirth of Big Band Jazz." This is a skilled condensation of the history of the movement, though I would quibble with a point here and there. For instance, had Redman by the time he left Henderson in 1927 really "incorporated Louis Armstrong's rhythmic innovations, the basis of 'swing,' into big band scoring" pervasively? My own counterassertion is that, despite by now virtually automatic claims to the contrary, Redman's Henderson scores "simply did not contain the patterns and figurations which commercial arrangers used constantly from the 1930s onwards."[1]

Next comes a page of around 600 words headed "The Workings of a Big Band." This is an outline of how large jazz ensembles operate in the mechanical sense, and the most significant historical point here is that with the advent of the Raeburn and Sauter-Finegan bands doubling by members of the saxophone section became more important and has of course remained so. The rest of this booklet is filled with Kirchner's usually enlightening historical, critical, and analytical remarks on each of the 75 tracks. These are headed with full discographical details, including identification of soloists, of composers and arrangers, the whole being interspersed with 54 photographs.

Given his background as a player and arranger, Kirchner has made his choices with a knowing professional ear. A vast amount of skill in performing jazz can be heard on these records, almost enough to suggest that the ability to improvise it really well, and in a considerable variety of manners, is now commonplace. Such a view would be seriously optimistic, yet on many of these performances it is the soloists who provide nearly all the musical interest. Herb Pomeroy's 1957 "Theme for Terry," for example, offers a sequence of admirable solos but nothing fresh orchestrally. Rather similar is Duke Pearson's "New Girl" of ten years later, with excellent Burt Collins trumpet and Lew Tabackin tenor set in writing which, although it has a personal slant, presents nothing that hints at even a minor new departure. Bob Belden's "Treasure Island" of 1989 is a comparable instance, only more so, with solos from Tim Hagans (trumpet) and Marc Copland (piano) which are fine personal statements. It is quite interesting, also, in Belden's composing and orchestration, to trace the influences of Gil Evans, of Miles Davis's 1963–70 groups, of Hancock, etc., yet one cannot find anything that is his alone.

Some writing here is less impressive by far, and fails to make its point *as* writing. The 1959 "Cottontail" by Terry Gibbs's Dream Band, for instance, is a meaningless tear-up, and it is surprising that so fine a craftsman as Al Cohn did the arrangement. Gerald Wilson's "Viva Tirado" is a dull Latin piece from 1962 whose repetitions latterly become wearisome. He is better represented here by his score of "Perdido," of which the 1960 Ellington band gives a magisterial performance. A different case is that of Clare Fischer. "Miles Behind" is surely the most engaging track on his 1968 *Thesaurus* Atlantic LP, and this for his ensemble writing rather than for solos by Warne Marsh and Conte Candoli. But he would have been more tellingly represented by his "Piece for Soft Brass, Woodwinds and Percussion" of 1965 for Kenton. As to Quincy Jones's 1961 "Meet B.B.," initially for Benny Bailey, this has no orchestral point, being merely a vehicle for Joe Newman's routine trumpet virtuosity. Jones's youthful precocity is well remembered, and on listening again to some of his long series of big band LPs from the 1950s to the 1970s—they have titles like *Quincy Plays for Pussy Cats* and *Quincy Jones Digests and Interprets the Wonderful Sounds that are Henry Mancini*—one can have no doubt about his wide range of skills. Yet for him, and especially for us, it is as well that he long since retired into pop music.

Despite George Russell's dictum that "a jazz writer is an improviser, too,"[2] composing, or even arranging, jazz creatively is a gift shared by very few beside the many who can improvise. Kirchner values innovation highly and always draws attention to it in his notes. But rather too often here are found performances like Sam Jones's "Antigua" of 1979, which presents nothing whatever that is new, yet is admirably played. Billy May's 1963 "Dat Dere" is the same: a catchy tune nicely dressed up for big band, stunningly performed, but without anything fresh. It appears significant, too, that Kirchner commends the "mature professionalism" of Holman's empty "Pizza Boy," faultlessly delivered by Frank Rosolino with Les Brown and His Band of Renown. One suspects he would say the same about "Savannah" from Curtis Fuller with Manny Albam in 1962 or about Les and Larry Elgart's "Soon" from 1967.

Of course, no line can be drawn between innovation and its absence, as is shown by a piece such as Maynard Ferguson's 1964 "On Green Dolphin Street," scored by Mike Abene. It seems ironic that the once-notorious high-note screamer should later have brought forward writing for his excellent band that was genuinely, if modestly, new, with fresh colors, textures, harmony. And to say that a band like Harry James's did not offer anything fresh is not to say that it had nothing at all, or to dismiss it as a mere copy of Basie. When James plays items such as Ernie Wilkins's "Jazz Connoisseur" of 1961 or particularly Thad Jones's 1967 "That's Thad" some listeners would rather hear him than latter-day Basie.

But if we seek the line of *evolution* in big band music or in any element of jazz then surely the direction is best marked by innovations, be they of technique or expression. In the latter regard I am as subjective as everyone else and so make no apology for extensively disagreeing with Kirchner's choices or for suggesting some very different items that might have appeared here instead. For now I would describe some of his selections as predictable, some as seeming like inspired discoveries, and others as inexplicable. It might be as well to deal with these last first, though not before acknowledging that anyone putting an anthology like this together may be restricted by circumstances quite outside their control. Sometimes use of a particular item is denied by the copyright owner; or too large a fee is demanded; or the copyright owner cannot be found. Yet such limitations do not quite explain why some pieces are here.

Remembering how influential sets like this can be, there seems no point to including the U.S. Air Force Airmen of Note's soporific "Noël" or the Boss Brass's "Portrait of Jennie." Buddy Rich, who comes with "Goodbye Yesterday," never did anything to move orchestral thinking in jazz forward, and while Henry Mancini was a neat arranger his decoration of "'Round about Midnight" is entirely expendable. Anything from Doc Severinsen and the Tonight Show Band (I have heard their complete Amhurst LPs) is flashy and retrogressive music. All these are a waste of space while the inclusion of Barnet's "Eugipelliv" and Russell's "Manhattan" are missed opportunities.

When Kenton temporarily retired at the end of 1948, Capitol were left without a big band and made attempts to persuade Barnet towards Stanley Newcomb's concept of progress. The results varied greatly and "Eugipelliv" was the worst record by that edition of Barnet's outfit; in fact

I cannot improve on Alun Morgan's dismissal of it as being "typical of late-1940 pretentiousness."[3] Almost anything else by this band would have been preferable, such as Gil Fuller's highly animated "Cu-Ba," Kai Winding's "Really" (alias "Bop City" alias "Dishwater"), "Claude Reigns," a stimulating piano-with-band vehicle for Claude Williamson, or, best of all, Tiny Kahn's sensitive arrangement of "Over the Rainbow." This beautiful and forgotten record should have supplanted the banal "Eugipelliv." Similarly "Manhattan" is a poor choice from *New York N.Y.,* an LP which, quite apart from being saddled with Jon Hendricks's trite spoken rhymes, contains easily Russell's weakest writing. This is truly a chance thrown away because there were so many other possibilities. How about one of the "Chromatic Universe" movements from *Jazz in the Space Age* or something from *Listen to the Silence* or *Vertical Form VI?* But more of Russell later.

Again, I believe it was a tactical error on Kirchner's part to let in people whose most original orchestral ventures were dealt with by Williams and Schuller. The obvious case is Gillespie, here represented by an unremarkable 1957 "I Remember Clifford" and "Chorale" from 1962. Similarly Herman's finest hours were spent with his First and Second Herds, and I can see no point in giving space to items like his 1972 "Summer of '42." If further work of Herman's stamp was deemed essential, how about something from one of Chubby Jackson's big band dates? These produced jazz that was "school of Herman," yet saw that music from a different angle. Good examples would be Tiny Kahn's 1950 scores of "Flying the Coop" or "Hot Dog."

What seems like another mistaken gesture was the inclusion of "Four in One" from Monk's 1963 Lincoln Center concert. Obviously he was a highly original theme writer and a pianist of remarkable independence, but he was no kind of orchestral thinker. Hall Overton's arrangements of this and other pieces for this and comparable occasions are notable feats of ingenuity, but Monk himself made no contribution to the evolution of jazz orchestral writing and so does not belong here.

And nor—to become seriously iconoclastic for two paragraphs—do I have much enthusiasm for the Clarke-Boland, Jones-Lewis, or latter-day Basie bands. All these were highly praised ensembles, and, on listening to the performances Kirchner chose, it is easy to understand why, not least during the solos from Derek Humble (alto), Ake Persson (trombone), and Sahib Shihab (baritone) on Clarke-Boland's "Now Hear My Meanin'." Yet although Boland's writing is very effective, and splendidly played in this 1963 piece, it contains nothing that we have not heard often before—even if those six trumpets really sting! The Jones-Lewis outfit had even more of this shouting vitality, and I have to say that it convinces me no more. A piece such as the 1976 "Cherry Juice" is, again, superbly performed and would obviously have made a great impact in person, but, despite Kirchner's notes, I can hear no significantly individual voice in Jones's writing, here or elsewhere. As so often, the chief musical strength lies in the soloing, for example Jones's own on "Willow Weep for Me." And I would rather hear Frank Foster in "Cherry Juice" than on any of his records with Basie.

The latter's artistic success from the late 1930s through to the "Little Pony"/"Beaver Junction" date of 1951 depended on the prowess of his soloists, the innovative nature of his rhythm section, and a remarkable brand of ensemble spontaneity. Much of this survives in Kirchner's first selection, "Rambo"—originally issued in the 78 rpm days as "Bambo." This is a 1946 J. J. Johnson composition and arrangement on which he takes a solo that finds him well on course for the bop trombone style he began to define later that year with the first of his Savoy quintet sessions.[4] It seems cruel to follow this vital performance with "Li'l Darlin'," which is my nomination for the dullest performance ever recorded by this uniformly tedious band. Of course, the disciplined precision with which the band's collective power was by then used conveyed a great feeling of security, and Basie was hugely popular for a long time. There is no arguing with that, least of all in the U.S.A., but the product of this reactionary outfit has no place in a set dealing with "the *evolution* of the jazz orchestra." Foster's "Blues in Hoss' Flat" is all too characteristic of the lack of musical interest, let alone adventure, for every solo and ensemble phrase is traditional in the most stale sense. The clamorous noise and excitement may briefly deceive us, yet there is no invention, no discovery here.[5]

Luckily plenty of both can be found in the writing of Handy, Sauter, Ellington, Russell ("Similau" for Shaw), Mulligan, Graettinger, Russo, Ellis, Toshiko Akiyoshi, Gil Evans, J. J. Johnson, John Lewis, Mingus, Abrams, and perhaps Johnny Richards. That is a good list, and enough to compensate for the surrounding disappointments, though one is not being unduly wise after the event in saying that the inevitable opening gambit was Parker with McShann. Kirchner chose an excellent specimen with 1941's "Swingmatism," a 16-bar blues in F minor with a decent arrangement by Willie Scott. The young master is glimpsed firmly on his way to bop, and the supporting performance, while not moving jazz forward at all, suggests a reflecting enthusiasm. To hear jazz being dragged into the twentieth century we need Raeburn. This is an historical joke because he was a completely undistinguished musician, a mere frontman, who had about as much to do with the jazz his band played as William McKinney had with the Cotton Pickers. And just as Redman, following John Nesbitt, worked out the Cotton Pickers' style, so Ed Finckel and particularly George Handy did likewise for Raeburn. Finckel wanted the band to sound like a modernized version of Basie's, playing what he called "orchestrated Lester Young." Pieces like his "Boyd meets Stravinsky" (which, because of its allusion to "Chant of the Weed," ought to have been titled "Raeburn meets Redman") are indeed aggressively updated swing. But Handy went much further, building a virtuosic, consciously modernistic ensemble emphasizing harmonic dissonance and some textural discontinuity. His "Dalvatore Sally" hints that the ambitions were formal as well as linguistic, as this was the first section of a four-movement suite, to be followed by "Hey Look, I'm Dancing," "Grey Suede, Special Maid" and "Keef" (= Key F). "Dalvatore Sally" is at first highly contrapuntal, with very different types of figuration going on simultaneously; yet the line of thought is repeatedly broken, and so the mood switches also. Such music was a genuine step forward in composing for the large jazz ensemble, and it is our loss that Handy was unable to develop his obvious gifts further after the Raeburn outfit's brief flight.

It might seem that nothing could be expected from an organization with such classics as "Have You Got Any Gum, Chum?" behind it. But although ignored by the history books of modern jazz, McKinley's, as Kirchner assures us, was among the most advanced big bands of the mid-1940s. Its having "Idiot's Delight" by Eddie Sauter in the library is hence no big surprise, although this consistently original composer, whose contributions started with Red Norvo's 1930s band, never received anything like his due even when writing for Goodman and Shaw. "Idiot's Delight" is all ensemble, somewhat discontinuous, with *pointilliste* orchestration, counterpoint, displaced accents, combining its two main sections in an entirely satisfactory climax: here is another advance in writing for the large jazz ensemble. To *whom* McKinley played "Idiot's Delight" can scarcely be imagined. Obviously it would offend the ballroom crowd — and perhaps hence the title.[6]

As Sauter is one who did continue developing his music it might have been apt to include instead a later piece such as "Kinetic Energy" or "Tropic of Kommingen," especially as the latter pursues ideas not dissimilar from those in "Idiot's Delight." However, these were recorded by the South West German Radio and TV Big Band, of which Sauter was then director,[7] and European activities raise matters I address at the end of this review.

One hardly could do justice to Ellington with five CDs, and to choose a mere five tracks to represent him is the most obviously impossible of the several impossible tasks Kirchner undertook in making this whole selection. Ellington had first used the voice as a wordless instrument twenty years before, of course, but "On a Turquoise Cloud" from 1947 was perhaps his most immaculate harnessing together of Kay Davis's lovely soprano voice, Jimmy Hamilton's then rather cold clarinet, and Lawrence Brown's nearly miraculous trombone playing. However, there were several such pieces, and I tend to prefer "Transblucency," based on the 1938 "Blue Light," partly because more is heard there from Ellington's piano. I further prefer the March 1946 radio transcription of this latter to the RCA-Victor record of the following July: this last is the better performance, yet the piece itself is cut by almost a minute, from the transcription's 3:55 to the RCA version's 2:57.

Kirchner's notes are again helpful on the modal improvising of Gonsalves in "Tourist Point of View," a fine instance of Ellington opening his music, in 1966, to new resources. Still, as Neil Tesser wrote in his notes for the Bluebird reissue of *Far East Suite* (far more intelligent than those for the initial RCA issue), this work is a jazz equivalent to Copland's *El Salón México* or Gershwin's *An American in Paris,* a matter of tourist recollections. And Ellington calling his first movement "Tourist Point of View" suggests that he was aware of the fact.

Turning elsewhere, "Undercurrent Blues" from 1949 is as good a big band sampling as could be found of Goodman's flirtation, at forty, with bop. There are idiomatic solos from Eddie Bert and especially Doug Mettome, but Chico O'Farrill's score barely touches bop. And his other writings, for Parker, Gillespie, Kenton, and Machito, prove that he never understood it. Incidentally, Goodman's finest involvement with bop— without it affecting his own playing—was the previous year's septet account of "Stealing Apples" with Fats Navarro and Wardell Gray. The young men play excellently but are actually surpassed by a Goodman brilliantly on his mettle. It is rather like the ending of *The Cincinnati Kid,* where, against all the odds, the Edward G. Robinson character outplays the Steve McQueen character.

Not that Barnet and Goodman were the only leaders of yesterday's big bands dallying with bop as the 1940s closed. Shaw's 1944–5 ensemble was still adventurous and played its Sauter, Buster Harding, and Ray

Conniff scores with attacking enthusiasm. "Lucky Number" was quite conventional, but the other Shaw piece included here, the long-unissued "Similau" by his 1949 band, is something quite otherwise. Basically this is an unenterprising 32-bar AABA popular song, yet it undergoes an extraordinary, in part polytonal, transformation by George Russell. Part of it is a Shaw solo in which he shows a full awareness of what Russell is doing, and this whole piece is simply fascinating. One had always wondered what else the latter was up to when he wrote "The Bird in Igor's Yard" for DeFranco, and here at last is part of the answer. This is one of the set's major discoveries and with it, as with "Idiot's Delight," Kirchner has put us in his debt.

It is no small tribute to Kenton to discover that arriving at a mere five tracks to define his contribution to orchestral jazz is almost as impossible as with Ellington. So there seems little point in including "Intermission Riff," except perhaps as a specimen of the basic Kenton sound. The other early architect of that sound was obviously Pete Rugolo, and though his "Cuban Carnival" might seem representative in view of Kenton's Latin leanings, there are at least a half-dozen other 1947 records that more sharply isolate Rugolo's originality as a composer. I would suggest "Chorale for Piano, Brass and Bongos," "Impressionism," "Monotony," "Abstraction," "Lament," and "Collaboration." Or, as a few small group recordings have been allowed into the set, like Carter's "Blue Star" (alias "Evening Star") and Davis's "Israel," I would favor Rugolo's "Fugue for Rhythm Section."

According to accepted wisdom, the ensemble which recorded "Young Blood" in 1952 was "the most swinging band Kenton ever had," and this is indeed a fine score, stunningly played with memorable solos from Conte Candoli, Richie Kamuca, and Lee Konitz. It moves, too, with the lithe swing recognizable from virtually all of Mulligan's other writings, for large or small groups. But the most original music Kenton ever played was composed by Robert Graettinger. Considering that the response of most jazz fans, including Kenton devotees, to this composer's complex, highly dissonant, and very emotional work has usually been one of facetiousness, it was a gesture of real independence on Kirchner's part to include one of his pieces. Graettinger's masterwork is "City of Glass," but Kirchner reasonably picked "A Trumpet" from the six-movement "This Modern World" suite of 1953. It is in part a vehicle for Maynard Ferguson and stands with Ellington's "Madness in Great Ones" (for Cat Anderson) from *Such Sweet Thunder* (1957) as almost the only case of extreme high-note trumpet virtuosity being employed to serious artistic purpose. It might even have been an idea for Kirchner to have included "Madness in Great Ones," thus bringing these two absolutely exceptional compositions together.[8]

Less extravagantly ambitious, Bill Russo's "Egdon Heath" still uses 1954 Kenton resources in an innovative manner, generating complicated and unfamiliar textures, remarkably free harmony, and no steady jazz pulse. Such writing, without wishing to stress the point unduly, ought to have had a larger place in this collection instead of items from Basie, Herman, Rich, Brown, Elgart, Albam, May, Mancini, Quincy Jones. . . . Even so, in Kirchner's place I believe that I might have gone for somewhat later music by Russo, such as a movement from his nine-movement *Seven Deadly Sins* of 1960.[9]

The presence of the Sauter-Finegan band's "The Loop" is justified by the innovative orchestral writing of both leaders. But although this is a very swinging 1954 performance, climaxed by a quotation from the "Northwest Passage" which Ralph Burns charted for Herman, Joe Venuto's xylophone solo reminds us that the ingenuity often served rather trivial ends. And there are questions to be asked about Johnny Richards's "Nipigon" of 1957, which contains further inventive orchestration yet is essentially mood music. True, it prompted my return to other records by this 1957–9 Richards bands, but I cannot help thinking that this collection's ends might have been met rather better with something from *Adventures in Time,* one of the finest LPs Kenton ever made (in 1962). Or, as an occasional smallish group is allowed in here, what about part of Richards's intriguing *Annotations of the Muses,* a 1955 essay which I have only ever seen on the exceedingly rare Legende label?

On "Weep" Mulligan is the main soloist, with good contributions from Bob Brookmeyer and Don Ferrara. In fact this piece is chiefly them, and I cannot hear any special merit in Gary McFarland's writing, smoothly accomplished though it is. Surely a clearer idea of the Concert Jazz Band's capabilities would have arisen from the same 1961 date's account of Russell's "All about Rosie" or of Carisi's "Israel." These, after all, are powerfully original pieces, the former miles ahead of "Manhattan."

Speaking of powerful originality brings us to Don Ellis, and his "Chain Reaction" of 1972 is one of this set's most refreshing experiences, not least because this band was swimming against the conservatism so active elsewhere. It was probably the best demonstration in its own time—late 1960s, early 1970s—that there were indeed further moves to be made with the large jazz ensemble and that somebody was making some of them. And, even with space at a premium in this anthology, one must question only a single track going to Ellis; picking it must have been another of Kirchner's impossible tasks. The point is not the unusual time-signatures and the electronics but the imagination with which they are deployed, the widened spectrum of orchestral colors, the rhythmic counterpoint of sections intriguingly set against each other, and other features that arise logically from within, from the music's expressive intent. A large ensemble was the only possible medium for what Ellis had to say and this music is essentially orchestral in concept, the proof being that each of his best pieces, such as "Chain Reaction," generates its own kind of inner tension, this in turn being due to each score unfolding as an organic whole, not as a stringing-together of formulae. Further, each item is packed with incidents peculiar to it alone, and the restless depths and kaleidoscopic variety of these dancing, shimmering, multivoiced textures are obviously reminiscent of Gil Evans, although that great recomposer's brooding sensibility is partly replaced by rhythmic insistence and his glowing, opalescent colors with more astringent tones.

After this exhilaration comes the terrible anticlimax of "Green Witch," a dreary scrap of jazz rock by the Rhythm Combination and Brass that is not worth a moment of anyone's time. Yet we then ascend steeply again for the Manchurian Candidate, who could almost be said to have taken the torch of jazz orchestral innovation from Ellis's hands. "Sumie" is an excellent small-scale 1976 example of Toshiko Akiyoshi's powers as a composer and of the similarly unique qualities of her band. It is slightly preferable, I feel, to the later, fractionally longer, version on an LP also called *Sumie* on RCA (F) PL37537. We should note that Akiyoshi has held this band together since 1973, writing all the music for its many (unpublicized, poorly distributed) LPs.[10] This is a great feat in itself quite apart from the originality of that music. Again Kirchner had an impossible task in choosing just one piece, and I assume he went for "Sumie" to illustrate the character of the band and of Akiyoshi as a composer. There is no quarrel with that, but as further possibilities I would simply mention "Relaxing at Zell-am-Zee" on *European Memoirs* (Baystate (J) RJL8036) and "Shades of Yellow" on *Farewell* (RCA (J) RVJ6078). But no single piece can demonstrate more than a few aspects of Akiyoshi's achievement.

Most people likely to read this will know why Kirchner included the 1949 Miles Davis nonet version of "Israel." The *Birth of the Cool* recordings came out of Gil Evans's bravely independent work for the Claude Thornhill band and in turn pointed towards his three great collaborations with Davis. From the first of these, *Miles Ahead,* comes "Blues for Pablo," but Kirchner has most intelligently let us hear Evans's preliminary move. This is the original Hal McKusick recording of the previous year (1956), and to hear this followed by Evans's richly expanded setting for Davis is a considerable lesson in orchestration. I have written about this music at more than sufficient length elsewhere[11] and so will only remark here on what a fertile augmentation of the *Birth of the Cool* instrumentation, crammed with further potentialities, Evans devised for his 1957 sessions with Davis.

Incidentally, Kirchner follows Evans-Davis with a track from Bill Potts's 1959 *Porgy and Bess* LP, and this juxtaposition serves as an almost mortifying reminder of the distance between an artist and a craftsman. Then, to ram the point home, we get Evans's "Barbara Song" of 1964. This makes us wish he had done an entire LP of Weill and defies both description and analysis, as pure poetry usually does. "Barbara Song" sounds like beauty half asleep and dreaming of itself.

And if that is Beauty, Mingus conceivably might have been content for his music, with its questionable architecture and wonderful gargoyles, to signify the Beast. Certainly in "Revelations" he follows Pound's ancient exhortation to "make it new" and no mistake. But I have, again, written about this music more than enough in other places[12] and will add only that it is a pity there was no room for a couple more of the exploratory 1957 Brandeis Festival pieces, maybe Giuffre's "Suspensions," Milton Babbitt's "All Set," or even the original version of Russell's "All about Rosie."

So great a trombonist is J. J. Johnson that it is hard, even now, to think of him as a fine composer as well. Yet there are many pieces like "El Camino Real," recorded in 1964, which prove that he is. Besides a perfect vehicle for his own playing, this is also an interestingly organized piece, superbly written and played. It was commissioned by John Lewis for performance at the 1959 Monterey Jazz Festival, and Lewis is up next with "Animal Dance," originally part of a 1961 ballet titled *Original Sin.* This 1965 recording sets the MJQ within an orchestral framework and Lewis, being quite unhypnotized by the standard procedures of big band scoring, offers some adventurous ensemble writing.

After this it is mainly downhill. Mancini and Severinsen have been mentioned, and "Heidi" by Oliver Nelson's Berlin Dream Band is an unnecessarily protracted vehicle for his alto saxophone in Coltrane mode. Sun Ra's "Street Named Hell," mainly a workout for timpani and other drums, is a reminder that he seldom got his muddled act together. In late years it seemed to be chiefly a matter of dressing up, and it may be that something from his *The Heliocentric Worlds of Sun Ra* on ESP would have served better. Possibly "Outer Nothingness" or "Outer Worlds" from Volume 1. At first I was put off Tom Pierson's "Planet of Tears" by the Coltrane imitations of Scott Robinson's soprano fore and aft. But Pierson has shaped this 1989 performance, of over 12 minutes, as a single whole and the final effect is satisfying even if there is not much distinction in the orchestral writing as such. Muhal Richard Abrams's "Hearinga," also of 1989, includes a curiously eccentric yet arresting trumpet solo from Jack Walrath, and there are some fairly surprising instrumental textures. So there is a modest reaching-out at the close.

But what did Kirchner omit? At first sight, very little. The one absence that is astonishing is Carisi's 1961 "Angkor Wat" and "Moon Taj," orchestral jazz of unforgettable beauty and great originality. These would have been at the top of my list with Ellington, Gil Evans, Sauter, Graettinger, Ellis, Russell and Toshiko Akiyoshi. For the rest one might have expected to find a movement from Dick Groves's *Little Bird Suite,* something from Alan Silva's Celestial Communications Orchestra, or "Teardrop" from Gunther Schuller's *Jumpin' in the Future* (GM Recordings GM3010D). Yet this, Carisi aside, is hardly a list.

Could the selection have been done quite differently? How about abandoning all the items I have described as extraneous, so making room for a smaller number of longer pieces, thereby including some of the major achievements of sustained composition for the large jazz ensemble? And as the subtitle reads "The Evolution of the Jazz *Orchestra*" was Kirchner confined to something like conventional big band instrumentation? How about Giuffre's "Mobiles" or a segment of his 1960 "Piece for Clarinet and Strings"? Indeed, a number of the most fruitful attempts to develop new forms of orchestral jazz have been on a rather large scale, as we might expect, so would not a movement from Phil Sunkel's "Jazz Concerto Grosso" have been relevant? The two brief excerpts from Charlie Haden's 1969 *Liberation Suite* have little impact, but with the lightweight material excised there could have been space for a more substantial passage. Also something from Carla Bley's *Genuine Tong Funeral,* and one or another of the "Communications" pieces recorded in 1968 by the Jazz Composers' Orchestra. One might also in these circumstances suggest one of Akiyoshi's larger (not merely longer) pieces such as "Two Faces of a Nation" from *European Memoirs* or "Minimata" (the *Insights* version, not the Newport one). And if we then think of such items as Heiner Stadler's "Clusterity" of 1966 (Tomato 269.652-

2) and Coltrane's "Greensleeves" from his 1961 *Africa Brass* we are already on the way to a substantially different body of music.

So what have *I* missed out? Stadler's "Clusterity" was recorded by the North German Radio and TV Big Band under Dieter Glawischnig, and I have already mentioned Sauter's activities in that country. Even if we set aside the futile Rhythm Combination and Brass, there still is a considerable European presence in Oliver Nelson's Berlin Dream Band and the Clarke-Boland outfit. And then there are Ted Heath and John Dankworth. The former is represented by an up-tempo 1955 reading of "The Man I Love" that is immaculately played yet completely unoriginal. It would have been more satisfactory if this band had been sampled some years earlier, when it was full of youthful fire and enterprise, as with Kenny Baker's "Bakerloo Non-Stop" of 1946 or one of the scores Tadd Dameron provided for it, such as "Lyonia" (1949). Dankworth is here with "Sailor" from his *The $1,000,000 Collection,* and this is a thoroughly effective miniature concerto for Kenny Wheeler—noticeably superior to Quincy Jones's "Meet B.B." Yet if this highly individual trumpeter and composer was to be featured, Kirchner would have done better to include a movement (or two) from *Windmill Tilter,* Wheeler's LP-long 1968 celebration of Don Quixote and an outstanding example of the programmatic jazz suite.

However, considering the welter of European material relevant to this *Big Band Renaissance* box, it greatly misrepresents the situation for Heath's and Dankworth's to be the sole purely European ensembles included. The simplest thing would have been to omit them, and then the selection could have been titled *Big Band Renaissance in America.* But although it seems unlikely that anybody at the Smithsonian Institution ever devoted a moment's thought to cultural activities outside the Americas, one could not be content about one of their influential record sets completely bypassing European manifestations in this particular field. It would of course be entirely possible to put together an anthology titled *Big Band Renaissance in Europe,* but we shall have to look elsewhere than to the Smithsonian for that.

All I can do here is to list a little of the potential material with brief notes. I should start with the four European musicians who ought to have been in Kirchner's selection even as it stands, beginning with the large ensemble called Django's Music. The great guitarist's activities as a composer are perhaps not a matter of total ignorance, and, though he was musically illiterate, he dictated off his guitar a whole series of surprisingly characteristic big band scores and got them recorded in Paris and

Brussels during the Nazi occupation. Once little known even in Europe, the almost complete body of these 1940–41 Reinhardt pieces has lately been issued by Hep. André Hodeir should have been here, too, perhaps with his "Autour d'un Récif" recorded by Tony Proteau's band as early as 1949, or, much better, with a movement from his "Anna Livia Plurabelle" of 1966 or from "Bitter Ending" (1972). A movement from Lars Gullin's "Aeros Aromatic Atomica" of 1976 ought to have made it, as should one of Martial Solal's big band pieces such as "Et si c'était vrai" (1983). It is bad that Solal is ignored as a great pianist and almost worse that scarcely anyone outside France is aware of his large and very independent body of work for big band.

Possibly of more specialized interest is the Jan Allan record titled *Jan Allan 70,* which apparently intended to be an echo of Evans-Davis yet turned into something quite different. It has been continuously available in Scandinavia for 25 years, has won several prizes, yet seemingly is unknown elsewhere. Is there such a thing as jazz which does not travel in the sense that some wines cannot? And might that also apply to Neil Ardley, a persistently original composer for big bands in Britain with "Greek Variations," "Symphony of Amaranths" and other major pieces, above all the electronically shaded "Kaleidoscope of Rainbows," a movement or two of which ought to figure in any anthology of progressive orchestral jazz, European or otherwise. Then there is the 12-tone jazz of Pavel Blatný, the large output of Gustav Brom, such figures as Mike Gibbs (something from his *Chrome Waterfall* LP?), Ib Glindemann, Friedrich Gulda (maybe part of his "Music for Four Soloists and Band No. 2"?), Willem van Manen (*De Ruyter Suyte?*), Palle Mikkelborg (*The Mysterious Corona?*), Andy Sheppard (*Soft on the Inside?*). Globe Unity? The Vienna Art Orchestra? I could go on. . . .

NOTES

1. Max Harrison: "Fletcher Henderson—an Unproven Case," *Jazz on CD,* March 1995: 50–2.
2. Russell's sleevenote for the initial U.S. issue of his 1956 *Jazz Workshop* LP (RCA-Victor LPM 2534).
3. Max Harrison, Alun Morgan, *et al: Modern Jazz: the Essential Records 1945–70* (London: Aquarius Books, 1975), 5.
4. Herewith a sample of the uncomprehending response such music encountered 50 years ago. I came across it by chance while looking for

something else, which is how one usually discovers such gems: "I have a feeling that "Rambo" is fairly horrible, but I haven't the stamina to play it again to find out"—Denis Preston: "Current Records," *Jazz Music* 3, no. 3 (1946): 27–30. This approaches the depth of Hughes Panassié's branding of Lester Young: "His sonority is small and frankly ugly, and in the lower registers frequently reminds one of an automobile horn"—*The Real Jazz* (New York: Smith & Durrell, 1942), 116. Presumably the world of jazz would be incomplete without such commentators.

5. While making these entirely negative comments on latter-day Basie I have not forgotten André Hodeir, "Basie's Way," *Toward Jazz* (New York: Grove Press, 1962), 109–16, or Martin Williams, "Horses in Midstream," *Annual Review of Jazz Studies 2* (1983): 1–6.
6. Compare "Idiot's Delight" with other Sauter scores for this band on McKinley's *Borderline* CD, Savoy SV0203.
7. Hear *The Historic Donaueschingen Jazz Concert of 1957* by Sauter, Hodeir, and the MJQ (MPS 68.161).
8. All Kenton's recordings of Graettinger's pieces are now gathered together on the CD *City of Glass,* Capitol 7243-8-32084-2-5. Unfortunately the movements of "This Modern World" have been placed in the wrong order. They should run: "A Horn," "Some Saxophones," "A Cello," "A Thought," "A Trumpet," and "An Orchestra," thereby alternating solo vehicles with ensemble pieces.
9. Concerning "Egdon Heath" one should question Gunther Schuller's assertion (in *Musings* [New York: Oxford University Press, 1986], 130) that Russo named this piece after a passage in Thomas Hardy's *The Return of the Native* (1878). When he lived in London (1962–5), Russo used to say that he had never heard of Hardy at the time of composition and had just chosen the title because he liked the sound of it.
10. Nobody at RCA in any country ever came near to grasping what, or who, they had under contract for so long. So random was their marketing that Akiyoshi's 1977 appearance at Newport was originally issued only in Germany (*Live at Newport,* RCA [G] PL40821) with the second volume only in Brazil (*Live at Newport II,* RCA [Br] 104 4145)!
11. In Bill Kirchner (ed.), *A Miles Davis Reader,* forthcoming from the Smithsonian Institution.
12. For example in Max Harrison, *A Jazz Retrospect* (London: Quartet Books, 1991).

ABOUT THE EDITOR

HENRY MARTIN (Ph.D. in music composition, Princeton; M.M. in music theory, University of Michigan; B.A. in piano performance, Oberlin Conservatory; and B.A. in mathematics, Oberlin) is Director of Music Theory and Composition at the Mannes-New School Jazz and Contemporary Music Program. His books include *Charlie Parker and Thematic Improvisation* (Scarecrow Press) and *Enjoying Jazz* (Schirmer Books). He has contributed numerous articles on music theory to such journals as *Perspectives of New Music* and *In Theory Only*. As a composer, his *Preludes and Fugues* won the National Composers Competition, sponsored by the League of Composers—International Society for Contemporary Music, and was issued on compact disc by GM Recordings in 1996.

ABOUT THE CONTRIBUTORS

GENE ANDERSON is Associate Professor of Music Theory and Director of Bands at the University of Richmond in Richmond, Virginia. With a Ph.D. in music theory from the University of Iowa, he has published articles in the *Indiana Theory Review,* the *Journal of the Science and Practice of Music,* and *American Music.* He is presently working on a full-length biography of Johnny Dodds.

WILLIAM BAUER is an Assistant Professor of Music at Rutgers University in Newark. In addition to writing about jazz, he composes music that draws upon a wise range of influences. He is currently completing his Ph.D. in Composition at the City University Graduate School. His dissertation consists of a woodwind quintet and an extended prose essay about the life and music of jazz singer Betty Carter.

GEOFFREY L. COLLIER received his doctorate in cognitive psychology from Columbia University. His dissertation studied rhythmic tapping in trained musicians in a laboratory setting. Prior to studying cognitive psychology, he was a musician in New York, teaching guitar and composing. He is currently Assistant Professor of Psychology at South Carolina State University.

JAMES LINCOLN COLLIER has written extensively on jazz history. His most recent book is *Jazz: The American Theme Song* (Oxford University Press).

TIM DEAN-LEWIS, jazz musician and theoretician, was born in Essex, England, and raised in New Jersey. Since his return to the U.K., he has lectured at the University of Brighton and is currently working on a book about the use of symmetry as an improvisational tool in jazz.

ARMEN DONELIAN has recorded for the SunnySide, Atlas, and Odin labels. He is on the faculty of the Mannes-New School Jazz Program, William Paterson State College, and the Manhattan School of Music. A graduate of Columbia University, six-time NEA Jazz Fellow, author of *Training the Ear* (Advance), and Steinway Affiliated pianist, Donelian has performed as a featured soloist, bandleader, and sideman with Sonny Rollins and many others.

PATRICK C. DORIAN is a member of the music department of East Stroudsburg University in Pennsylvania, where he has taught instrumental ensembles, jazz improvisation, and music theory since 1987. He taught instrumental music in the public schools for fourteen years and since 1992 has been IAJE Co-chair for Summer Jazz Studies and Educational Jazz Festivals. Along with Phil Woods, he has directed the COTA Cats, a summer student jazz ensemble, for the Delaware Water Gap Celebration of the Arts for fifteen years. He holds degrees from Northwestern University and Ithaca College.

MAX HARRISON studied with Anthony Milner, Iain Hamilton, and finally with Mátyás Seiber. He for many years worked in classical music publishing in London as an editor, arranger and orchestrator, but writing about music finally took over. He produced hundreds of reviews of classical concerts for *The Times,* of classical records for *The Gramophone,* as well as appearing in numerous other publications both in Britain and on the Continent. Harrison has also written extensively about jazz.

JAMES KURZDORFER currently teaches music theory, music appreciation, and jazz ensemble at Villa Maria College of Buffalo, and is doing post-graduate work in music theory at State University of New York at Buffalo. He was the original bassist of the jazz fusion group Spyro Gyra and remains an active member of the Western New York area jazz scene.

STEVE LARSON is Associate Professor of Music Theory at the University of Oregon. His publications appear in *American Music, College Music Symposium, In Theory Only, Indiana Theory Review, Journal of Aesthetic Education, Journal of Music Theory, Journal of Music Theory Pedagogy, Music Perception, Perspectives of New Music, Proceedings of the Cognitive Science Society, Proceedings of the Third International Conference on Music Perception and Cognition, The New Grove Dictionary of American Music,* and *The New Grove Dictionary of Jazz.* His jazz compositions and piano improvisations may be heard on the compact disc *Portfolio* (with flutist Cynthia Folio), Nebula NU 5009).

DAVID LIEBMAN, jazz saxophonist, composer and educator, has played with Miles Davis and Elvin Jones as well as leading his own groups. He has nearly 75 records under his own name, is featured on 150 others, and has several books and videos well known in the jazz field. He is founder and artistic director of the International Association of Schools of Jazz.

STEVEN STRUNK is a composer and Professor of Music at The Catholic University of America in Washington, DC. He has contributed articles to *ARJS* and *The New Grove Dictionary of Jazz.*

KEITH WATERS is a jazz pianist who has recorded and performed throughout the United States, Europe, and in Russia. He has appeared in concert with James Moody, Bobby Hutcherson, Sheila Jordan, Chris Connor, Eddie Harris, and others. He has contributed articles on jazz as well as classical music to a variety of journals and publications. Currently he is a faculty member of the University of Colorado at Boulder.

ABOUT THE INSTITUTE
OF JAZZ STUDIES

The Institute of Jazz Studies of Rutgers, the State University of New Jersey, is a unique research facility and archival collection, the foremost of its kind. IJS was founded in 1952 by Marshall Sterns (1908–1966), a pioneer jazz scholar, professor of medieval English literature at Hunter College, and the author of two essential jazz books: *The Story of Jazz* and *Jazz Dance*. In 1966, Rutgers was chosen as the collection's permanent academic home. IJS is located on the Newark campus of Rutgers and is a branch of the John Cotton Dana Library of the Rutgers University Libraries.

IJS carries on a comprehensive program to preserve and further jazz in all its facets. The archival collection, which has quadrupled its holdings since coming to Rutgers, as of 1991 consists of more than 100,000 sound recordings in all formats, from phonograph cylinders and piano rolls to video cassettes and laser discs; more than 5,000 books on jazz and related subjects, including discographies, bibliographies, and dissertations; and comprehensive holdings in jazz periodicals from throughout the world. In addition, there are extensive vertical files on individuals and selected topics, a large collection of photographs, sheet music, big band arrangements, realia, and memorabilia.

IJS serves a broad range of users, from students to seasoned scholars, authors, and collectors. The facilities are open to the public on weekdays by appointment. In order to allow the widest possible access, there is no charge for routine use of reference materials. Researchers requiring extensive staff assistance, however, are assessed a charge. Due to limited audio facilities, as well as to preserve the record collection, listening and taping are limited to serious research projects.

In addition to students, scholars, and other researchers, IJS routinely assists teachers, musicians, the media, record companies and producers, libraries and archives, arts agencies, and jazz organizations.

For further information on IJS programs and activities, write to:

Institute of Jazz Studies
Dana Library
Rutgers, The State University
Newark, NJ 07102